The Greatest Sailing Stories Ever Told

Twenty-Seven Unforgettable Stories

EDITED BY

CHRISTOPHER CASWELL

LYONS
PRESS

Guilford, Connecticut

An imprint of Globe Pequot, the trade division of
The Rowman & Littlefield Publishing Group, Inc.
4501 Forbes Blvd., Ste. 200
Lanham, MD 20706
www.rowman.com

Distributed by NATIONAL BOOK NETWORK

British Library Cataloguing in Publication Information available

Library of Congress Cataloging-in-Publication Data Available

ISBN 978-1-4930-6547-9 (paperback)

♾™ The paper used in this publication meets the minimum requirements of American
National Standard for Information Sciences—Permanence of Paper for Printed Library
Materials, ANSI/NISO Z39.48-1992.

Contents

Introduction

Man has sailed from the day that a daring cave dweller first spread a ragged animal skin and harnessed the wind to move a log across the water. Man has raced from the time a second caveman thought he could do it better.

Over the centuries, man has set sail for a multitude of reasons: adventure, exploration, trade, and war. And, while the boats have changed, man's love affair with sail has not. From the towering canvas on the Cape Horn square-riggers to the clouds of nylon and Dacron on modern America's Cup racers, sailing has remained as both a challenge and a joy.

Sailing is more a state of mind and heart than it is just another method of getting from Point A to Point B. For many sailors, even the act of hoisting sail puts them in a mellow mood, and a destination is often far down the list of importance.

With the sea covering more than 140 billion square miles, it is clearly one of the last frontiers and, as such, sailors are the astronauts of liquid space. The stories on the following pages cover the wide spectrum of the human condition: hopes, dreams, passion, fear, and heroism.

It has been interesting to note that weather played a major part in many of these stories, which should really be no surprise because weather is a major factor for sailors. Too little wind is just as memorable as too much wind, storms can be frightening, and waves can range from sparkling summer swells that toss back a spritzing of spray to towering black mountains that threaten your very existence.

Sailors have an insatiable appetite for reading about the adventures of others on the sea: an abiding interest whether the tales are about long-distance racing or cruising to a nearby cove. Many of these stories are excerpted from larger works and, if the short version intrigues you, I hope you will be encouraged to search out the complete book. Some are true stories that made newspaper headlines, others are works of pure fiction, and yet others fall into a twilight zone of reminiscences and reflections on the world of sail.

To gather a collection of stories and label it "greatest" is a challenge, and there will always be far more stories omitted than included. So if your favorite story is not found here, my apologies, but, hopefully, you will have discovered some new sailing stories to enjoy. Those included were selected not just for historic or literary reasons, but for pure reading enjoyment. My goal was to provide a collection that will satisfy the sailor and the armchair adventurer alike.

One of the joys of producing a book such as this is that it forced me to read a number of books that I had left too long on my library shelves, and for that, the project has brought hours of pleasure along with the work of making decisions.

I would like to picture the reader of this book in one of two places. The first is in a comfortable chair in front of a roaring fire, and the second is tucked in a cozy pilot berth aboard a sailboat, with rain pattering on the deck and the smell of coffee on the galley stove.

Either way—or wherever you choose to read—I hope you will conjure up the smell of salt air, of wind on your face and the sound of rigging moving in tune with the sea.

Close Encounter

From *Close to the Wind*

BY PETE GOSS

THIS STORY OF Pete Goss, an ex-Royal Marine, is one of sheer determination, incredible courage, and heroism of the highest caliber. Pete Goss was first drawn to the challenging long-distance ocean races at the age of twenty-four, and his first transatlantic boat was so weary when it arrived at the finish line in America that its keel fell off. Sacrificing everything including his home and car to build his boat, the *Aqua Quorum,* he set off on one of the most grueling races, the Vendee Globe, a nonstop single-handed yacht race around the world.

In this excerpt from his book, *Close to the Wind,* Goss gives up his chances to win the race when he hears the faint Mayday of a competitor. Deep in the raging Southern Ocean far below Australia, in winds gusting near hurricane strength and in seas the height of six-story buildings, he knows that the oldest tradition of the sea must be followed: when someone is in trouble, you help.

It won't give away anything to say that he saves the near-dead sailor from certain death in a life raft somewhere in the vast wilderness of the merciless sea. But it should prove satisfying that his actions brought Goss France's highest award for gallantry, the Legion d'Honneur; he was awarded the Medal of the British Empire by the Queen; and, perhaps just as important, he was named Yachtsman of the Year by a public who viewed Pete Goss as a true hero. When he crossed the finish in France, a crowd of 150,000 were on hand to cheer not the race winner, but its hero.

CHRISTMAS DAY 1996 BEGAN with a bright blue sky and a crisp, refreshing, twenty-knot wind from the north. My position was about 1,400 miles south of Perth, Western Australia. Perfect. I had been making good speed all night under the number two staysail and one reef in the main as we surged along over the large northerly swell that had set in. It would have been idyllic if it hadn't been for the barometric pressure, which was dropping fast. A fall of thirty-six millibars in twenty-four hours, and most of that had been in the last twelve. The forecast looked horrifying—the isobars on the weather chart were so close together that they seemed to merge into a solid black line. I had a deep sense of impending doom and felt very uneasy—I couldn't settle, couldn't relax. I had seen livestock back in the West Country bunch together and move restlessly about the field before a bad storm; I could relate to the feeling, except I was on my own. I had experienced many severe blows over the years but this one, for some reason, held a heavy sense of foreboding. I could almost taste it in the air.

Thoughts of Christmas were pushed to one side. I tried to ignore the feeling of uneasiness but it followed me around the boat as I checked that everything was as it should be. Fear was not an emotion which I associated with the sea. Of course, I respected the ocean but for me it was no longer an alien environment, it had become my way of life over the years and I was comfortable in its presence. I knew that *Aqua Quorum* and I were up to the job—it was the waiting for what were bound to be pretty grim conditions that brought on the whispers, the anxieties. It was time to have a cuppa, get busy, apply logic. Once the storm arrived the rest would be easy.

I could feel it now, I togged up and got on deck. The wind started to back—within three hours it had gone round to the southwest and was rising at an alarming rate. I could only just keep up. No sooner had I gybed and sorted everything out than the number two needed dropping. And I mean dropping, it was over the side and in the sea. Damn! It was a real struggle to drag it on to the deck as we hurtled along. I folded it up and left it lashed there. I knew it should have gone below but I just didn't have time—the wind was rising faster than I had ever experienced. I clambered back to the mast, put the third reef in and still the wind rose. Hell's teeth! I reduced the sail area and immediately it was too much and needed reducing further. I could sense the autopilot struggling to cope as we hurtled along. No time to tidy the reefing lines. I flaked out the staysail halyard and freed the clutch; couldn't afford niceties. The sail flogged like a bastard as we careered off down an odd sea, often submerged. It was hard work to manage the most basic of jobs and my elbow was playing up, too.

I whipped off the staysail and shoved it below taking loads of water with it—so much of the stuff was sweeping the decks that it was hard to judge a good moment. I made the staysail halyard off on the storm jib, thankful that I had already hanked it on in readiness for the occasion, made my way back to the mast and tried to pull it up. It was no good, the wind was too strong. I had to winch it all the way. It felt very hot inside my Musto oilies, I'd been hard at it for a couple of hours now. I went back to the cockpit for a breather to find that the wind was up to forty-five knots and rising. Fuck me—and it was only just beginning. The hair stood up on the back of my neck.

I forgot about taking a breather. I had to get the main down and get it down quickly. Up to the mast, I flaked out the halyard, checked everything over; if it went wrong now I'd have a hell of a job getting it back under control. Not happy with the sheet, I nipped back, winched it in a bit and eased the halyard. The sail fell away and jammed on the spreaders, pinned by gusts of goodness knows what strength. It was a real old struggle and I had to work between the gusts that were whipping the water into a white frenzy. I tied it off with enough rope to moor the *Queen Mary,* removed the halyard, made it off on the end of the boom and took it up tight. I then rigged up a couple of lines from the end of the boom to either side of the cockpit and winched them up bar tight.

I worked my way round the boat, tidying everything away and making sure that all was shipshape. I pulled both dagger boards up and added a line to stop them falling out if we got rolled upside down. I tied off the blades on the wind generator as the automatic brake didn't seem man enough in these conditions. I knew the number two sail should be removed from the deck and stowed below but decided to leave it—the bow was under water most of the time now and discretion was the better part of valour in this case.

I had to crawl on hands and knees back to the cockpit. The wind was still rising and I felt as though I was a passenger in a car, with the driver pressing hard on the accelerator with no regard for a rapidly approaching corner. I rolled from my knees into the cockpit and clipped on my additional safety line before releasing the other. The wind was a screaming banshee lashing the ocean into a frenzy of spume and spray that felt like a shotgun blast on my hands and face. It had settled at a vicious fifty knots, topped up with regular gusts that blasted their way through us at sixty knots, flattening the sea as they passed. Still the storm hadn't settled—it continued to rise.

I stumbled below and for the first time in my life fitted the washboards in anger. I shook off the worst of the water, grabbed a Mars bar and once again called up the weather chart. There was nowhere to go, the best thing was just to run before it and hope the storm dissipated before inflicting too much damage. Looking at the chart I suspected that Raphael and Patrick might be experiencing even worse conditions and I silently wished them well—we were all caught up in something far greater than we had ever experienced before. The energy of the storm was incredible—they were hurricane conditions. The hull hummed and shook as we surfed off down a wave at twenty-seven knots. I braced myself for the impact at the bottom and we dropped for what seemed an eternity before the crash came. The wind in the rigging rose and fell from a high-pitched screech to a low and sorrowful moan that worked its way into my soul.

I clambered back on deck and marvelled at the conditions as we flew along under the storm jib alone. The sail was little more than the size of a tablecloth and yet the sheet was tight and as unyielding as a steel rod. It resonated when I hit it with a winch handle. There was a roar as a big sea broke behind us. I ducked beneath the canopy and held on for grim death as good old *Aqua Quorum* accelerated out of it. This was fantastic. I grabbed the camera and fired off a few shots for the kids. I had never managed to take a good wave shot in all my years at sea. The lens somehow flattened them out, but I suspected that these monsters might be impressive. And still the wind rose.

My main concern was the waves. A large and menacing sea had been whipped up from the southwest and was being made worse by a northerly swell which would take a while to dissipate. Individually they presented nothing more than one would expect—it was when they combined that they erupted into an unpredictable brute of tumbling water. At times we were planing across the face of a northerly swell, leaning to windward on the occasional steep face when a southwesterly sea slammed into us. The transom was lifted by the combined force of the two waves and we turned and dropped dangerously into a pit. I spent a while finding the best line, set the autopilot and tumbled below. There was no steering out of the bad ones. I was better off shut below in the safety of the hull.

I was worried. I felt my control of the situation ebbing away as the conditions deteriorated. Unusually, the first knockdown was to windward. Two waves erupted on my port quarter, *Aqua Quorum* slewed round until she was dead downwind, the keel on full power pulled her over and the wave did the rest as we accelerated into what felt like a brick wall. I was braced against the chart table, hands against the cabin roof, feet on the floor in a star position, and I watched through the skylight as the spreaders dragged in the water. They pulled her back to windward, she was up, the storm jib filled and she was off again. Water poured into the cockpit and cascaded below.

I considered going to bare poles to slow the boat's headlong rush but instinct told me that speed, alarming as it may have been, was the one defence I had. We hurtled into a hole at forty-five degrees and stopped dead. I waited for the seemingly inevitable pitch-pole as we went completely under. The cabin went dark as the sea cut out the light. I was thrown against the chart table and looked out of the back of the boat at the sky as gallons of water poured into the accommodation from the cockpit. The flare box hit me on the shin and the pain gave me something to focus on, dispelling the fear as *Aqua Quorum* struggled to recover. The rudders were out of the water and I held on and hoped. There is always one bad blow on any long race and you know that if you get through it you will make the finish. I had no doubt that this was the one.

There was a tremendous crash and *Aqua Quorum* was knocked down again. I was thrown across the cabin as the boat groaned under the strain. Through the din I heard the satcom system bleeping away. I couldn't believe it was still able to work on what had practically become a yellow submarine. I struggled across to the chart table and called up the message. Mayday, mayday, mayday. It was a distress call being passed on by Marine Rescue and Control Centre (MRCC) Australia. The vessel in trouble was the yacht *Algimouss*. Poor sods. I wondered who they were and hoped I wouldn't be joining them. I assumed that she was somewhere near the Australian coast. I extricated a chart from the mess, plotted their position and did a double take. They were about 160 miles away. Who the hell would be daft enough to be down here? It never occurred to me that it might be one of us. The name *Algimouss* meant nothing to me as race communications had used the name of the skipper rather than the name of the boat.

The satcom bleeped again. This time the message was from Philippe Jeantot. The mayday *was* from one of us. *Algimouss* was Raphael Dinelli's boat and he was in trouble. Philippe asked if I could help. I took another look at the chart and realised that things were pretty bad: not only was Raphael 160 miles away from me but he was also to windward in atrocious conditions. But I had to go, I knew that. It was that simple; the decision had been made for me a long time ago by a tradition of the sea. When someone is in trouble you help.

However, I needed a minute to grasp the enormity of it. How could we make headway in this weather? Would *Aqua Quorum* hold together? The reality of what lay ahead grabbed at my guts. It was a cold and clammy grasp. Having made the decision I sat down to contemplate the consequences. It was only for thirty seconds, a minute—I'm not sure. I thought about what I was about to put on the line: my family, my boat, my life. In my own little world it was a profound moment that I shall never forget. To me, and I am sure it is different for everyone, if you keep chipping away at life you will eventually get to a clear and simple crossroads. I knew I had to stand by my morals and principles. Not turning back, whatever the stakes, would have been a disservice to myself, my family and the spirit of the sea. I fired off a quick fax to Philippe and expressed my doubts as to our ability to make our way back to Raphael—but I was going anyway.

I ventured on deck and the fight began. I had to think of it as a fight. I shouted at the wind and waves, and the anger helped to strengthen my resolve. We had to gybe. Oddly it was easy and went like clockwork. I brought *Aqua Quorum* up to face the wind, feeling the full force of the hurricane, as the wind across the deck immediately increased by the twenty-five-knot speed that I had been travelling downwind. The first gust put the guardrail under and the lower spreaders touched the water. I couldn't believe the energy that was whistling past. I winched in the storm jib hard, put the helm down again and waited to see what would happen. *Aqua Quorum* was game, it was as if she knew what was at stake. The mast slowly came upright and she began to move to windward. I couldn't believe that she was making about eight knots—sometimes more—as she climbed steeply to the wild, toppling crests at the apex of each huge wave, before accelerating down the fifty-foot slope on the other side and into the next trough. It wasn't quite the course I needed—eighty degrees to the wind was the best we could do—but it was a start, and the wind would ease soon. It had to.

Meanwhile it screamed deafeningly through the rigging, sounding like a jet taking off, as *Aqua Quorum* gamely struggled away.

It was impossible to breathe if I faced windward—the breath was sucked from my lungs—and I couldn't open my eyes.

Now that we were committed, I knew that we would do it somehow. The things I learned with the Royal Marines took over: be professional at all times, never give up and make intelligent use of everything on hand. I had asked a lot of my boats in the past, but never this much. I decided to take no prisoner. *Aqua Quorum* would do it or she would break up in the attempt; a man was out there and there could be no half measures. Night closed and we struggled on. The huge, breaking seas and the waves were horrifying.

I had to fire off a fax to Tracey as I didn't want her to hear about all this from someone else. I made the mistake of telling her not to worry which was something I had never done before. She told me later that it was the only time during the race that she became really concerned.

25 DEC 1996 15:56 FROM INMC VIA SENTOSA LES
Hi Tracey, Happy Xmas — I am in bad storm 60knts wind but fine, I stress fine. Another competitor is in distress & I am trying to make my way back to rescue him, I stress I am fine & storm may just be easing so don't worry. Wanted you to know before press start baying. Can't tell you how much I love you. Hope the Xmas meal/day has been good. Love to all. Pete XXXXX
FROM 423420410=AQUA X 25-DEC-1996 15:56:42
MSG214085 SENTOSA C IOR

Below it was an indescribable mess: water slopped about and a litre bottle of cooking oil had burst. Everything was coated with the stuff and it was slippery. I slithered and slid about—it was getting as dangerous below as it was on deck. My infected elbow took a bad blow and would cause problems from then on. A wave swept the deck with such ferocity that all the rope clutches opened. God, what next?

I crawled into the cockpit and we were knocked down again, this time beyond ninety degrees, and I felt myself falling out of the boat. *Aqua Quorum* came up, a spinnaker pole had burst its lashings at one end, the head car metal fitting at the top of the mainsail had broken, and both the mainsail and the number two, which were lashed to the deck, were ripped. I decided not to venture beyond the mast.

I was wet and very cold as I hadn't had the chance to put on my full thermals. I was also hungry. I got below, grabbed some food and shoved it down. Raphael needed someone in good shape. Come on, keep going, take charge. I could feel the first signs of hypothermia coming on, being soaked through and not wearing my heavy thermals. I put the kettle on and dragged my warmest thermals over the wet ones. A big wave hit the boat and the kettle hit the deckhead. I re-filled it and flashed up the stove again. This time I held the kettle down but with the next big wave both the kettle and I hit the deckhead. I crawled into my sleeping bag and tied myself into the bunk before dropping into semiconsciousness. The tea would have to wait.

I awoke with a jolt as we were knocked down again. We were being knocked down every half hour or so now. I was disoriented, tired and confused in the darkness. The cabin filled with a nauseating smell. My stores under the chart table had broken free and an aerosol can of oil was emptying itself. There were big sparks coming from under the table—the can had wedged itself across the live generator terminals and was causing a short circuit. A fire was all I needed.

The wind had lost its edge; I felt the worst was behind us. Hold on, Raphael. We had eighty miles to go and I could make the course. I updated Philippe, gulped some water, ate what I could and went back to my sleeping bag. I had to conserve energy because I felt my limits were not far off. I thought of Raphael out there and wondered how he could possibly survive. The wind was easing, we had got through round one, and I needed to make good use of my time in the corner before round two began. I worked as fast as I could; the wind was down to thirty-five knots now and I needed more sail up. I checked the deck and stowed the torn number two. I tackled the repair to the mainsail, drilling holes for the needle to save time. It took two and a half hours, every minute dragging. Raphael would be in a bad way by now—he had to be. I talked my way through possible first aid treatment as I sewed.

Job done, I went below and stowed the sailmaker kit, put a quick cup of tea on and . . . vrooooom . . . it was a Royal Australian Air Force rescue plane. They told me over the VHF radio that they had dropped Raphael two life rafts, he seemed well and was in an immersion suit. His yacht *Algimouss* was submerged. I took her position and asked if there were any other vessels involved in the rescue. 'No, sir, we're pinning our hopes on you,' came the reply. Fine. We'd do it.

Round two began as the aircraft's engines faded into the distance. I spent a quiet few minutes working out my next actions as *Aqua Quorum* continued to bash her way to windward. I needed a new strategy because the fight had changed. My opponent was wily and I must adapt. More thought was required now and instinct and determination were not enough. I broke the way ahead into clearly defined chunks and mentally walked the course a few times. I felt as though I was actually there, each time throwing in a new problem and coming up with a practical solution. Every visualised run culminated in a successful rescue.

Phase one was a simple yacht race to Raphael's general location. Phase two would take a little more effort to crack. It was a big area and it would be like looking for a needle in a haystack, particularly as it would be getting dark. Phase three would be the pick-up. This could present all sorts of complications. No worries though. I had plenty of time for some more reruns of this phase. First of all I needed information and so I faxed Philippe and asked for a detailed twelve-hour weather forecast for my area. Philippe played a vital role throughout the operation.

Very soon a special forecast came through from Météo France: a front would arrive in the afternoon, the wind would head me all day, visibility would reduce and winds of forty knots were expected. This would add a good four hours to the passage and make it very hard to find Raphael. There was no room to manoeuvre. I just had to get on deck and sail like the devil. The rest of the day was spent concentrating on the boat speed—nothing dramatic, just sailing—and it was a relief, apart from the frustration of being headed off the course by the hour. I continually got updates on Raphael's position and drift. MRCC Australia confirmed that an RAAF plane would aid the rescue in the morning. This gave me great comfort for we had a safety net if I couldn't find him in the dark.

Provided Raphael could cope with the cold I felt we had him. I was now twenty miles directly downwind of him and started short-tacking up his drift line. It began to get dark. This could actually be a blessing if the raft had a light as it would make him easier to spot. The wind just would not settle and the autopilot found it hard to keep as close to the wind as I would have liked in the confused sea, so I went back to the helm. Some five hours later, we were five miles downwind of where Raphael should be, given his drift. I slowed *Aqua Quorum* down and popped up the mast to the first set of spreaders to try and catch a glimpse of him. In those seas, I needed a lot of luck.

I went below and saw that another message had come in. It was a position update and it had changed considerably. We had overshot the mark by seven miles. Philippe also informed me that he had seen a photograph taken from the RAAF plane. *Algimouss* had been dismasted and was submerged. There was nothing to be seen apart from the life raft and he thought the yacht may have sunk by now anyway. There was no point in looking for a mast. The needle in the haystack got smaller.

I sailed back to the exact position I had been given and, as I was to windward, I dropped the main and zigzagged down his drift line under storm jib, keeping the speed down to between three and five knots. It was very dark and the front had arrived. A sense of desperation set in as the wind rose and visibility fell. I stood on the bow, blasting the foghorn and firing rocket flares. If only I could attract Raphael's attention, he could the let off a flare and we would have cracked it. 'Come on, Raphael. Wake up,' I shouted into the darkness. There was no response, just an enveloping greyness that soaked up my attempts to penetrate it.

I reached the end of his projected drift line. He was here, I knew it. I could feel it and yet emptiness pervaded. Come on, come on, we didn't tackle that storm for this. Give us a break, Neptune, surely we deserved one now. I decided to carry on the run until I had doubled his drift. We had to exhaust each avenue. Nothing.

Right. We turned round, got the main up and worked back. We'd bloody well do this all night if we had to. You'll never grind us down, damn you. The main kept jamming in the lazy jacks. My elbow ached and there was no strength. I had to be methodical. Persistence would pay. I nipped below and another position came in. It had changed and the drift was different. All that for nothing. I started to replot the position, but there were now two charts swimming before my eyes as if I were drunk. I just couldn't work it out. The first plot put him a crushing sixty miles away. Whoa, hang on, that wasn't right. I went on deck and stuck my head in a bucket of water. It was the first time I was thankful that the Southern Ocean was cold. I went back to the chart table and started again. It made sense now. He was six miles away and the plot was quite recent. Dawn had arrived. I rammed down some cold beans, a mug of cold water, and went back to concentrating on boat speed. It seemed an eternity before we arrived at the new waypoint and the show started again.

Slowly, slowly. Concentrate, don't miss him. Come on, Raphael, bang off a flare or something. You have got to help yourself now. I am not enough. I tried the Navico hand-held VHF in desperation. It is waterproof and I could use it on deck. I got a response. 'Aqua Quorum, Aqua Quorum. This is Rescue 252. We have started our descent and should be with you in four minutes.' Thanks, guys. The relief was heady. Soon the RAAF plane flew past. They had a visual. He was three miles away and they would drop a smoke flare by him. I still couldn't see him. They turned and flew back toward me. As they passed over Raphael they flashed their lights. I took the best bearing of my life. They informed me there were two life rafts, Raphael was in the first and he had waved at them. Good lad, he must have the constitution of an ox. Phase three suddenly became simple.

I dropped the main, felt the wind and . . . there he was! As the life raft came into sight I judged the best approach. Port side. I had grablines all round the boat and a long line with two fenders on it aft just in case I overshot. Fifty, forty, thirty, twenty metres. It was going to be a good one. Thank heavens for all the practice. I ran forward and threw off the headsail halyard. Raphael gripped the grabline. Got him!

Wow, a true professional here. He insisted on passing me three distress beacons and a box of stores. There was a bottle of champagne. Oh go on, then, seeing as you've brought a drink. We both heaved and he was on deck. Just like that. The best Christmas present I've ever had, all wrapped up in an immersion suit.

My new passenger lay face down on the deck and tried to move, but he was too stiff and cold. It was hardly surprising—he had spent two days waiting for me to rescue him. I gently turned him over to reveal a nose and two very inflamed eyes surrounded by thick, yellowish wax. A feeble 'thank you' could be heard from inside the immersion suit. All I could see was his eyes and I shall never forget them. I had no idea that a pair of eyes could convey such a depth of relief and gratitude. I was cheered to see that Raphael could converse and that he tried to help himself—the last thing I wanted was a medical case. I dragged him back to the cockpit by his ankles; his feet were agonisingly painful because of the cold, and he couldn't walk. We worked together to get him under the cockpit overhang. I nipped up to the foredeck and raised the storm jib to steady the violent roll of *Aqua Quorum* in the swell. I set the autopilot and got back to Raphael.

His survival suit was inflexible and encrusted with salt, and it took five minutes to undress him. His hands and feet were in the worst condition: cold, colourless and useless. Skin came away on contact and I wondered if there would be long-term damage. The next

step was to get him below through the small hatch, which was difficult to negotiate at the best of times. He was very stiff—it was as
though rigor mortis was setting in—and it took a couple of attempts
before he tumbled through. Now he was below in my cramped, wet
little hell hole. It was a palace to him and he smiled weakly. I gave
him a quick clean with wet-wipes and towelled him down—no
major injuries, just bruising.

I put a dry set of thermals on him, pulled a woolly hat over
his head and eased him into my best sleeping bag. He couldn't
straighten out so I propped him in a sitting position against my kit-
bag and put a support under his knees. Every movement was slow
and painful for him. I bunged on the kettle and informed the
RAAF plane of the casualty's condition and thanked them for their
help. They asked my intentions. Crumbs, I hadn't thought that far.
I'd probably drop him off in Hobart. I asked the RAAF what I
should do with the life raft. Leave it, they said. I went on deck and
cast it off—it would probably bob around the Southern Ocean forever. The kettle was boiling and I made a very sweet cup of tea in a
cyclist's drinking bottle; I had it on board for just such an occasion
as it has a nipple on the top and you can't spill the contents. I
helped Raphael slowly and painfully wrap his frozen hands round
it. He took a sip and a look of pleasure lit up a face haggard beyond
its twenty-eight years. He told me later that it was as though he had
landed in England.

I filled my grandmother's old hot-water bottle and placed it
under his feet. As Raphael began to warm up he started to talk in a
mixture of broken English and French, which I found hard to understand. He wanted to share his ordeal, repeating himself many times
during the telling of how he fought off death for forty-eight hours. I
told him that he was a very lucky man to have survived. It was strange
to have another human on board after so long by myself. It was both
a pleasure and an intrusion. I had a bizarre urge to start tidying up.
Aqua Quorum could certainly do with it. What a boat! I felt a great
surge of pride at the fantastic job she had done.

Raphael was very weak and stiff and unable to get out of his bunk without help. His body had seized up after days of being huddled in a life raft in icy temperatures. Going to the toilet was a major task—I had to carry him to the bucket and support him there. The race doctor was a great help during this time, prescribing medication and giving advice. I administered muscle-relaxant drugs and gave Raphael physiotherapy in the form of stretching. It exhausted him but improved his mobility, and after five days he could get out of his bunk unaided. When he slept, the roll of the boat seemed to bring back memories of his ordeal and he had the odd nightmare.

The fax continued to pour out an endless stream of messages. Many were from Raphael's family and he did his best to translate them for me. His parents said that I was now part of the Dinelli family and a fax from his elder brother in Paris said: 'We have another brother now in Pete.' I was very touched by the warmth of those messages.

Four days after the rescue Raphael proposed by fax to his girlfriend Virginie on her birthday. I think that perhaps his close brush with death on the deck of *Algimouss* made him realise what was important in his life. She faxed back her acceptance and suggested that I be best man. I was honoured. It was time to have a go at the champagne. The satcom had endless messages for us and demands for our story poured in from the press. It appeared that our little adventure had caused quite a stir. For the moment I only communicated with the race doctor, Jean-Yves, about Raphael's condition. I was also concerned with trying to get the damage on board sorted out before I arrived in Hobart. I wanted a quick turnaround so that I could get on with the race, having lost many miles and a lot of time. I was told that the race committee would give me an allowance for the time lost during the rescue, but I felt it was all a bit hypothetical.

Apart from a quick handshake at the start of the race, I didn't really know Raphael, but we hit it off immediately. I was to discover over the next days that we were kindred spirits. I have since been told that it is unusual for the relationship between a casualty and the rescuer to be a successful one because of complex feelings of guilt, gratitude and debt. Not so with us. We felt we were facing the same foe. Any one of the competitors could have been in the path of the freak wave that capsized Raphael and destroyed *Algimouss*. There but for the grace of God . . .

However, all I really wanted to do once I had him sorted out and in a sleeping bag was to grab some sleep myself—I was already tired when we went into the storm, and by the time of the actual pick-up two days later I was exhausted. The trouble was that Raphael was on a survivor's high and kept rabbiting away. I just couldn't shut him up.

At first he kept repeating aspects of his rescue over and over again and it took a while to piece his ordeal together. His was a tale of quite extraordinary determination. There is no way that he should have survived for the length of time that he did. He had accepted that he was probably going to die, but he never gave up and kept pushing death before him, day by day, hour by hour, minute by minute. The man is a giant.

Raphael had been overtaken by an intense storm. The wind was blowing at hurricane strength—sixty-five knots and over—and increasing in the gusts to eighty knots. His boat was surfing on waves as high as a sixty-foot, six-storey building. It was too dangerous on deck and he was sheltering down below and trying to control the headlong rush of *Algimouss* with his autopilot. It was hopeless. He was trapped inside the upturned hull of *Algimouss* after being capsized by a huge wave which crashed across the boat, flipping it on its side and turning it upside down. He was strapped below in his seat with everything flying everywhere. He worked his way free and activated his satellite emergency radio beacons, praying that someone would hear his mayday. The mast broke and was pile-driving through the hull—water poured in through the holes it made. After freeing himself, he spent the next three hours in the galley with the water rising up to his thighs. The diesel tanks were leaking and the fumes were making him violently sick.

The mast eventually freed itself from the tangled rigging, passed through the side of the hull and the boat righted itself. He clambered into the cockpit, which was awash, clipped himself to the submerged hull, faced the fifty-foot seas and fought it out. Each wave that struck choked and froze him, the icy water working its way down inside his survival suit. He could feel his body locking up with the cold, and started dancing on the flooded deck to keep his circulation going. 'I must have looked like a madman,' he said later.

He had nothing to eat or drink as he clung on there for twenty-four hours. Huge waves were running and each time they swept the boat he could feel her starting to give up and begin to settle lower under his feet for her final trip to the bottom. He talked to her, shouted at her, and again and again she dragged herself back to the surface. He thought about Virginie and their daughter Philippine. He made plans for the future, determined to be positive. The ropes which attached his life raft to the hull parted in the savage winds, and he was forced to watch his last hope of survival blow away.

He held out through that night and thought that all was lost until the RAAF, who played such a brave and vital part in his rescue, turned up and dropped him another life raft. He clambered on board, taking with him some food and a bottle of champagne which had washed to the surface. Inside the life raft was a message in French saying that Pete Goss and *Aqua Quorum* were ten hours away, due south. Five minutes later *Algimouss* finally succumbed to the Southern Ocean and sank beneath the waves to begin her long journey, 3,500 metres down to the sea bed. Then began the struggle for survival in the life raft until we finally arrived on the scene.

For me it did not end with picking up Raphael. It was probably the toughest physical and mental ordeal I had ever been through and I didn't realise the extent of the toll it had taken until a few days later when I was sitting on deck, enjoying the sunshine and the brightness of the day. I had just given Raphael a decent physio session and he was asleep. Suddenly I found tears rolling down my cheeks. I don't think I was crying in the normal sense of the word—I certainly wasn't grieving for anything. It was a release of the tension that I had bottled up during the previous five days. I was thoroughly exhausted. I had been shocked when I changed out of my thermals after the rescue—I barely recognised my body for bruises and weight loss. I reckon I lost at least half a stone in thirty hours. The tears didn't take long to clear. I had just explained how I felt in a fax to Tracey:

> **29 DEC 1996 05:27 FROM INMC VIA SENTOSA LES TO 001441503230779**
> Hi Tracey, Raphael is asleep. I have just given him a physio session & he is improving although still not well. I just wanted to express my feelings to you as a shoulder to cry on ... I feel quite traumatised at the moment, very tired & a bit emotional about the whole thing. It was a very bad experience & I now have to get myself back together, drop off Raphael and try to start all over again having lost my stride. I don't think it will be easy & I'm not looking forward to it ... I'm on top of it but it just helps to share it. AQ is fine & I do little repair jobs every day—she is brilliant & it was she who saved the day ... Tell the kids I love them loads & thank them for the cards they sent me. I had a good Christmas because I saved a man's life & he is OK. I am sailing home as fast as I can to give them a big hug. Thanks, Tracey. I feel better now, you know how it is. Love you loads 'n loads. Pete.
> **FROM 423420410=AQUA X 29-DEC-1996 05:28:14**
> **MSG232858 SENTOSA C IOR**

There was a language barrier between Raphael and me—he spoke only schoolboy English and I couldn't speak French. At first we communicated by using pictures and sign language but by the end of the ten days that it took us to get to Hobart we were having pretty deep conversations. As the journey went on Raphael's English grew better and better, the words just seemed to come. First, his understanding of what I was saying increased, and then, he began to reply more and more fluently.

We talked about our families and pretty much everything else—from life generally, to boat design and the ideas he had in mind for his next Vendée, and personal relationships. Sometimes it would take a whole day to get one fairly simple point across, but we would always get there in the end.

Our paths leading up to the Vendée start line were pretty similar. Like me he had been endlessly beset by one financial crisis after another. I told him about having to sell our home, and how I was worried about how Tracey and I were going to manage to pay the heating bills when I got back after the race. England was in the grip of a particularly vicious winter and Tracey was struggling to keep our rented cottage warm. Raphael told me about his struggle to find a boat and fund his campaign—only to be refused official status in the Vendée at the last moment by the race committee because he hadn't been able to complete his qualifying passage. He decided he would sail the course as an unofficial entrant, an outsider. Nothing was going to stop him taking part in the Vendée. Like me, he had dreamed long and hard about the race.

As Raphael gradually became a little more mobile he busied himself below with some light tidying up and trying to sort out the mess caused as *Aqua Quorum* fought her way back through the storm to find him. Food packages had burst and the contents were strewn everywhere. While he was putting my stores in order he found a number of cassette tapes which were hidden away along with some other surprise Christmas presents—my other tapes had long since been destroyed by water cascading below during a storm. The Walkman was still working and so Raphael and I took turns in enjoying the tapes—we discovered a shared pleasure in music. Next he came across a Christmas card from my children which had survived the soaking that had ruined all my other Christmas cards, along with the presents, early in the race. When I read the greetings from Alex, Olivia and Eliot I had a lump in my throat.

I had my share of finds as well. While I was working on the generator on New Year's Day I stumbled across a shrink-wrapped

Christmas pudding wedged up in a corner of the engine. Perfect tim-
ing. We celebrated New Year's Eve with Christmas pud and some
half-bottles of wine that had escaped the bashing. Raphael and I got
very drunk. Among the Christmas presents were a couple of party
hats—a pair of headphones dressed up like a Christmas cracker with
the word 'BANG!' printed across them for Raphael, and a bobble hat
with rude words and funny sayings sewn on for me. As midnight
neared we pledged that we would race together in the future when
things were on a more even keel. The constant crashing and bouncing
caused by the gale which raged outside barely seemed to matter as we
toasted in the New Year. It was a great party.

The Story of Sailing

From *My World—and Welcome to It*

BY JAMES THURBER

A N AMERICAN HUMORIST probably best known for *The Secret Life of Walter Mitty,* Thurber joined Harold Ross's newly established *The New Yorker* where his wry humor showed great sensitivity to human foibles.

He was, however, no sailor and his attempt to understand sailors and their lingo led to the following piece.

PEOPLE WHO VISIT YOU IN Bermuda are likely to notice, even before they notice the flowers of the island, the scores of sailing craft which fleck the harbors and the ocean round about. Furthermore, they are likely to ask you about the ships before they ask you about the flowers, and this, at least in my own case, is unfortunate, because although I know practically nothing about flowers, I know ten times as much about flowers as I know about ships. Or at any rate, I did before I began to study up on the subject. Now I feel that I am pretty well qualified to hold my own in any average discussion of rigging.

I began to brush up on the mysteries of sailing a boat after an unfortunate evening when a lady who sat next to me at dinner turned to me and said, "Do you reef in your gaff-topsails when you are close-hauled or do you let go the mizzen-top bowlines and crossjack braces?" She took me for a sailor and not a landlubber, and of course I hadn't the slightest idea what she was talking about.

One reason for this was that none of the principal words (except *reef*) used in the sentence I have quoted is pronounced the way it is spelled: *gaff-topsails* is pronounced "gassles," *close-hauled* is pronounced "cold," *mizzen-top bowlines* is pronounced "mittens," and *crossjack braces* is pronounced "crabapples" or something that sounds a whole lot like that. Thus, what the lady really said to me was, "Do you reef in your gassles when you are cold or do you let go the mittens and crabapples?" Many a visitor who is asked such a question takes the first ship back home, and it is for these embarrassed gentlemen that I am going to explain briefly the history and terminology of sailing.

In the first place, there is no doubt but that the rigging of the modern sailing ship has become complicated beyond all necessity. If you want proof of this, you have only to look up the word *rigging* in the *Encyclopaedia Britannica*. You will find a drawing of a full-rigged modern ship and under it an explanation of its various spars, masts, sails, etc. There are forty-five different major parts, beginning with *bowsprit* and going on up to *davit topping lifts*. Included in between are, among others, these items: the fore-topmast staysail halyards (pronounced "fazzles"), the topgallant mastyard-and-lift (pronounced "toft"), the mizzen-topgallant brace (pronounced "maces"), and the fore-topmast backstays and topsail tye (pronounced "frassan-tossle"). The tendency of the average landlubber who studies this diagram for five minutes is to turn to *Sanscrit* in the encyclopedia and study up on that instead, but only a coward would do that. It is possible to get something out of the article on rigging if you keep at it long enough.

Let us creep up on the formidable modern sailing ship in our stocking feet, beginning with one of the simplest of all known sailing craft, the Norse Herring Boat. Now when the Norse built their sailing boats, they had only one idea in mind: to catch herring. They were pretty busy men, always a trifle chilly, and they had neither the time nor the inclination to sit around on the cold decks of their ships trying to figure out all the different kinds of ropes, spars and sails that might be hung on their masts. Each ship had, as a matter of fact, only one mast. Near the top of it was a crosspiece of wood and on that was hung one simple square sail, no more complicated than the awning of a cigar store. A rope was attached to each end of the crosspiece and the other ends of these ropes were held by the helmsman. By manipulating the ropes, he could make the ship go ahead, turn right or turn left. It was practically impossible to make it turn around, to be sure, and that is the reason the Norsemen went straight on and discovered America, thus proving that it isn't really necessary to turn around.

As the years went on and the younger generations of Norsemen became, like all younger generations, less hardworking and more restless than their forebears, they began to think less about catching herring and more about monkeying with the sails of their ships. One of these restless young Norsemen one day lengthened the mast of his ship, put up another crosspiece about six feet above the first one and hung another but smaller sail on this new crosspiece, or spar (pronounced, strange as it may seem, "spar"). Thus was the main topsail born.

After that, innovations in sails followed so fast that the herring boat became a veritable shambles of canvas. A Norseman named Leif the Sailmaker added a second mast to his ship, just in front of the first one and thus the foremast came into being and with it the fore mainsail and the fore topsail. A Turk named Skvar added a third mast and called it the mizzen. Not to be outdone, a Muscovite named Amir put up a third spar on each of his masts; Skvar put up a fourth; Amir replied with a fifth; Skvar came back with a sixth, and so it went, resulting in the topgallant foresail, the top-topgallant mizzen sail, the top-top-topgallant main topsail, and the tip-top-top-gallant-gallant mainsail (pronounced "twee twee twee twa twa").

Practically nobody today sails a full-rigged seven-masted ship, so that it would not be especially helpful to describe in detail all the thousands of different gaffs, sprits, queeps, weems, lugs, miggets, loords (spelled "leewards"), gessels, grommets, etc., on such a ship. I shall therefore devote what space I have left to a discussion of how to come back alive from a pleasant sail in the ordinary twenty- or thirty-foot sailing craft such as you are likely to be "taken for a ride" in down in Bermuda. This type of so-called pleasure ship is not only given to riding on its side, due to coming about without the helmsman's volition (spelled "jibe" and pronounced "look out, here we go again!"), but it is made extremely perilous by what is known as the flying jib, or boom.

The boom is worse than the gaff, for some people can stand the gaff (hence the common expression "he can stand the gaff"), but nobody can stand the boom when it aims one at him from the floor. With the disappearance of the Norse herring fisherman and the advent of the modern pleasure-craft sailor, the boom became longer and heavier and faster. Helmsmen will tell you that they keep swinging the boom across the deck of the ship in order to take advantage of the wind, but after weeks of observation it is my opinion that they do it to take advantage of the passengers. The only way to avoid the boom and have any safety at all while sailing is to lie flat on your stomach in the bottom of the ship. This is very uncomfortable on account of the hard boards and because you can't see a thing, but it is the one sure way I know of to go sailing and come back in the boat and not be washed up in the surf. I recommend the posture highly, but not as highly as I recommend the bicycle. My sailing adventures in Bermuda have made me appreciate for the first time the essential wonder of the simple, boomless bicycle.

The Fisherman's Cup Races:
Last Act

From Wanderer

BY STERLING HAYDEN

A NAUTICAL VERSION OF the rivalry between the Hatfields and the McCoys was the long-running battle between two famed fishing schooners: the *Bluenose,* skippered by Captain Angus Walters of Nova Scotia; and Captain Ben Pine's *Gertrude L. Thebaud* from Gloucester. The two raced, officially and unofficially, for more than twenty years.

In 1938, a young Sterling Hayden served both as the navigator and as the daredevil mastheadman aboard the *Thebaud* in that year's race. With the tall blond looks of a Viking god, he was quickly discovered by Hollywood and, though he only wanted to earn enough to buy his own schooner, he was soon a movie star. His career started and stopped many times: during World War II when he fought with Italian partisans and after the war when he was blacklisted as a communist. Best known as General Jack D. Ripper in *Dr. Strangelove,* as the fall guy of *The Asphalt Jungle,* and as the bad cop in *The Godfather,* he once took his children in defiance of a divorce decree and set sail across the Pacific with them.

Through it all, his one true love was the sea and, whether he was sailing a schooner in the Pacific, living aboard a barge in France, or looking over San Francisco Bay from his home in Sausalito, he was, first and foremost, a sailor.

OUT OF GLOUCESTER, A WEEK before the first race, forty men and one tall ship bound on a trial run. Pitted against the clock. Against some wind as well—ragged brawling wind blowing a southeast gale. Storm warnings fly beneath a dull gray sky, and leaves skirmish. (Out on the Banks, no dories will work this day, and up in Boston, girls clutch skirts and hats go tumbling to leeward.)

Half past ten, says a belfry clock. Captain Ben Pine stands by the wheel. You would swear he was part of his ship—in spite of the blue-vested suit, the brown felt hat and a red bow tie. More like a coach he looks than like a racing-schooner skipper.

A motor launch tows the *Thebaud* free of the wharves and holds her head to the wind. "You can set your mainsail now," Ben says softly. Forty men to the halyards—peak to starboard, throat to port. Twenty men to a side—to lay back hauling, grunting at first, then gasping. Big new halyards an inch and a half in a diameter. The canvas flogs. All over the harbor you hear it. (Plenty of empty seats in Gloucester's schools. Plenty of hooky players hiding out in wharves.)

"Now go ahead on your foresail." Ben spits in his hands and paces in front of the wheel, feeling the wind and gauging the heft of the ship. Putting pieces together like an artist, working with wood and wind, buoys and rocks and anchored vessels, painting a wind-blown scene.

"Run up your jumbo and jib." His voice edged now, the coach look lost. The decks a tangle of gear; of mooring warps, gaskets, lifts, sheets, runners, tackles and halyards. (Paid for by townsmen who donated money or labor, by riggers and shipwrights and sailmakers who worked for almost nothing.) Ben spits as he gauges and measures. The towline is gone, and the bow cants fast to starboard. She starts to move through the water. Most skippers would be content to run for the open sea, but not Ben Pine.

Cordage bites into grooved oak rails. Like an iron-capped lance, her bowsprit flies toward Sherm Tarr's office window. A sharp puff rams home in her sails and lays the vessel over. Her rail smokes.

Dead toward the dock she goes. Anyone who doesn't know schooners would swear something is wrong.

She goes now. Better than ten she goes. Up aloft, you hear a deep rumbling roar—and the hissing of spray. Square in mid-channel lies an old-time sailing vessel—a brigantine with a lascar crew, hailing from Ceylon. Her name stands out—*Florence C. Robinson*.

With a thrust of his fist, Ben orders a man aloft. Up he goes on the run till he reaches the masthead, where he heaves himself over the hounds, breathing hard, and goes to work with the topsail. "Stand by!" Ben's voice betrays his calm. One final look—full circle—with an arm flung wide for balance. Now he claws at the wheel, fighting it over. "Helm's alee!" For the first time, he really yells out.

She slashes into the wind. Canvas booms and sheet blocks dance under booms. Straight into the eye of the wind. (Not six feet separate her from the queer brig with the crew all wrapped in skirts and blankets—tumbling up on deck in response to a shipmate's warning.)

She passes across the wind, flung down to port. "Leggo your main sheet, boys." Ben is right where he wants to be. "Clear that coil—now let her run to the knot." The sheet runs snaking out till the knot fetches up in the block.

She swings toward the harbor entrance, and all around the harborside spurts of white stab from whistles—a pleasant sound, on a southeast day with rain.

Half a mile inside the breakwater she really begins to pitch, though the force of the wind is blunted. Both topsails are set. Down in the galley, they're mixing hot water with rum, butter and cinnamon.

Up aloft you hang on. Beyond the breakwater the wild Atlantic growls. Plumes of spray pounce on lighthouse windows. Your main-masthead is six feet higher than where Jack Hackett lives, thirty feet away. His voice is high and loud. "Oh dyin' Jaysus, boy, if she catches one o' them seas just right she'll pitch us clear to Newfoundland!" Up here, you feel the motion more. You feel her reach out over a sea and hang; then down she goes with a sickening rush, and the second after the crash your mast goes buckling forward with a sideways motion. You wonder how wood can take it. (This goes on for an hour and more. Then both topsails are furled so as not to do any damage.)

Boudreau comes up from the galley, wiping his lips, leaning in to the weather rail, shoulders hunched. His yellow oilskins shine. He rests one knee on the deck and jams one booted leg out stiff against a hatch as he watches the vessel go. Low in the water she flies; two feet of sifting water conceal her rail. Her long bow threads through breaking seas, reaching high, plunging down, always with the roar in the shrouds. He thrashes his arms and screams: "Fourteen, goddamn it, boys, fourteen she goes or I hope to die with a hard-on!"

Ben by the lee of the wheel, fondling the spokes, feeling her go—knee deep in water. Satisfied.

Captain Angus Walters swung his big salt-banker *Bluenose* in past the Boston lightship, strapped her down and sent her rampaging up harbor in time for a welcoming luncheon thrown by the governor on behalf of the Commonwealth. Those who were there pronounced it a dandy affair; plenty of dames, plenty of booze, plenty of platitudes. Captain Angus wasn't there. He stayed by his vessel instead. "Let 'em spout," he barked. "I'm gettin' ready to race."

The mayor of Gloucester passed the word to the better saloons down on Duncan Street that he expected a little decorum, a little restraint . . . during the racing. When they heard this, the boys in the red jackboots and the checked shirts smiled. Saloon keepers are smart: by the time the *Bluenose* arrived there wasn't a piece of movable furniture in a single waterfront bar.

October came in like a lamb, mewed for a few days, roared like a lion for the better part of two weeks, then trailed off into November. The first two races were sailed in moderate winds and sunshine. *Thebaud* took the first one by thirty seconds, and *Bluenose* waltzed off with the second. During the scheduled three-day hiatus that followed, Gloucester got down on its knees and prayed for a living gale. While Gloucester was busy praying, Angus Walters took advantage of the moonless midnight hours to scan the weather forecasts and juggle around with his ballast. When the Clerk of the Weather predicted a breeze of wind—into the *Bluenose* went an extra ton or two of pig-iron ballast. When the clerk called for light airs—back on the wharf went the pigs. Pretty clever. It was also against the rules that governed the races. But Captain Elroy Proctor of the Master Mariners Association and Miss Ray Adams, Ben Pine's partner, were pretty clever too. They sprinkled a layer of sand over the ballast pile, and Angie was caught red-handed. "Some cute," said Gloucester. What Angus said did not appear in the *Gloucester Times.* Everybody shrugged. After all, the little Lunenburger was more than just a rack racing skipper: he was renowned as a dairyman, and, like all businessmen, he wanted to win and to hell with your goddamn rules.

The day of the third race dawned with rain and a driving easterly gale. All but one of the *Thebaud's* crew smiled, and I was the one who didn't. The reason was simple enough: only the day before, I had been turned from mastheadman to navigator because my predecessor had got all but lost in the second race. To make things worse, Captain Pine was in the hospital with a sinus attack.

A cannon on the Coast Guard boat let go with a puff of smoke and the race was on. Both schooners hit the starting line going twelve knots and the Canadian pulled ahead. Captain Cecil Moulton hung to the *Thebaud's* wheel with his boots full of water and his cap rammed down on his eyes. We averaged thirteen and a half to the first mark, where forty brawny Gloucestermen lay back chanting and straining on swollen manila sheets. "Haul, you bastards, haul!" cried Harry the cook, buried waist deep in the hatch, clutching his derby in one hand, a mug of rum in the other.

The *Bluenose* tore past the plunging buoy two lengths ahead of us and swung hard on the wind. Her long black snout, streaming spray, reached over a steep sea, then fell like a maul into the trench beyond. Her scarred old timbers shuddered. Her spars pitched hard against their tracery of shrouds. High far aloft, her foretopmost backstay parted and the wire rained down on deck. Fiery Angus—never a man noted for patience—laid down on the wind-honed waters a savage barrage of four-letter words.

With this stay gone, they were forced to strike their big jib topsail. The smaller *Thebaud* forced by to windward, slogging her way uphill now, through charging white-plumed seas. This was the windward leg. Fifteen miles away, dead into the eye of the wind, lay a small white buoy. The visibility was about two hundred yards at best—less in the squalls, of course. Back and forth the two great wagons tacked, sawing away at the base course. When they came about, you could hear the flogging of canvas halfway to Scollay Square. I'm all right, I kept reassuring myself, so long as the wind doesn't shift. If we can't find the buoy, they'll not blame me too much, what with this horsing around, first to the southeast, then to the northeast—with Christ knows what for a current setting beneath the keel. But if the wind should haul and we run for the mark—and I have to conjure a fixed course—what in hell then?

The wind hauled. I pored over the chart, gauging and guessing and praying. I crossed myself twice, exhaled with resignation and called out to Cecil: "Let her go east by south and a quarter south."

"East by south and a quarter south it is!" his voice came through the hatch. I wished I were Irving Johnson. I wished myself back on the masthead, where there was nothing to do but curse, work and spit downwind—all the while thinking how tough you were. I took the binoculars and made my way forward past the prone bodies of thirty men—half of whom were skippers of lesser craft. I climbed halfway up the lee fore rigging, locked my legs through the ratlines and smoked. For forty minutes, she blazed a trail with her rail buried deep in foam. The harder I looked, the less I saw. Either that, or there were buoys everywhere: dozens of baby buoys bouncing around plunging like pistons between helmeted seas.

"That's it, isn't it, Hayden?" Cooney the sailmaker called from his place in the bows.

"I think so," I called back calmly, seeing nothing yet, stealing a glance at him from under my binoculars. The *Bluenose* was far astern. The buoy lay dead ahead. If Cecil hadn't knocked her off a touch, we might have run it down. You lucky bastard, I muttered under my breath; and, swinging down to the deck, I sauntered aft, looking the world in the eye, vindicated, my belly afire with pride.

Rounding the mark, we flew downwind like a gull, bound for the finish line. The Coast Guard boat, with its cargo of seasick race committeemen, had quit and run for the cover of Boston. We clocked ourselves across the line. But fishermen are casual about some things. Nobody knew for certain whether we should leave the marker to port or starboard; so we finished twice for good measure, then jogged along slowly, the gang all on their feet, tired—but not too tired to line the rail and give three cheers when the big Queen of the North Atlantic came booming down on the line.

A late October day and the racing is finished, forever. Five thousand people are gathered under the Gloucester sun, with Legion and high-school bands, with the governor himself on hand, along with half a dozen subgovernors, surplus mayors and councilmen. Natives mingle with tourists in for the day, newsmen audit the scene with cameras and pencils and cabled microphones. This is an occasion: it marks the formal dedication of the big, new red-brick fish pier, financed in part by the PWA—with greetings from FDR.

Moored to the dock in the place of honor lie the two great racing schooners, victor and vanquished: *Bluenose* and *Thebaud*. The former had retained her title as champion of the North Atlantic, taking the last two races by a wide margin in what Gloucester called with contempt "New York Yacht Club weather." Both ships are dressed in flags this hot and windless day, and the traffic on Main Street is snarled. Tomorrow it will be over and the saloons will blossom with tables and chairs and benches.

A politician speaks. Hear him now, a comical cutout figure, full of brass, tempered in booze, bursting with plans for the future—

his future: "And so, friends, we are met this glorious fall day, not just to dedicate this marvel of brick and mortar, but to pay our respects to those men, living and dead, who for more than three hundred years have gone down to the terrible sea in frail barks to reap from it a harvest of fish. Now, friends, and fellow citizens of this great commonwealth, and our neighbors from across the gulf, it is altogether fitting that—"

From the fish hold of the *Bluenose* comes the sound of a trumpet muted by three-inch pine. A journalist stalks through the mob. His shirt is drenched and he harbors a terrible thirst as he swings to the deck of the *Bluenose*. Fishermen guard each hatch, for the party below is by invitation only—given by the crews of the schooners in their own honor, and maybe that of the press. No one else is welcome.

He shows his card: Tom Horgan, Associated Press. They give him a nod and down the ladder he goes to the cavernous hold. Here ninety men are assembled out of the sun, away from the politicians and tourists, the kids and the wives. They're assembled this day to bury some hatchets and kill a few kegs of rum. Up and down this cave, long bundles of sail are spread, with flags nailed to the inner hull. Hymie Rodenhauser, one of the *Bluenose*'s mastheadsmen, straddling a keg in a cradle, is blasting loose with his trumpet. A bedlam of laughter and singing and wild gesticulations seen through a pall of smoke.

Horgan is handed a cup. He raises his fist. "To the *Bluenose!* I say we drink to this ship!" A hand is slammed on his back. "I say we pretty damn well better drink to this ship, Tom, or else get our ass knocked off." The man who says this is pleasantly drunk. His head is large, with a domed brow and bright eyes, a big nose that leads to an upturned mouth. His hands are those of an artist. His name is Lawrence Patrick Joseph O'Toole ("Of the South Boston O'Tooles," he says). Along this coast he is a legend; if you want him any time, look down on T Wharf, where he hangs out, living with Horgan sometimes, or with any one of a thousand friends. People like to have him around because he makes them happy. He doesn't drive a car and he is always broke, and the worse things are, the more he laughs, painting away at his pictures of people and ships, or carving a figurehead.

Tom Horgan drains his cup. "Larry, you miserable bastard, why aren't you up on the dock making a speech or something?" O'Toole looks around and places a finger to his lips. "Sh-h-h," he whispers, "to the health of the poor old *Thebaud.*"Their cups meet. A man comes by with a pail full of rum. It slops when he ladles it out. O'Toole scoops deep with his cup.

Now they edge their way to a corner where a friend sits mute on a blown-out stays'l. "All right," says Tom, "I shall now propose a toast: To the best damn man to sail out of Gloucester in many a fucked-up year."

"Hear! Hear!" says O'Toole. "That's right."

The friend seems a little embarrassed. "Oh no," he smiles with a deprecatory nod, "don't say that."

"Whaddaya mean, 'Oh no'? You know who said that? Ben Pine said that. Don't be so goddamned modest."

"Then, I drink to Ben," says the friend, killing what's left in his cup.

A figure bursts into the hold, blowing the cook's tin whistle. "All right you bassards, up, up, everybo'y up on the goddamn deck! Hear me? The governor's gonna make us his honorin' speech, an' the mayor wants every friggin' one o' you on th' deck . . . An' leave the booze down here . . . An' no more friggin' noise! Hear?"

No one moves. "Drink up!" roars O'Toole. You can hear the Legion band playing the National Anthem. All rise. When the anthem expires, they sit—among them, three friends: Horgan, O'Toole and Hayden.

Requiem. Midnight. The dock is deserted, the flags make an arch in the rigging, and the night around is cool, calm and clear. Aloft on the *Thebaud's* mainmast, a man lies flat in the crosstrees, staring up at the stars. His legs are crossed at the ankles, one fist is full of a halyard. Up past the head of the pier, the streetlights blink when crossed by nodding branches.

(We approach this man . . . gently . . . intent on asking some questions . . . on probing his mind just a little.)

"Hey. [*softly*] Hey, you on a mainmasthead—"

"Yes?"

"You're sober, we trust."

"I'm sober enough."

"Where, if you don't mind the asking, where will you go from here, now that the racing is ended?"

"Oh hell," he sighs heavily, "I don't have the least idea." His eyes keep staring up.

"They say that, during the course of the races, you really distinguished yourself."

"Do they?"

"Yes. [*A rustling of paper is heard*] Yes, they do. We quote from the *Boston Post*, dated October 24, 1938: The mettle of the *Thebaud's* crew was tested when a block on the end of the main gaff began tearing out under the pressure of wind-tautened wet canvas. Sterling W. Hayden, the youngest and tallest of the Gloucesterman's crew, went inching out along the spar to secure the block along with Jack Hackett. The two men struggled there on this perilous perch, clinging against the blast of the gale, and—"

A hand is raised in the darkness. "Stop. That's enough."

"But there's more."

"I know; I read it all right, don't worry about that; made me feel good, I admit."

"Well, of course. [*Now a further rustling is heard*] And how about this? Again from the *Post*—under a big headline at the top of the second page, next to a picture of a face, close-up and grinning, showing some wind-tossed hair. THEBAUD SAILOR LIKE MOVIE IDOL. Gloucester Youth, 22, Born Sea Rover . . . Fine Masculine Specimen . . . Neat seamanship may decide the victor of the fishermen's races, but when it comes to masculine pulchritude, Sterling W. Hayden, tall, blond, and lithe, wins by 100 fathoms over fellow members of both crews. He stands straight as a ramrod and is six feet five inches tall ... More than a few of the scores of women who viewed the vessels yesterday at the fish pier inquired as to his identity ... "

"They did, eh?"

That's what it says in the paper.

The figure sweeps to an upright position and strikes a match off a shackle. "Yeah, yeah. I read that one, too. They shouldn't print stuff like that." Oh? why not?

"Because it makes you feel embarrassed. Besides, it's not even true."

What do you mean?

"Never you mind what I mean."

The Making of a Yachtsman

From *Yachtsman's Choice*

BY CONRAD MILLER

A S THE EDITOR OF *Rudder Magazine* in the early 1960s, Conrad Miller helped shape the magazine as a literate and informative periodical. The following piece suggests that yachtsmen are not born, but bred.

I AM A YACHTSMAN.

I am not a boater, nor an inboarder, nor an outboarder, nor a sailing enthusiast nor any kind of newfangled water sportsman. I'm a yachtsman.

Why do I claim the title yachtsman? Because I was raised in, on, and around boats. My father, brothers, and sisters all loved boats. We sailed under canvas, cruised under power, and generally gunk-holed around Barnegat from my pre-kindergarten days. To my family, boats were always a way of life—not a way of making a living, but an avocation more serious than idle hobby.

Amateur boatmen loving the water are yachtsmen. I don't like to hear people called boaters, or outboarders or sailboaters. The honorable word "yacht" has been altered by landsmen and status seekers to mean a large, private ship, very likely carrying a cargo of champagne and a crowd of rich stockbrokers complete with lady friends.

That, as Henry Mencken would say, is palpable buncombe.

A yacht is any boat used for sport, relaxation, or pleasure, and a yachtsman is one who operates a boat for fun and enjoyment. Only a pinched wouser or secluded reformer would claim it is sinful to operate a boat for pure enjoyment and relaxation. That's what boats, nay, yachts are for—enjoyment, health, fun.

What pushed the word "yachtsman" off into a corner with other half-bad words like "profit," "conservative" or "patriot"? Maybe they are old-fashioned words, but they are still good ones. Accurate, descriptive words have an honest place in the language even though given new, twisted meanings by journalists with leanings.

I am a yachtsman because when I was a school kid I used to sneak boating books and magazines behind the covers of the algebra text. I'd pretend to be studying, while drinking up boating lore and longing to be afloat. Boats, even the thought of them, were a release, an escape. Dreaming of water, beaches, and sails released me from the classroom and reality. My marks probably suffered, but my spirit did not.

Not that reality was unpleasant. I was raised in a home where boats were a common topic. Every winter morning I would go downstairs at 7:30 and grab *The New York Times,* not to read the news from Washington or other world capitals, but to glean news of frostbite sailing on Long Island Sound. Just reading about boats helped tide things over until spring when I could be afloat again.

How I counted the winter days waiting for the next issue of *Rudder!* William Albert Robinson was sailing *Svaap* around the world then and writing his adventures for *Rudder.* My dream was to follow in his footsteps.

During high school days (in the 1930s) my favorite books were Schoettle's classic *Sailing Craft,* and a salty, wonderfully mad book of the sea titled *Liverpool Jarge.*

Liverpool Jarge is a book you either read and throw aside in disgust, or read over and over again in delight. My younger brother, Fritz, and I read and reread *Liverpool Jarge* so many times the book became shredded. We used to quote whole salty passages and even complete pages of it to each other, laughing till we cried. Guests in the house would think we were crazy. But we were not crazy, just yachtsmen in the making.

As kids, we cruised our open, 16-foot sloop, *Vat-69,* on Barnegat Bay. The *Vat* was a stubby-masted, gaff-rigged sloop lacking freeboard, style, or speed. She was wet in the tiniest chop, but we kids loved our yacht and cruised it Huckleberry Finn style.

One night Fritz and I had been sailing off Waretown, where Barnegat's water is steep and choppy. It was late, and we were tired from a day of open cruising in the tiny sloop. The wind increased from the east; a dank drizzle started. To top our misery, the thermos jug broke, dumping the last of the hot coffee into the bilge. We were soaked, cold, unhappy. Fritz managed to light the kerosene lantern and rummaged in his duffle for something.

"What are you looking for?" I asked.

"The book," he replied. "I want to read a little of the gospel aloud."

"Good grief!" I shouted. "Things are wet and lousy, but we're not in danger. Belay the reading."

"'Alagazoo, Zip Bang. You're asleep,' he says. 'You can't move.' "'The hell I can't,' says Bull Taylor, very cross. And with that he fetches Jarge a cuff under the chops that knocks him clean across the deck, and he has to be carried below. That night, Jarge . . .'"

I burst out laughing. We both laughed, and he read until we had forgotten our soaked surroundings. Fritz was reading from our beloved *Liverpool Jarge*.

Since World War II there has been an emphasis on safe boating. Serious safety programs are needed because of new boat owners, many not raised on the water and lacking that inbred caution.

Safety programs remind me of things we did as youngsters. Perhaps they sound wild now, but I really think most were well-planned adventures. Anyway, they were part of a yachtsman's making.

In our 16-foot gaff-rigger, with sail and paddle alone, we used to challenge Manasquan inlet. This may shock some moderns who hesitate to tackle the nasty inlet with twin 300-horse engines.

Our secret, of course, was to play the tides. We would study and plot the tide flow. Then we'd ride the ebb tide out to the ocean in the morning and catch the flow back in the afternoon.

We stayed close to shore and always planned to beach the boat if a thunderstorm came up while we sailed the ocean waves. One August afternoon we had a chance to prove our strategy. A mean-looking black squall towered to the west of Bay Head. Getting back through the inlet was impossible. The tide was still ebbing fast, and sail power does not buck that kind of current.

We sailed close to the breakers, doused all sail, lashed things secure. Then with paddles we took the 16-footer through the surf and to the beach. A few feet from the sloping sand we dived and dragged the bow up the white beach. A dozen willing swimmers and sun bathers helped us pull the boat clear of the surf.

I remember sailing away after the squall passed. We pushed and paddled the boat out past the breakers, made sail, and headed north to the inlet. We were pleased with ourselves and proud of our boat handling. We were yachtsmen in the making.

Years later, on a less happy, darker day I was wading through the surf near Oran, North Africa. My thoughts flashed back to that pleasant landing operation at Bay Head. Thinking about it helped.

One summer at Mantoloking my brothers and I learned a lot about yachts and the gentlemen who build them.

The Mantoloking Boat Works was always referred to by us young scallywags as Scotland Yard, because our good friend, the chief boat-builder, was a Scotsman named Dave Beaton. Dave had a charming Scotch burr and a twinkle in his eye never to be forgotten. He loved boats and people. He particularly loved young yachtsmen in the making.

Dilapidated was the word for the old catboat, *Joy,* lying in the grass at Scotland Yard. The old yacht was so dry and the seams so open that grass grew in her bilge. She suffered from considerable rot, had broken frames and no rudder. But my brothers and I wanted her more than anything else. Dave said she'd been abandoned by her owner and if we'd pay the $25 yard bill she was ours, complete with a good sail. Pop staked us to the price and said he'd pay for paint, caulking, and materials.

Then we started.

For weeks we caulked, sanded, painted, fixed, and repaired. Slowly the *Joy* took shape. A yacht grew in place of the wreck.

Dave gave us lots of encouragement and expert guidance. One day he said, "Boys, you'll have to have a rudder made before you can sail the *Joy.*"

"Right, Dave," we agreed. "Pop will make it for us. Cabinet work is Pop's hobby, and hardwood importing is his business, so he has the skill and material to build a good, big rudder."

So we asked Pop to make us a sound, substantial rudder for the catboat *Joy.*

And he made the rudder. Oh, dear Lord what a rudder! Never has such a rudder been seen before or since. To this day, *that* rudder is discussed by all who saw it. Especially it is discussed by the good Scot, Dave Beaton. The episode was almost thirty years ago, yet Dave always mentions "that rudder" when we meet today.

Pop is a cabinet maker by hobby. He imports hardwood by the thousands of tons as a business. What could be more natural then, that he pull a thick three-inch piece of beautiful, flame-grain mahogany from the rack and carve it into a rudder? That's just what he did. The rudder was one big lovely slab of the most flawless, thick mahogany I've ever seen. It was magnificent. It could have been a dining table in a baron's hall.

Dave took one look at that beautiful, golden wood, the flawless workmanship, the expensive flame grain. Then he looked at the miserable old *Joy*. It was too much for the good Scot.

"You can't do it! You can't do it!" cried Dave. "Mr. Miller, you just can't put a hundred dollar rudder on a twenty-five dollar boat!" Dave walked away shaking his head. "When you sell the *Joy*, please sell me the rudder," he pleaded.

We said we would.

But we never kept the promise. The *Joy* was lost in a northeast storm the following winter, and that beautiful mahogany rudder drifted somewhere down Barnegat Bay.

It was all in the making of a yachtsman.

All at Sea

From *Two-and-a-Half-Ton Dream*

BY RAY WHITAKER

I T IS THE AVERAGE SAILOR, the one who will never set any records or win any major trophies, who really populates the sailing world. It is you and I who wonder what that noise is in the middle of the night, who scuff the hull when docking, who always forget the square knot is over-then-under and end up with a granny.

Anyone who has spent a night aboard their boat at anchor will recognize the following scenario. It is, perhaps, a more accurate portrait of the common sailor than all the stories of round-the-world races, harrowing storms, and legendary voyages.

I SHUT MY EYES. IT WAS wonderful just to relax. I knew it wouldn't be long before I was asleep.

Then I heard the noise. It was a sort of grating sound. It stopped after a moment or two. I lay, wide awake now, wondering what it was, and whether it would come again. I felt a niggling uneasiness. If there were going to be strange noises during the night, I wanted to know what made them.

The noise came again, after an interval of perhaps a couple of minutes. There was another interval, and then it sounded a third time.

I still didn't know what it was, but my resolve of a few minutes before to find out was failing. I was beginning to nod off. Whatever it was, it probably didn't matter very much. I decided to ignore it.

'Darling—' said a very drowsy voice from the other bunk.

'What? I thought you were asleep.'

'I was. But there's a queer sort of noise.'

'I know.'

'It woke me up.'

'I'm sorry.'

'What's making it?'

'I haven't a clue.'

'Does it matter?'

'Not in the least.'

'There isn't anything wrong, is there?'

'Of course there isn't.'

'But you don't know what's making it?'

'Not exactly.'

'Then how do you know there isn't anything wrong?'

'Oh—go to sleep.'

Silence again for a while, absolute and complete, apart from the faint soughing of the wind outside. Then the same noise came again. This time I realized what it was, and kicked myself for not having done so before.

'Darling, there's that noise again.'

'I heard it. It's nothing to worry about; it's only the anchor chain dragging over the bottom.'

'Does that matter?'

'Of course it doesn't.'

'You're sure it's only the chain dragging, and not the anchor?'

'Of course it isn't the anchor.'

'That's all right then. . . . Goodnight, darling.'

'Goodnight.'

Peace. The chain dragged again, but it was quite a pleasant sound, now that I knew what it was.

This time I really began to drift off to sleep—

'Darling—'

Somehow I struggled back to consciousness.

'What is it *now?*'

'You're *sure* it's not the anchor?'

'Absolutely certain.'

'That was an awfully long drag just now.'

'It's all *right.*'

'I do hope so . . . Darling—'

'For heaven's sake—'

'I'm sorry to be such a nuisance, but I wish you'd have a look and *see* that we're still in the same place. We don't want to drift out to sea, do we?'

I groaned, but I knew I was going to have to obey. The same sort of thing happened at home. Whenever there was an argument about whether I should get up and fix a rattling window or not, or let the cat in, I never won it. Besides, I knew I'd got to take a look now for my own peace of mind. The seeds of doubt had been sown.

I groaned again, and heaved myself off my bunk. My body felt like lead. It was chilly now in the cabin. I pushed back the sliding roof and stuck my head out, shivering.

The rain had almost stopped at last, but the night air was very cold indeed. A small, draughty breeze was blowing. I stared around me. After the pitch darkness of the cabin, it seemed comparatively light outside, and I was able to check *Puffin*'s position by the boats lying near her. I could hear the fast-running ebb tide chuckling faintly round her rudder, but she was perfectly stationary and steady. She was quite all right, as I'd known she would be.

I cowered back inside and shut the roof. It was much too cold out there.

'We haven't moved an inch,' I said. 'Does that satisfy you?'

No answer.

'So!' I muttered bad-temperedly to myself. 'She's so worried that she goes to sleep and forgets it. All she wanted was to get me out of my bunk. Women!'

I lay down again, feeling as righteously indignant as my weariness would let me. I pulled the blankets up over me.

The chain dragged again, and there was the faint tap-tap of a halyard against the mast. I knew what that was, so it didn't bother me at all. In fact it was a rather soothing sound.

'Darling—'

'Oh, no!'

'There's a tapping sound.'

'I know there is. It's a rope on the mast.'

'Why is it doing that? It wasn't a little while ago.'

'The wind is getting up again, that's all.'

'Wind? There's not going to be another storm, is there?'

'Of course there isn't.'

'Is that thing going to go on doing that all night?'

'I don't know.'

'It's a bit irritating, isn't it?'

'Is it? *I* find it rather soothing.'

'Is it? Well—perhaps it is.'

'Goodnight,' I said. 'For the last time.'

'Goodnight, darling.'

Once more I tried to settle down. But, dog-tired though I was, I somehow couldn't relax this time. I couldn't get warm. And the wind seemed to have risen quite a bit. *Puffin* was curtseying gently now. The halyard was tapping louder, and after a while it got on my nerves.

I said: 'I suppose I'd better fix it.'

Sue didn't answer. When I dragged myself out of my blankets and opened the hatch again, she didn't stir.

It was like winter outside. My feet were bare, and the wet deck felt like liquid ice. Just for good measure, I stubbed my toe on the jibsheet fairlead as I went forward. Mouthing savage oaths, I took the jib halyard and wrapped it round everything else on the mast. Shuddering with the cold, I went below again and lay down.

Just as I got horizontal once more, Sue stirred and sighed.

'Did you do it, darling?'

'Yes, I did it.' I pulled the blankets wearily up to my chin. *What a night*, I thought. *What next?*

'Next' was an odd sort of knocking, somewhere aft.

'What's that?' I asked aloud.

'What's what?' said Sue, awake again.

'That knocking sound.'

'That's what I meant. You said you'd fixed it.'

'I fixed the damned halyard.'

'But you said that wasn't worrying you—you said it was soothing.'

I couldn't trust myself to answer. I lay listening. The knocking still came, and it irritated me for two reasons. One was I didn't know what it was, and the other was its irregularity. You listened for it, and it didn't come. Then, just when you had decided it had stopped, there it was again.

There was no help for it.

'This row's going to drive me mad,' I said.

'Mm?'

'Go to *sleep*. It's all right for some people.'

'Mm.'

I got up with a horrible conviction that this sort of thing was going to go on all night. I stumbled out into the freezing night and stood in the cockpit, listening.

Not a sound.

Knock, damn you, knock! I told it.

Obligingly, it knocked. The noise still puzzled me for a moment. Then I discovered that it was the tiller banging against the boom crutch.

I lashed the tiller amidships and went back below. I didn't waste my breath on telling Sue what it was. I knew I wouldn't get an answer.

'What was it, darling?'

'It was the tiller banging against the boom crutch,' I said wearily.

'Oh—is *that* all?'

I sat down heavily on my bunk. It hardly seemed worth lying down. I knew that, as soon as I did, something else would devilishly demand my attention. I tried to think what else there was that could keep me from my sleep.

My morale was very low. I could feel myself going rapidly to pieces. One more unidentified noise would, I felt sure, be enough to reduce me to a gibbering, hysterical wreck . . .

Then I realized that everything was perfectly peaceful, and had been for some time. No dragging chain. No flapping halyard. No bumping tiller. *Puffin* had even stopped her curtseying, although, by the sound of it, the wind was still rising. She was sitting there as steady as a rock.

Hardly daring to hope, I lay down. I pulled the blankets over me, almost furtively.

I must have gone off that time, because when I came to again, dazedly, I found I was lying on the floorboards. I tried to sit up, but with a drunken sort of lurch I fell against the side of Sue's bunk. I wondered what the devil had happened. Everything seemed queerly lopsided.

Then the awful truth dawned on me. *Puffin* was aground. We must have been out of the channel when we dropped anchor. I remembered the patch of mud I had seen drying soon after high water.

I realized, too, why it was that she had seemed too stable, in spite of the weather, when I had fallen asleep. She must have been sitting on the bottom then. And now she had fallen over on her side.

I lay limply back on the slanting cabin floor. This was too much. It was the end. Let me just once get ashore, and I'd never set foot in a boat again. I almost wept at the thought of my beautiful, comfortable, horizontal bed at home . . .

Sue didn't stir. She was lucky. She was on the lower side of the boat, quite comfortably wedged between her bunk and the planking. She was still sleeping peacefully, and I had very mixed feelings about that. I was glad she wasn't as badly off as I was, but at the same time I resented her blissful obliviousness of my predicament. I half-hoped, selfishly, that she would wake up, so that she could share my misery. At the same time I prayed that she *wouldn't* wake up, because she would be scared stiff if she knew what was happening.

I knew I was in for a bad time, but I didn't realize just how bad. What followed was sheer purgatory. As *Puffin* heeled further and further over, she became a complex and diabolical system of knobs and sharp angles. There was nowhere to sit and nowhere to lie. Her angle of heel threw everything bewilderingly out of true in the darkness, so that it was difficult to keep one's balance even when sitting up, and the pull of gravity seemed to be increased tenfold.

For over two nightmare hours I lay pressed heavily into the angle between the cabin floor and the side of Sue's bunk until I couldn't stand it any longer. I dragged myself up, switched on the torch again, and looked at Sue. She had turned on to her back, and was lying quite happily half up the side of the boat. And the little devil was smiling in her sleep.

It was no good. The cabin had become a torture chamber. I pulled on my shoes, hauled myself to my feet, opened the hatch— even that was an extraordinarily difficult operation, with *Puffin* lying as she was now—and heaved my weary carcase out into the cockpit.

The cockpit, though, was equally uninhabitable. There was no room to stretch out, and I couldn't sit up either. If I tried to sit on the port-side seat, I slid off, and on the starboard side the cockpit coaming cut cruelly into my back. It was pretty obvious by now that the only habitable place aboard *Puffin* was the starboard-side bunk, and Sue was in it.

In the end I hauled the dinghy alongside and got into it, just for the blessed relief of being on an even keel again. It *was* a relief too, but I soon realized that sitting in a dinghy was no way to spend half a sub-arctic May night. To try to get some warmth back into my shuddering body and frozen hands, I cast off and rowed like a lunatic around the anchorage . . .

The tide *had* turned. It was setting strongly up the creek. And, now that it was running up against the wind, the water was quite rough. Some of the lighter craft I passed were surging about, caught between the opposing forces of wind and tide. The night seemed much more alive than it had been when I'd rowed ashore. It was full of movement and the cold wet slap of waves against boats' hulls . . .

I spent a long time rowing round, searching for *Puffin*. My one consolation was that, by the time I found her, she might be afloat again. My only object in life now was to get aboard and crawl into my bunk and give up the ghost.

She wasn't afloat. When I finally found her, she was still well over on her side. But even that didn't seem to matter any more. I struggled on board, secured the dinghy, stumbled into the cabin, and laid myself miserably down on the cabin floor.

Some time later I roused sufficiently—it was a violent shivering attack that woke me up—to realize that *Puffin* was on an even keel and afloat again. I hauled myself thankfully on to my bunk and pulled the blankets over me with palsied fingers.

I was awakened next time by a bump. It must have been quite a bump for, out to the world though I was, it brought me erect in my bunk with a jerk. I sat there rubbing my forehead and wondering what in God's name was happening now.

Things seemed to be getting violent outside. The wind was loud in the rigging, and *Puffin* was rolling quite heavily. Every now and then her chain dragged noisily.

I didn't care. Whatever happened, I wasn't going to get up again.

I lay down. As I did so, there came a sizeable wallop from somewhere aft. It was repeated a minute later. I knew that sort of thing just couldn't be allowed to go on. I wondered if some boat had broken adrift from her mooring and was bumping against us. That could be dangerous. Feeling suicidal, I got up to find out.

It was the damned dinghy. I got out into the cockpit in time to see it sheering away into the darkness after its last attack. No doubt it was retreating to the full length of its painter in order to get up maximum speed for its next onslaught. Sure enough, it came surging in. I fended the little brute off and then stood staring after it, wondering what to do about it.

It was the tide running against the wind that was causing the trouble. Both *Puffin* and the dinghy were ranging about a good deal. It was when their orbits intersected that the bumps came.

I had read a good deal about errant dinghies; without ever finding out just what to do about them, short of taking them on board. That was impossible, with so small a boat as *Puffin*. I suspected that the authorities I'd consulted on the subject had never been able to find any satisfactory alternative solution themselves.

I tried giving the dinghy the full length of her painter. She vanished into the darkness astern and, when some little time had passed without her reappearing again, I began to wonder whether those same authorities hadn't overlooked the simplest solution of all.

They hadn't. I was just diving back into the cabin when there came a fearful crash on the starboard quarter. It was incredible to think that an eight-foot dinghy could pack such a punch. It shook

Puffin from stern to stern. The things in the galley clashed together violently, and something fell over up forward. About the only item on board that remained oblivious to the collision was the female corpse in the starboard bunk.

Once again I turned bleakly back into the cockpit. The only thing I could think of now was to secure the dinghy on a very short painter instead of a very long one. If that didn't work, I was sunk.

It didn't work. On the short painter the dinghy hit *Puffin* twice as often, if less violently, and spent most of the intervals between the bumps scraping and groaning against the rudder-post and transom. The bumps were endurable now, though, and, after listening miserably for a while to the quick succession of thuds, wheezes, groans and scrapes that busy little boat was producing, I decided the only thing to do was to leave it at that.

I crawled back inside. I lay down. I slept, after telling myself I was definitely going to sell the damn boat back to Charlie the first moment I could. I'd *give* it to him.

It wasn't a bump that wakened me next time. It was a shaking. I didn't know what it was, and I didn't care. I hunched my shoulders against it. I didn't care if we sank with all hands, I wasn't going to get up for anything.

'Wake up, sleepy head! It's after nine o'clock—and I've made the tea.'

I turned on my back and opened my eyes. Sue was bending over me. She had a mug in her hand. The sun was streaming in through the hatch behind her, and what I could see of the sky was a cloudless, bland blue.

'You *have* had a good night, haven't you?' Sue said. 'So have I. Darling—I think sleeping on a boat is simply gorgeous. So calm. So peaceful.'

I groaned and shut my eyes again.

'Darling—your tea!'

'Leave me alone,' I said. 'I'm tired.'

Epilogue

From *Song of the Sirens*

BY ERNEST K. GANN

ITH A LITERATE AVIATOR AS A FATHER, I grew up with Ernie
Gann's writing about flying and pilots: *Fate Is the Hunter* was
(and is) a classic bestseller about flying, while I can watch
The High & The Mighty time after time as John Wayne brings
the airliner safely home.

But there was another side to Ernie Gann, and that was his love affair with the sea. His success in writing allowed him to dally with all manner of boats, from fishing boats on San Francisco Bay to a cute yacht
trawler in the San Juan Islands which came when Gann was weary of feeding and caring for hordes of guests on previous boats. His instructions to
the designer were for a boat that "drinks six, eats four, and sleeps two."

His most enduring nautical love affair was with the brigantine *Albatros,* which he owned for many years. When he finally sold *Albatros,* it was
with a deep sense of loss, although, in this passage, he assuages it with the
immediate construction of a new yacht, *Black Watch.*

But *Albatros* without Gann was a doomed ship, or perhaps it was always doomed and Gann was lucky enough (*Fate Is the Hunter?*) to let her go.
But while aboard *Black Watch* in the Greek islands, Gann finds out that *Albatros*
has been lost in the Gulf of Mexico. Sailing as a school ship, she went down
quickly after being hit by a white squall (hence the name of the movie starring
Jeff Bridges about the incident), taking the skipper's wife, four students, and a
friend and shipmate of Gann.

It is at this point that we join Gann as he ponders the permanence—and the tragedy—of the sea, and finds a renewal of his faith in the
sea from an apparent Siren. His words are particularly touching since he
dedicated *Song of the Sirens* to his son, George, an officer aboard a tanker
who would later be swept overboard and lost at sea.

⛵ ⛵ ⛵ ⛵

ONE OF THE GREATEST BLESSINGS the oceans bestow upon man is a sense of everlasting permanence. The oceans *do* change, but they take their time about it and a thousand years is only an interval. Time apparently stands still for the oceans—the light and play of liquid, the sounds and scent of salt air, and the inhabitants are basically the same as they were long ago. Thus modern man needs the oceans more than ever, for the minute slice of earth upon which he dwells changes constantly and sometimes overwhelmingly. Where is the house of my childhood? Where is the building in which I found my first job, the church in which I was married, the park where the team played, the fields where we used to hunt, and the ponds where there were so many fish? Torn down, burned down, occupied by a shopping center, laid out in a housing development, polluted—all changed since only yesterday. This is very hard on normal man's deep yearning for stability. Many simply cannot endure such accelerating progress and try desperately to lose themselves in nostalgia or hurl themselves into personal tragedy. Familiarity with the oceans can do much to reassure that part of us which instinctively fears change.

Perhaps that is why, when at last I parted with the *Albatros* and was obliged to admit that I was no longer her master or owner, I sought immediate distraction in the building of a new vessel. She was to be designed specifically for research, upon the sea and particularly along its fringes. I was certain such a vessel would serve as a magnet for all manner of individuals. I wanted the new vessel to be designed as a workboat and she had best be a sailing ketch for the long oceanic passages. She must have sufficient power to handle the strong tides of the northern latitudes as well as endurance for the suffocating calms of the southerly seas. She would be built in Denmark by a small firm hoary with experience in building heavy wooden vessels of commercial design. Hopefully she would incorporate all of the qualities and inherit none of the faults of the sixteen preceding sirens. By matching the proceeds from the sale of the *Albatros* against reasonable Danish prices I could almost afford such a dream.

It had taken nearly a year to build the *Black Watch* and now another year had passed, and having come a long way, we were prowling the waters of the Aegean. We had retraced our course through Norwegian fiords, crossed the North Sea, and Scotland via the Caledonian Canal, which is one of the most delightful passages any sailor can make, and we had repeated Boswell's tour of the Hebrides with his very book in hand, and we had been hove to for three days in a September screamer of a gale off the Irish coast, and we had been swallowed by the Mediterranean at Gibraltar and spit right out again. We had nosed into little gunk-holes the ages have chewed into the flanks of Corsica and Sardinia, and in Malta we had hobnobbed with what was left of the British Raj and met in the best clandestine style with a Maltese underground leader who vowed to overthrow the government. We had fought our way up the Dalmatian coast against an unforgiving *bora* and eventually swung about to pass through the Ionian Sea and the Gulf of Corinth to the Aegean. The summer was over and Greece in September is often a land of new rains falling on ancient ruins. The parched earth rejoices in the first scattered droplets to be sucked from the barren sky in months, and the Greek people renew their love affair with life. Ironically it was then that the terrible news found us.

The *Albatros* had capsized in the Gulf of Mexico. She had gone down so quickly it was a miracle anyone had escaped. I grieved for Sheldon, whose heavy sense of responsibility must now be torturing him. He had been operating her as a school ship and had made several highly successful cruises in that employment. The only significant changes he had made were below to improve accommodations for his students and teachers. I knew him to be a most thoroughly competent seaman—how then, after so many thousands of miles, could the *Albatros* now be on the bottom of the sea? With her had gone Sheldon's wife, our treasured friend Ptacnik, who had remained aboard as cook although he had at first intended to sail in the *Black Watch*, and four students. Sheldon himself and the balance of his company had been rescued by a freighter after spending only twenty-four hours in the two lifeboats. One report said the *Albatros* had been overcome by a "white squall," and that once it had passed the sea became quiet again. From the air I had seen the so-called white squalls, which are peculiar to the Gulf of Mexico, and I knew them to be a species of marine tornado. Although they actually cover but a small area the intensity of the winds may be as high as 100 miles an hour and a vessel caught all standing might easily be overwhelmed.

Sheldon was a man of deep convictions and honest courage. Now I longed to reach out and touch his hand, for how many times had I crept into the same after cabin and secretly whispered for mercy. There was, I knew, no wrath so dreadful as a storm at sea. It confounds the best of men, perhaps because in the wastes of the ocean he is so alone. I had flown through the interior of thunderstorms many times and my bowels were therefore accustomed to restraining one of man's primary reactions to fear, yet always we knew that the ordeal would not long endure and most of the time our radios could reach for our mental comfort to other men who stood vigil in peace and quiet. At sea the nightmare of almost any storm seems to continue forever and the total massing of cruelty may be divided by the size of the vessel.

When the *Albatros* went down something happened to the sense of permanency which I had always drawn from the sea. For a time I simply could not conceive of her not sailing somewhere in the world, if only because I had devoted four years of my life to her well-being and had striven with all my will and resource to assure her long and healthy future. I wept for a loss which was not even mine, for dreams are important to all men and Sheldon's had been viciously annihilated.

A cloak covered my spirits and I could not shake it off. The haunting sense of loss would subside for a week or more and then it would return and I was trying to learn how to be patient until it went away again.

I was so disenchanted with the sea that I could think only of its discomforts and dangers, and even the very deck upon which I stood represented a tremendous waste of time, energy, and fortune. What indeed had the life of a sailor done for me except to pay me poorly when I was paid at all, allow me to lose innumerable hours of sleep, and be so far removed from the center of things that on going ashore I must each time first adjust myself and then go about the tedious business of making new friends. I was a stranger everywhere; there were no roots in the oceans, and in little vessels such as must always be my lot there was no honest home to be found afloat. Well then, a pox on all salt water and the sooner the *Black Watch* was sold out from under me the better. There would be no more blustery days like this one when we came swirling southward before a hard and hot *meltemi,* sailed full blast through the narrow passage which separates Fournoi from an adjacent islet, and rounded up in this cul-de-sac, where we hoped for a night's sleep if the anchor decided not to drag.

There were still four of us in the *Black Watch.* When the deck gear was made up and all secured for the night I stood on the foredeck and watched the anchor chain with suspicion. The yellow light of evening was already fading, yet heat from the great cinder of Fournoi whirled down upon us, the still-hot breath of the *meltemi* augmented by hills cooked too long in the sun. The others had gone below to prepare the evening meal and I was left alone with my brooding. Our anchor seemed secure and yet I unaccountably lingered about the foredeck. Perhaps all of my movements then were a sum of delays because I was so recently advised of the *Albatros* catastrophe. Perhaps my physical cogs were slipping, because to divert my thoughts toward more rewarding fields I had deliberately become lost in Greek antiquity and my own pace had unconsciously seemed to match those more reflective times. I was staring down at the ruffled water when I first heard the singing. It was a feminine voice, thin, high, very clear and gay—the voice of a Circe or a sprite, I thought, according to a man's wish and imagination. It was a voice drifting down the wind from the ages; it was a cry of life from the fringes of the sea, of zest for all the temple of Poseidon offered.

At first I was unable to find the source of the singing, although I carefully searched the arid bowl which rose up from the sea and shaped the cove of Fournoi. There were a few white plaster houses and the inevitable goats, but there had not been a sign of human life. Yet there, as if singing for my heart alone, was the voice. It seemed so near and clear I dared not believe I had not really heard it.

I walked aft to the quarter-deck and picked up my binoculars. Again I searched the shore, then stopped in disbelief. For I focused upon a lone fig tree which was swaying violently in the wind. And in the tree was a young girl, skirt billowing, singing joyously, yet as if her very life depended on it.

I slipped below to advise my shipmates, who were weary of the wind. "Come on deck. I'll show you something you won't believe."

Perhaps three or four minutes had passed before we were all on deck. I handed the binoculars to Post and said, "That tree just there—to the left of the larger rock pile. Tell me what you see." I spoke with pride, as if the girl were mine to exploit.

"A donkey," Post said flatly. There are donkeys everywhere in Greece, so I understood her lack of enthusiasm.

"No, no. In the tree."

"I do not see the donkey in the tree. He is under it in the shade, as donkeys always are."

I snatched the binoculars away from her without apology and focused on the tree. There was no girl in it or even about it. We are looking at the wrong tree, I thought. Then one by one I inspected the few trees visible from the cove of Fournoi. They were all swinging in the wind, but none of them supported a young girl. Nor was she to be seen anywhere on the land.

"Just what are we looking for?"

"A girl . . . a young girl, singing in that tree . . ." I spoke with the binoculars still at my eyes because I sensed an uneasiness in the voices of my shipmates and I dared not risk looking into their faces. "She has a strange, haunting little voice . . ."

"Oh yes, of course, well, well . . ." My shipmates drifted away and I saw they were trying very hard not to reveal their embarrassment. When they were gone I thought that I should be more secretive about the kind of things I observed on shore.

Again I examined the tree in which I was so certain the singing girl had been. Nothing. Had I really seen a vision?

In the binoculars I saw the donkey raise his head and look in my direction. Then he brayed.

For several days afterward there was, inevitably, some badinage about my having seen a girl singing in a fig tree, and I tried to convince myself that she had been a product of my melancholy and had never really existed. Yet I could not forget her.

We passed northwestward through the Aegean as far as the Turkish coast, and the searing *meltemi* winds kept us preoccupied no matter what our course. There were innumerable other distractions, none of which succeeded in removing my thoughts from Fournoi. I had rescued a goat from certain drowning after he had foolishly decided to swim the channel at Meganisi, and I had an abscessed tooth removed on the Island of Samos by a Swiss dentist using borrowed Greek equipment. The operation had been performed before an open window which faced on the dusty street and a large proportion of the island's population was able to enjoy the afternoon entertainment. To ease my pain I thought about the singing girl of Fournoi.

On every Greek island there is a minimum of one Greco-American who has returned to his native land to rest on his social security checks, which arrive with faithful regularity from that other generous land across the sea. He is from Detroit or Philadelphia or Cleveland or St. Paul, and nothing will do but you must accept his hospitality and tell him, while he anxiously fingers his worry beads, why his favorite ball team is not at the top of the league. All of this takes a very long time and considerable concentration in the heat of the Greek sun, yet even then my memory of the singing girl simply would not go away.

A month later, running before an identical *meltemi* wind, we sailed back to Fournoi. One of the reasons for our return was punitive. My mind had betrayed me here and to chastise it I would forever prove that there was no singing girl of Fournoi. Once again we had anchored and once again I stood on the foredeck watching the chain suspiciously. I did my best to ignore the shore and finally walked aft. It was drinking time and the custom held on the *Black Watch* as firmly as on the *Albatros*.

Suddenly I halted. There . . . *there!* I dared not look around but moved quickly aft to the binocular box exactly as I had done before. I called down to my shipmates: "Come! On deck! Immediately!"

I took out the binoculars and turned them on the shore. Halfway up the side of the bowl. There! There she was singing in the fig tree, her skirts billowing in the wind just as they had done a month ago.

Post was beside me now, and Steffensen, who had also sailed in the *Albatros*.

"Yes! Yes, I hear her!" Steffensen said.

I handed the binoculars to Post, and after a moment she said wonderingly, "Yes . . . I see her now."

And Anderson, who was the last to come on deck, saw her too.

For a time we stood quietly, listening and sometimes looking through the binoculars to reassure ourselves. Except for her donkey there was again no other sign of life on the entire hillside. She sang alone then, not for us or for anyone else that we could see, a wild song to match the wind and the skittering waves of the cove.

In the binoculars we could see her head tilted back as if she sang to the sky. Her tune was difficult to classify because of the vagaries of the wind, which alternately muted and brought her voice full volume. It sounded improvised as if she sang purely on inspiration, yet her lyrics were in distinct cadence and there was nothing shy about her style. Holding to a branch of the fig tree with one hand, she would make a sweeping gesture with her free hand to encompass her audience of none. It was a regal gesture to be seen at La Scala rather than to be impressing the dry rocks on a somewhat larger rock in the middle of the Aegean. Not once did I see her look our way. She seemed oblivious to our presence; nor did she concentrate on any other sector of her view. The wind was her audience, the sky, and the sea far beyond us.

Nightfall came quickly and we thought surely that the singing girl of Fournoi would abandon her concert. Yet after dinner when we came on deck she was still there, somewhere in the darkness beyond our anchor light, singing as boisterously as before. There were short pauses which we took to be the end of things and then she could be heard again. And after a while my thoughts again followed their familiar way to the loss of the *Albatros,* but somehow my utter dejection had passed. Somehow my faith in the permanency of the sea had been restored by this daughter of Poseidon on a faraway isle in a faraway sea. And I knew that I was in love again and always would be.

Soon after my mood had changed, the singing ceased and there was no more. During the night there was only the sound of the sea and the wind and in the morning the singing girl of Fournoi did not reappear.

The Boat Journey

From *South*

BY SIR ERNEST SHACKLETON

I n August 1914, twenty-eight men aboard the ship *Endurance* began what was to be the "last of the great explorations"—the crossing of the vast Antarctic landmass. But rather than a glorious expedition, the journey turned into one of the most remarkable survival stories ever recorded. Sir Ernest Shackleton, the legendary leader of the expedition, kept his crew together throughout a hellish two-year odyssey in one of the most inhospitable regions on earth. Their ordeal began when *Endurance* was trapped in the Antarctic pack ice and ultimately crushed. Undeterred, Shackleton and crew began an impossible journey over the barren, frozen wasteland. In this passage Shackleton describes his attempt in April 1916, with five others of his crew, to sail the twenty-two-and-a-half-foot ship's boat, *James Caird*, from Elephant Island some 800 miles across the stormy and frigid ocean to South Georgia to find help for his crew remaining on Elephant Island.

THE INCREASING SEA MADE IT necessary for us to drag the boats farther up the beach. This was a task for all hands, and after much labour
we got the boats into safe positions among the rocks and made fast
the painters to a big boulder. Then I discussed with Wild and Worsley
the chances of reaching South Georgia before the winter locked the
seas against us. Some effort had to be made to secure relief. Privation
and exposure had left their mark on the party, and the health and
mental condition of several men were causing me serious anxiety.
Blackborrow's feet, which had been frost-bitten during the boat
journey, were in a bad way, and the two doctors feared that an operation would be necessary. They told me that the toes would have to be
amputated unless animation could be restored within a short period.
Then the food-supply was a vital consideration. We had left ten cases
of provisions in the crevice of the rocks at our first camping-place on
the island. An examination of our stores showed that we had full rations for the whole party for a period of five weeks. The rations could
be spread over three months on a reduced allowance and probably
would be supplemented by seals and sea-elephants to some extent. I
did not dare to count with full confidence on supplies of meat and
blubber, for the animals seemed to have deserted the beach and the
winter was near. Our stocks included three seals and two and a half
skins (with blubber attached). We were mainly dependent on the
blubber for fuel, and after making a preliminary survey of the situation, I decided that the party must be limited to one hot meal a day.

A boat journey in search of relief was necessary and must not
be delayed. That conclusion was forced upon me. The nearest port
where assistance could certainly be secured was Port Stanley, in the
Falkland Islands, 540 miles away, but we could scarcely hope to beat
up against the prevailing northwesterly wind in a frail and weakened
boat with a small sail area. South Georgia was over 800 miles away,
but lay in the area of the west winds, and I could count upon finding
whalers at any of the whaling-stations on the east coast. A boat party
might make the voyage and be back with relief within a month, provided that the sea was clear of ice and the boat survived the great

seas. It was not difficult to decide that South Georgia must be the objective, and I proceeded to plan ways and means. The hazards of a boat journey across 800 miles of stormy sub-Antarctic ocean were obvious, but I calculated that at worst the venture would add nothing to the risks of the men left on the island. There would be fewer mouths to feed during the winter and the boat would not require to take more than one month's provisions for six men, for if we did not make South Georgia in that time we were sure to go under. A consideration that had weight with me was that there was no chance at all of any search being made for us on Elephant Island.

The case required to be argued in some detail, since all hands knew that the perils of the proposed journey were extreme. The risk was justified solely by our urgent need of assistance. The ocean south of Cape Horn in the middle of May is known to be the most tempestuous storm-swept area of water in the world. The weather then is unsettled, the skies are dull and overcast, and the gales are almost unceasing. We had to face these conditions in a small and weather-beaten boat, already strained by the work of the months that had passed. Worsley and Wild realized that the attempt must be made, and they both asked to be allowed to accompany me on the voyage. I told Wild at once that he would have to stay behind. I relied upon him to hold the party together while I was away and to make the best of his way to Deception Island with the men in the spring in the event of our failure to bring help. Worsley I would take with me, for I had a very high opinion of his accuracy and quickness as a navigator, and especially in the snapping and working out of positions in difficult circumstances—an opinion that was only enhanced during the actual journey. Four other men would be required, and I decided to call for volunteers, although, as a matter of fact, I pretty well knew which of the people I would select. Crean I proposed to leave on the island as a right-hand man for Wild, but he begged so hard to be allowed to come in the boat that, after consultation with Wild, I promised to take him. I called the men together, explained my plan, and asked for volunteers. Many came forward at once. Some were not fit enough for the work that would have to be done, and others would not have been much use in the boat since they were not seasoned sailors, though the experiences of recent months entitled them to some consideration as seafaring men. McIlroy and Macklin were both anxious to go but realized that their duty lay on the island with the sick men. They suggested that I should take Blackborrow in order that he might have shelter and warmth as quickly as possible, but I had to veto this idea. It would be hard enough for fit men to live in the boat. Indeed, I did not see how a sick man, lying helpless in the bottom of the boat, could possibly survive in the heavy weather we were sure to encounter. I finally selected McNeish, McCarthy, and Vincent in addition to Worsley and Crean. The crew seemed a strong one, and as I looked at the men I felt confidence increasing.

The decision made, I walked through the blizzard with Worsley and Wild to examine the *James Caird*. The 20-ft. boat had never looked big; she appeared to have shrunk in some mysterious way when I viewed her in the light of our new undertaking. She was an ordinary ship's whaler, fairly strong, but showing signs of the strains she had endured since the crushing of the *Endurance*. Where she was holed in leaving the pack was, fortunately, about the water-line, and easily patched. Standing beside her, we glanced at the fringe of the storm-swept sea that formed our path. Clearly, our voyage would be a big adventure. I called the carpenter and asked him if he could do anything to make the boat more seaworthy. He first inquired if he was to go with me, and seemed quite pleased when I said "Yes." He was over fifty years of age and not altogether fit, but he had a good knowledge of sailing-boats and was very quick. McCarthy said that he could contrive some sort of covering for the *James Caird* if he might use the lids of the cases and the four sledge-runners that we had lashed inside the boat for use in the event of a landing on Graham Land at Wilhemina Bay. This bay, at one time the goal of our desire, had been left behind in the course of our drift, but we had retained the runners.

The carpenter proposed to complete the covering with some of our canvas, and he set about making his plans at once.

Noon had passed and the gale was more severe than ever. We could not proceed with out preparations that day. The tents were suffering in the wind and the sea was rising. We made our way to the snow-slope at the shoreward end of the spit, with the intention of digging a hole in the snow large enough to provide shelter for the party. I had an idea that Wild and his men might camp there during my absence, since it seemed impossible that the tents could hold together for many more days against the attacks of the wind; but an examination of the spot indicated that any hole we could dig probably would be filled quickly by the drift. At dark, about 5 P.M., we all turned in, after a supper consisting of a pannikin of hot milk, one of our previous biscuits, and a cold penguin leg each.

The gale was stronger than ever on the following morning (April 20). No work could be done. Blizzard and snow, snow and blizzard, sudden lulls and fierce returns. During the lulls we could see on the far horizon to the north-east bergs of all shapes and sizes driving along before the gale, and the sinister appearance of the swift-moving masses made us thankful indeed that, instead of battling with the storm mid the ice, we were required only to face the drift from the glaciers and the inland heights. The gusts might throw us off our feet, but at least we fell on solid ground and not on the rocking floes. Two seals came up on the beach that day, one of them within ten yards of my tent. So urgent was our need of food and blubber that I called all hands and organized a line of beaters instead of simply walking up to the seal and hitting in on the nose. We were prepared to fall upon this seal *en masse* if it attempted to escape. The kill was made with a pick-handle, and in a few minutes five days' food and six days' fuel were stored in a place of safety among the boulders above the high-water mark. During this day the cook, who had worked well on the floe and throughout the boat journey, suddenly collapsed. I happened to be at the galley at the moment and saw him fall. I pulled him down the slope to his tent and pushed him into its shelter with orders to his tent-mates to keep him in his sleeping-bag until I allowed him to come out or the doctors said he was fit enough. Then I took out to replace the cook one of the men who had expressed a desire to lie down and die. The task of keeping the galley fire alight was both difficult and strenuous and it took his thoughts away from the chances of immediate dissolution. In fact, I found him a little later gravely concerned over the drying of a naturally not over-clean pair of socks which were hung up in close proximity to our evening milk. Occupation had brought his thoughts back to the ordinary cares of life.

There was a lull in the bad weather on April 21, and the carpenter started to collect material for the decking of the *James Caird*. He fitted the mast of the *Stancomb Wills* fore and aft side the *James Caird* as a hog-back and thus strengthened the keel with the object of preventing our boat "hogging"—that is, buckling in heaving seas. He had not sufficient wood to provide a deck, but by using the sledge-runners and box-lids he made a framework extending from the forecastle aft to a well. It was a patched-up affair, but it provided a base for a canvas covering. We had a bolt of canvas frozen stiff, and this material had to be cut and then thawed out over the blubber-stove, foot by foot, in order that it might be sewn into the form of a cover. When it had been nailed and screwed into position it certainly gave an appearance of safety to the boat, though I had an uneasy feeling that it bore a strong likeness to stage scenery, which may look like a granite wall and is in fact nothing better than canvas and lath. As events proved, the covering served its purpose well. We certainly could not have lived through the voyage without it.

Another fierce gale was blowing on April 22, interfering with our preparations for the voyage. The cooker from No. 5 tent came adrift in a gust, and although it was chased to the water's edge, it disappeared for good. Blackborrow's feet were giving him much pain, and McIlroy and Macklin thought it would be necessary for them to operate soon. They were under the impression then that they had no chloroform, but they found some subsequently in the medicine-chest after we had left. Some cases of stores left on a rock off the spit on the day of our arrival were retrieved during this day. We were setting aside stores for the boat journey and choosing the essential equipment from the scanty stock at our disposal. Two ten-gallon casks had to be filled with water melted down from ice collected at the foot of the glacier. This was a rather slow business. The blubber-stove was kept going all night, and the watchmen emptied the water into the casks from the pot in which the ice was melted. A working party started to dig a hole in the snow-slope about forty feet above sea-level with the object of providing a site for a camp. They made fairly good progress at first, but the snow drifted down unceasingly from the inland ice, and in the end the party had to give up the project.

The weather was fine on April 23, and we hurried forward our preparations. It was on this day I decided finally that the crew for the *James Caird* should consist of Worsley, Crean, McNeish, McCarthy, Vincent, and myself. A storm came on about noon, with driving snow and heavy squalls. Occasionally the air would clear for a few minutes, and we could see a line of pack-ice, five miles out, driving across from west to east. This sight increased my anxiety to get away quickly. Winter was advancing, and soon the pack might close completely round the island and stay our departure for days or even for weeks. I did not think that ice would remain around Elephant Island continuously during the winter, since the strong winds and fast currents would keep it in motion. We had noticed ice and bergs going past at the rate of four or five knots. A certain amount of ice was held up about the end of our spit, but the sea was clear where the boat would have to be launched.

Worsley, Wild, and I climbed to the summit of the seaward rocks and examined the ice from a better vantage-point than the beach offered. The belt of pack outside appeared to be sufficiently broken for our purposes, and I decided that, unless the conditions forbade it, we would make a start in the *James Caird* on the following morning. Obviously the pack might close at any time. This decision made, I spent the rest of the day looking over the boat, gear, and stores, and discussing plans with Worsley and Wild.

Our last night on the solid group of Elephant Island was cold and uncomfortable. We turned out at dawn and had breakfast. Then we launched the *Stancomb Wills* and loaded her with stores, gear, and ballast, which would be transferred to the *James Caird* when the heavier boat had been launched. The ballast consisted of bags made from blankets and filled with sand, making a total weight of about 1000 lb. In addition we had gathered a number of round boulders and about 250 lb. of ice, which would supplement our two casks of water.

The stores taken in the *James Caird,* which would last six men for one month, were as follows:

30 boxes of matches.
6½ gallons paraffin.
1 tin methylated spirit.
10 boxes of flamers.
1 box of blue lights.
2 Primus stoves with spare parts and prickers.
1 Nansen aluminum cooker.
6 sleeping bags.
A few spare socks.
A few candles and some blubber-oil in an oil-bag.

Food:
3 cases sledging rations = 300 rations.
2 cases nut food = 200 rations.
2 cases biscuits = 600 biscuits.
1 case lump sugar.
30 packets of Trumilk.
1 tin of Bovril cubes.
1 tin of Cerebos salt.
36 gallons of water.
112 lb. of ice.

Instruments:
Sextant.
Binoculars.
Prismatic compass.
Sea-anchor.
Charts.
Aneroid.

The swell was slight when the *Stancomb Wills* was launched and the boat got under way without any difficulty; but half an hour later, when we were pulling down the *James Caird,* the swell increased suddenly. Apparently the movement of the ice outside had made an opening and allowed the sea to run in without being blanketed by the line of pack. The swell made things difficult. Many of us got wet to the waist while dragging the boat out—a serious matter in that climate. When the *James Caird* was afloat in the surf she nearly capsized among the rocks before we could get her clear, and Vincent and the carpenter, who were on the deck, were thrown into the water. This was really bad luck, for the two men would have small chance of drying their clothes after we had got under way. Hurley, who had the eye of the professional photographer for "incidents," secured a picture of the upset and I firmly believe that he would have liked the two unfortunate men to remain in the water until he could get a "snap" at close quarters; but we hauled them out immediately, regardless of his feelings.

The *James Caird* was soon clear of the breakers. We used all the available ropes as a long painter to prevent her drifting away to the northeast, and then the *Stancomb Wills* came alongside, transferred her load, and went back to the shore for more. As she was being beached this time the sea took her stern and half filled her with water. She had to be turned over and emptied before the return journey could be made. Every member of the crew of the *Stancomb Wills* was wet to the skin. The water-casks were towed behind the *Stancomb Wills* on this second journey, and the swell, which was increasing rapidly, drove the boat onto the rocks, where one of the casks was slightly stove in. This accident proved later to be a serious one, since some sea-water had entered the cask and the contents were now brackish.

By midday the *James Caird* was ready for the voyage. Vincent and the carpenter had secured some dry clothes by exchange with members of the shore party (I heard afterwards that it was a full fortnight before the soaked garments were finally dried), and the boat's crew was standing by waiting for the order to cast off. A moderate westerly breeze was blowing. I went ashore in the *Stancomb Wills* and had a last word with Wild, who was remaining in full command, with directions as to his course of action in the event of our failure to bring relief, but I practically left the whole situation and scope of action and decision to his own judgment, secure in the knowledge that he would act wisely. I told him that I trusted the party to him and said good-bye to the men. Then we pushed off for the last time, and within a few minutes I was aboard the *James Caird*. The crew of the *Stancomb Wills* shook hands with us as the boats bumped together and offered us the last good wishes. Then, setting our jib, we cut the painter and moved away to the north-east. The men who were staying behind made a pathetic little group on the beach, with the grim heights of the island behind them and the sea seething at their feet, but they waved to us and gave three hearty cheers. There was hope in their hearts and they trusted us to bring the help that they needed.

I had all sails set, and the *James Caird* quickly dipped the beach and its line of dark figures. The westerly wind took us rapidly to the line of pack, and as we entered it I stood up with my arm around the mast, directing the steering, so as to avoid the great lumps of ice that were flung about in the heave of the sea. The pack thickened and we were forced to turn almost due east, running before the wind towards a gap I had seen in the morning from the high ground. I could not see the gap now, but we had come out on its bearing and I was prepared to find that it had been influenced by the easterly drift. At four o'clock in the afternoon we found the channel, much narrower than it had seemed in the morning but still navigable.

Dropping sail, we rowed through without touching the ice any-where, and by 5:30 P.M. we were clear of the pack with open water before us. We passed one more piece of ice in the darkness an hour later, but the pack lay behind, and with a fair wind swelling the sails we steered our little craft through the night, our hopes centred on our distant goal. The swell was very heavy now, and when the time came for our first evening meal we found great difficulty in keeping the Primus lamp alight and preventing the hoosh splashing out of the pot. Three men were needed to attend to the cooking, one man holding the lamp and two men guarding the aluminium cooking-pot, which had to be lifted clear of the Primus whenever the move-ment of the boat threatened to cause a disaster. Then the lamp had to be protected from the water, for sprays were coming over the bows and our flimsy decking was for no means water-tight. All these opera-tions were conducted in the confined space under the decking, where the men lay or knelt and adjusted themselves as best they could to the angles of our cases and ballast. It was uncomfortable, but we found consolation in the reflection that without the decking we could not have used the cooker at all.

The tale of the next sixteen days is one of supreme strife amid heaving waters. The sub-Antarctic ocean lived up to its evil winter reputation. I decided to run north for at least two days while the wind held and so get into warmer weather before turning to the east and laying a course for South Georgia. We took two-hourly spells at the tiller. The men who were not on watch crawled into the sodden sleeping-bags and tried to forget their troubles for a period; but there was no comfort in the boat. The bags and cases seemed to be alive in the unfailing knack of presenting their most uncomfort-able angles to our rest-seeking bodies. A man might imagine for a moment that he had found a position of ease, but always discovered quickly that some unyielding point was impinging on muscle or bone. The first night aboard the boat was one of acute discomfort for us all, and we were heartily glad when the dawn came and we could set about the preparation of a hot breakfast.

This record of the voyage to South Georgia is based upon scanty notes made day by day. The notes dealt usually with the bare facts of distances, positions, and weather, but our memories retained the incidents of the passing days in a period never to be forgotten. By running north for the first two days I hoped to get warmer weather and also to avoid lines of pack that might be extending beyond the main body. We needed all the advantage that we could obtain from the higher latitude for sailing on the great circle, but we had to be cautious regarding possible ice-streams. Cramped in our narrow quarters and continually wet by the spray, we suffered severely from cold throughout the journey. We fought the seas and the winds and at the same time had a daily struggle to keep ourselves alive. At times we were in dire peril. Generally we were upheld by the knowledge that we were making progress towards the land where we would be, but there were days and nights when we lay hove to, drifting across the storm-whitened seas and watching, with eyes interested rather than apprehensive, the uprearing masses of water, flung to and fro by Nature in the pride of her strength. Deep seemed the valleys when we lay between the reeling seas. High were the hills when we perched momentarily on the tops of giant combers. Nearly always there were gales. So small was our boat and so great were the seas that often our sail flapped idly in the calm between the crests of two waves. Then we would climb the next slope and catch the full fury of the gale where the wool-like whiteness of the breaking water surged around us. We had our moments of laughter—rare it is true, but hearty enough. Even when cracked lips and swollen mouths checked the outward and visible signs of amusement we could see a joke of the primitive kind. Man's sense of humour is always most easily stirred by the petty misfortunes of his neighbours, and I shall never forget Worsley's efforts on one occasion to place the hot aluminium stand on top of the Primus stove after it had fallen off in an extra heavy roll. With his frost-bitten fingers he picked it up, dropped it, picked it up again, and toyed with it gingerly as though it were some fragile article of lady's wear. We laughed, or rather gurgled with laughter.

The wind came up strong and worked into a gale from the northwest on the third day out. We stood away to the east. The increasing seas discovered the weaknesses of our decking. The continuous blows shifted the box-lids and sledge-runners so that the canvas sagged down and accumulated water. Then icy trickles, distinct from the driving sprays, poured fore and aft into the boat. The nails that the carpenter had extracted from cases at Elephant Island and used to fasten down the battens were too short to make firm the decking. We did what we could to secure it, but our means were very limited, and the water continued to enter the boat at a dozen points. Much baling was necessary, and nothing that we could do prevented our gear from becoming sodden. The searching runnels from the canvas were really more unpleasant than the sudden definite douches of the sprays. Lying under the thwarts during watches below, we tried vainly to avoid them. There were no dry places in the boat, and at last we simply covered our heads with our Burberrys and endured the all-pervading water. The baling was work for the watch. Real rest we had none. The perpetual motion of the boat made repose impossible; we were cold, sore, and anxious. We moved on hands and knees in the semi-darkness of the day under the decking. The darkness was complete by 6 P.M., and not until 7 A.M. of the following day could we see one another under the thwarts. We had a few scraps of candle, and they were preserved carefully in order that we might have light at meal-times. There was one fairly dry spot in the boat, under the solid original decking at the bows, and we managed to protect some of our biscuit from the salt water; but I do not think any of us got the taste of salt out of our mouths during the voyage.

The difficulty of movement in the boat would have had its humorous side if it had not involved us in so many aches and pains. We had to crawl under the thwarts in order to move along the boat, and our knees suffered considerably. When a watch turned out it was necessary for me to direct each man by name when and where to move, since if all hands had crawled about at the same time the result would have been dire confusion and many bruises. Then there was the trim of the boat to be considered. The order of the watch was four hours on and four hours off, three men to the watch. One man had the tiller-ropes, the second man attended to the sail, and the third baled for all he was worth. Sometimes when the water in the boat had been reduced to reasonable proportions, our pump would be used. This pump, which Hurley had made from the Flinders bar case of our ship's standard compass, was quite effective, though its capacity was not large. The man who was attending the sail could pump into the big outer cooker, which was lifted and emptied overboard when filled. We had a device by which the water could go direct from the pump into the sea through a hole in the gunwale, but this hole had to be blocked at an early stage of the voyage, since we found that it admitted water when the boat rolled.

While a new watch was shivering in the wind and spray, the men who had been relieved groped hurriedly among the soaked sleeping-bags and tried to steal a little of the warmth created by the last occupants; but it was not always possible for us to find even this comfort when we went off watch. The boulders that we had taken aboard for ballast had to be shifted continually in order to trim the boat and give access to the pump, which became choked with hairs from the moulting sleeping-bags and finneskoe. The four reindeer-skin sleeping-bags shed their hair freely owing to the continuous wetting and soon became quite bald in appearance. The moving of the boulders was weary and painful work. We came to know every one of the stones by sight and touch, and I have vivid memories of their angular peculiarities even to-day. They might have been of considerable interest as geological specimens to a scientific man under happier conditions. As ballast they were useful. As weights to be moved about in cramped quarters they were simply appalling. They spared no portion of our poor bodies. Another of our troubles, worth mention here, was the chafing of our legs by our wet clothes, which had not been changed now for seven months. The insides of our thighs were rubbed raw, and the one tube of Hazeline cream in our medicine-chest did not go far in alleviating our pain, which was increased by the bite of the salt water. We thought at the time that we never slept. The fact was that we would doze off uncomfortably, to be aroused quickly by some new ache or another call to effort. My own share of the general unpleasantness was accentuated by a finely developed bout of sciatica. I had become possessed of this originally on the floe several months earlier.

Our meals were regular in spite of the gales. Attention to this point was essential, since the conditions of the voyage made increasing calls upon our vitality. Breakfast, at 8 A.M., consisted of a pannikin of hot hoosh made from Bovril sledging ration, two biscuits, and some lumps of sugar. Lunch came at 1 P.M., and comprised Bovril sledging ration, eaten raw, and a pannikin of hot milk for each man. Tea, at 5 P.M., had the same menu. Then during the night we had a hot drink, generally of milk. The meals were the bright beacons in those cold and stormy days. The glow of warmth and comfort produced by the food and drink made optimists of us all. We had two tins of Virol, which we were keeping for an emergency; but finding ourselves in need of an oil-lamp to eke out our supply of candles, we emptied one of the tins in the manner that most appealed to us, and fitted it with a wick made by shredding a bit of canvas. When this lamp was filled with oil it gave a certain amount of light, though it was easily blown out, and was of great assistance to us at night. We were fairly well off as regarded fuel, since we had 6½ gallons of petroleum.

A severe south-westerly gale on the fourth day out forced us to heave to. I would have liked to have run before the wind, but the sea was very high and the *James Caird* was in danger of broaching to and swamping. The delay was vexatious, since up to that time we had been making sixty or seventy miles a day; good going with our limited sail area. We hove to under double-reefed mainsail and our little jigger, and waited for the gale to blow itself out. During that afternoon we saw bits of wreckage, the remains probably of some unfortunate vessel that had failed to weather the strong gales south of Cape Horn. The weather conditions did not improve, and on the fifth day out the gale was so fierce that we were compelled to take in the double-reefed mainsail and hoist our small jib instead. We put out a sea-anchor to keep the *James Caird*'s head up to the sea. This anchor consisted of a triangular canvas bag fastened to the end of the painter and allowed to stream out from the bows. The boat was high enough to catch the wind, and, as she drifted to leeward, the drag of the anchor kept her head to windward. Thus our boat took most of the seas more or less end on. Even then the crests of the waves often would curl right over us and we shipped a great deal of water, which necessitated unceasing baling and pumping. Looking out abeam, we would see a hollow like a tunnel formed as the crest of a big wave toppled over on to the swelling body of water. A thousand times it appeared as though the *James Caird* must be engulfed; but the boat lived. The south-westerly gale had its birthplace above the Antarctic Continent, and its freezing breath lowered the temperature far towards zero. The sprays froze upon the boat and gave bows, sides, and decking a heavy coat of mail. This accumulation of ice reduced the buoyancy of the boat, and to that extent was an added peril; but it possessed a notable advantage from one point of view. The water ceased to drop and trickle from the canvas, and the spray came in solely at the well in the after part of the boat. We could not allow the load of ice to grow beyond a certain point, and in turns we crawled about the decking forward, chipping and picking at it with the available tools.

When daylight came on the morning of the sixth day out we saw and felt that the *James Caird* had lost her resiliency. She was not rising to the oncoming seas. The weight of the ice that had formed in her and upon her during the night was having its effect, and she was becoming more like a log than a boat. The situation called for immediate action. We first broke away the spare oars, which were encased in ice and frozen to the sides of the boat, and threw them overboard. We retained two oars for use when we got inshore. Two of the fur sleeping-bags went over the side; they were thoroughly wet, weighing probably 40 lb. each, and they had frozen stiff during the night. Three men constituted the watch below, and when a man went down it was better to turn into the wet bag just vacated by another man than to thaw out a frozen bag with the heat of his unfortunate body. We now had four bags, three in use and one for emergency use in case a member of the party should break down permanently. The reduction of weight relieved the boat to some extent, and vigorous chipping and scraping did more. We had to be very careful not to put axe or knife through the frozen canvas of the decking as we crawled over it, but gradually we got rid of a lot of ice. The *James Caird* lifted to the endless waves as though she lived again.

About 11 A.M. the boat suddenly fell off into the trough of the sea. The painter had parted and the sea-anchor had gone. This was serious. The *James Caird* went away to leeward, and we had no chance at all of recovering the anchor and our valuable rope, which had been our only means of keeping the boat's head up to the seas without the risk of hoisting sail in a gale. Now we had to set the sail and trust to its holding. While the *James Caird* rolled heavily in the trough, we beat the frozen canvas until the bulk of the ice had cracked off it and then hoisted it. The frozen gear worked protestingly, but after a struggle our little craft came up to the wind again, and we breathed more freely. Skin frost-bites were troubling us, and we had developed large blisters on our fingers and hands. I shall always carry the scar of one of these frost-bites on my left hand, which became badly inflamed after the skin had burst and the cold had bitten deeply.

We held the boat up to the gale during that day, enduring as best we could discomforts that amounted to pain. The boat tossed interminably on the big waves under grey, threatening skies. Our thoughts did not embrace much more than the necessities of the hour. Every surge of the sea was an enemy to be watched and circumvented. We ate our scanty meals, treated our frost-bites, and hoped for the improved conditions that the morrow might bring. Night fell early, and in the lagging hours of darkness we were cheered by a change for the better in the weather. The wind dropped, the snow-squalls became less frequent, and the sea moderated. When the morning of the seventh day dawned there was not much wind. We shook the reef out of the sail and laid our course once more for South Georgia. The sun

came out bright and clear, and presently Worsley got a snap for longitude. We hoped that the sky would remain clear until noon, so that we
could get the latitude. We had been six days out without an observation, and our dead reckoning naturally was uncertain. The boat must
have presented a strange appearance that morning. All hands basked in
the sun. We hung our sleeping-bags to the mast and spread our socks
and other gear all over the deck. Some of the ice had melted on the
James Caird in the early morning after the gale began to slacken, and
dry patches were appearing in the decking. Porpoises came blowing
round the boat, and Cape pigeons wheeled and swooped within a few
feet of us. These little black-and-white birds have an air of friendliness
that is not possessed by the great circling albatross. They had looked
grey against the swaying sea during the storm as they darted about
over our heads and uttered their plaintive cries. The albatrosses, of the
black or sooty variety, had watched with hard, bright eyes, and seemed
to have a quite impersonal interest in our struggle to keep afloat amid
the battering seas. In addition to the Cape pigeons an occasional
stormy petrel flashed overhead. Then there was a small bird, unknown
to me, that appeared always to be in a fussy, bustling state, quite out of
keeping with the surroundings. It irritated me. It had practically no
tail, and it flitted about vaguely as though in search of the lost member. I used to find myself wishing it would find its tail and have done
with the silly fluttering.

We reveled in the warmth of the sun that day. Life was not so
bad, after all. We felt we were well on our way. Our gear was drying,
and we could have a hot meal in comparative comfort. The swell was
still heavy, but it was not breaking and the boat road easily. At noon
Worsley balanced himself on the gunwale and clung with one hand
to the stay of the mainmast while he got a snap of the sun. The result
was more than encouraging. We had done over 380 miles and were
getting on for half-way to South Georgia. It looked as though we
were going to get through.

The wind freshened to a good stiff breeze during the afternoon, and the *James Caird* made satisfactory progress. I had not real-

ized until the sunlight came how small our boat really was. There was some influence in the light and warmth, some hint of happier days, that made us revive memories of other voyages, when we had stout decks beneath our feet, unlimited food at our command, and pleasant cabins for our ease. Now we clung to a battered little boat, "alone, alone, all alone, alone on a wide, wide sea." So low in the water were we that each succeeding swell cut off our view of the sky-line. We were a tiny speck in the vast vista of the sea—the ocean that is open to all and merciful to none, that threatens even when it seems to yield, and that is pitiless always to weakness. For a moment the consciousness of the forces arrayed against us would be almost overwhelming. Then hope and confidence would rise again as our boat rose to a wave and tossed aside the crest in a sparkling shower like the play of prismatic colours at the foot of a waterfall. My double-barrelled gun and some cartridges had been stored aboard the boat as an emergency precaution against a shortage of food, but we were not disposed to destroy our little neighbours, the Cape pigeons, even for the sake of fresh meat. We might have shot an albatross, but the wandering king of the ocean aroused in us something of the feeling that inspired, too late, the Ancient Mariner. So the gun remained among the stores and sleeping bags in the narrow quarters beneath our leaking deck, and the birds followed us unmolested.

The eighth, ninth, and tenth days of the voyage had few features worthy of special note. The wind blew hard during those days, and the strain of navigating the boat was unceasing, but always we made some advance towards our goal. No bergs showed on our horizon, and we knew that we were clear of the ice-fields. Each day brought its little round of troubles, but also compensation in the form of food and growing hope. We felt that we were going to succeed. The odds against us had been great, but we were winning through. We still suffered severely from the cold, for, though the temperature was rising, our vitality was declining owing to shortage of food, exposure and the necessity of maintaining our cramped positions day and night. I found that it was now absolutely necessary to prepare hot milk for all hands during the night, in order to sustain life until dawn. This meant lighting the Primus lamp in the darkness and involved an increased drain on our small store of matches. It was the rule that one match must serve when the Primus was being lit. We had no lamp for the compass and during the early days of the voyage we would strike a match when the steersman wanted to see the course at night; but later the necessity for strict economy impressed itself upon us, and the practice of striking matches at night was stopped. We had one water-tight tin of matches. I had stowed away in a pocket, in readiness for a sunny day, a lens from one of the telescopes, but this was of no use during the voyage. The sun seldom shone upon us. The glass of the compass got broken one night, and we contrived to mend it with adhesive tape from the medicine-chest. One of the memories that comes to me from those days is of Crean singing at the tiller. He always sang while he was steering, and nobody ever discovered what the song was. It was devoid of tune and as monotonous as the chanting of a Buddhist monk at his prayers; yet somehow it was cheerful. In moments of inspiration Crean would attempt "The Wearing of the Green."

On the tenth night Worsley could not straighten his body after his spell at the tiller. He was thoroughly cramped, and we had to drag him beneath the decking and massage him before he could unbend himself and get into a sleeping-bag. A hard north-westerly gale came up on the eleventh day (May 5) and shifted to the south-west in the late afternoon. The sky was overcast and occasional snow-squalls added to the discomfort produced by a tremendous cross-sea—the worst, I thought, that we had experienced. At midnight I was at the tiller and suddenly noticed a line of clear sky between the south and south-west. I called to the other men that the sky was clearing, and then a moment later I realized that what I had seen was not a rift in the clouds but the white crest of an enormous wave. During twenty-six years' experience of the ocean in all its moods I had not encountered a wave so gigantic. It was a mighty upheaval of the ocean, a thing quite apart from the big white-capped seas that had been our tireless enemies for many days. I shouted, "For God's sake, hold on!

It's got us!" Then came a moment of suspense that seemed drawn out into hours. White surged the foam of the breaking sea around us. We felt our boat lifted and flung forward like a cork in braking surf. We were in a seething chaos of tortured water; but somehow the boat lived through it, half-full of water, sagging to the dead weight and shuddering under the blow. We baled with the energy of men fighting for life, flinging the water over the sides with every receptacle that came to our hands, and after ten minutes of uncertainty we felt the boat renew her life beneath us. She floated again and ceased to lurch drunkenly as though dazed by the attack of the sea. Earnestly we hoped that never again would we encounter such a wave.

The conditions in the boat, uncomfortable before, had been made worse by the deluge of water. All our gear was thoroughly wet again. Our cooking-stove had been floating about in the bottom of the boat and portions of our last hoosh seemed to have permeated everything. Not until 3 A.M., when we were all chilled almost to the limit of endurance, did we manage to get the stove alight and make ourselves hot drinks. The carpenter was suffering particularly, but he showed grit and spirit. Vincent had for the past week ceased to be an active member of the crew, and I could not easily account for his collapse. Physically he was one of the strongest men in the boat. He was a young man, he had served on North Sea trawlers, and he should have been able to bear hardships better than McCarthy, who, not so strong, was always happy.

The weather was better on the following day (May 6), and we got a glimpse of the sun. Worsley's observation showed that we were not more than a hundred miles from the north-west corner of South Georgia. Two more days with a favourable wind and we would sight the promised land. I hoped that there would be no delay, for our supply of water was running very low. The hot drink at night was essential, but I decided that the daily allowance of water must be cut down to half a pint per man. The lumps of ice we had taken aboard had gone long ago. We were dependent upon the water we had brought from Elephant Island, and our thirst was increased by the fact that we were now using the brackish water in the breaker that had been slightly stove in in the surf when the boat was being loaded. Some sea-water had entered at that time.

Thirst took possession of us. I dared not permit the allowance of water to be increased since an unfavourable wind might drive us away from the island and lengthen our voyage by many days. Lack of water is always the most severe privation that men can be condemned to endure, and we found, as during our earlier boat voyage, that the salt water in our clothing and the salt spray that lashed our faces made our thirst grow quickly to a burning pain. I had to be very firm in refusing to allow any one to anticipate the morrow's allowance, which I was sometimes begged to do. We did the necessary work dully and hoped for the land. I had altered the course to the east so as to make sure of our striking the island, which would have been impossible to regain if we had run past the northern end. The course was laid on our scrap of chart for a point some thirty miles down the coast. That day and the following day passed for us in a sort of nightmare. Our mouths were dry and our tongues were swollen. The wind was still strong and the heavy sea forced us to navigate carefully, but any thought of our peril from the waves was buried beneath the consciousness of our raging thirst. The bright moments were those when we each received our one mug of hot milk during the long, bitter watches of the night. Things were bad for us in those days, but the end was coming. The morning of May 8 broke thick and stormy, with squalls from the north-west. We searched the waters ahead for a sign of land, and though we could see nothing more than had met our eyes for many days, we were cheered by a sense that the goal was near at hand. About ten o'clock that morning we passed a little bit of kelp, a glad signal of the proximity of land. An hour later we saw two shags sitting on a big mass of kelp, and knew then that we must be within ten or fifteen miles of the shore. These birds are as sure an indication of the proximity of land as a lighthouse is, for they never venture far to sea. We gazed ahead with increasing eagerness, and at 12:30 P.M., through a rift in the clouds, McCarthy caught a glimpse of the black cliffs of South Georgia, just fourteen days after our departure from Elephant Island. It was a glad moment. Thirst-ridden, chilled, and weak as we were, happiness irradiated us. The job was nearly done.

We stood in towards the shore to look for a landing-place, and presently we could see the green tussock-grass on the ledges above the surf-beaten rocks. Ahead of us and to the south, blind rollers showed the presence of uncharted reefs along the coast. Here and there the hungry rocks were close to the surface, and over them the great waves broke, swirling viciously and spouting thirty and forty feet into the air. The rocky coast appeared to descend sheer to the sea. Our need of water and rest was wellnigh desperate, but to have attempted a landing at the time would have been suicidal. Night was drawing near, and the weather indications were not favourable. There was nothing for it but to haul off till the following morning, so we stood away on the starboard tack until we had made what appeared to be a safe offing. Then we hove to in the high westerly swell. The hours passed slowly as we waited the dawn, which would herald, we fondly hoped, the last stage of our journal. Our thirst was a torment and we could scarcely touch our food; the cold seemed to strike right through our weakened bodies. At 5 A.M. the wind shifted to the north-west and quickly increased to one of the worst hurricanes any of us had ever experienced. A great cross-sea was running, and the wind simply shrieked as it tore the tops off the waves and converted the whole seascape into a haze of driving spray. Down into valleys, up to tossing heights, straining until her seams opened, swung our little boat, brave still but labouring heavily. We knew that the wind and set of the sea were driving us ashore, but we could do nothing. The dawn showed us a storm-torn ocean, and the morning passed without bringing us a sight of the land; but at 1 P.M., through a rift in the flying mists, we got a glimpse of the huge crags of the island and realized that our position had become desperate. We were on a dead lee shore, and we could gauge our approach to the unseen cliffs by the roar of the breakers against the sheer walls of rock. I ordered the double-reefed mainsail to be set in the hope that we might claw off, and this attempt increased the strain upon the boat. The *James Caird* was bumping heavily, and the water was pouring in everywhere. Our thirst was forgotten in the realization of our imminent danger, as we baled unceasingly, and adjusted our weights from time to time; occasional glimpses showed that the shore was nearer. I knew that Annewkow Island lay to the south of us, but our small and badly marked chart showed uncertain reefs in the passage between the island and the mainland, and I dared not trust it, though as a last resort we could try to lie under the lee of the island. The afternoon wore away as we edged down the coast, with the thunder of the breakers in our ears. The approach of evening found us still some distance from Annewkow Island, and, dimly in the twilight, we could see a snow-capped mountain looming above us. The chance of surviving the night, with the driving gale and the implacable sea forcing us on to the lee shore, seemed small. I think most of us had a feeling that the end was very near. Just after 6 P.M., in the dark, as the boat was in the yeasty backwash from the seas flung from this iron-bound coast, then, just when things looked their worst, they changed for the best. I have marveled often at the thin line that divides success from failure and the sudden turn that leads from apparently certain disaster to comparative safety. The wind suddenly shifted, and we were free once more to make an offing. Almost as soon as the gale eased, the pin that locked the mast to the thwart fell out. It must have been on the point of doing this throughout the hurricane, and if it had gone nothing could have saved us; the mast would have snapped like a carrot. Our backstays had carried away once before when iced up and were not too strongly fastened now. We were thankful indeed for the mercy that had held that pin in its place throughout the hurricane.

We stood off shore again, tired almost to the point of apathy. Our water had long been finished. The last was about a pint of hairy liquid which we strained through a bit of gauze from the medicine-chest. The pangs of thirst attacked us with redoubled intensity, and I felt that we must make a landing on the following day at almost any hazard. The night wore on. We were very tired. We longed for day.

When at last the dawn came on the morning of May 10 there was practically no wind, but a high cross-sea was running. We made slow progress towards the shore. About 8 A.M. the wind backed to the north-west and threatened another blow. We had sighted in the meantime a big indentation which I thought must be King Haakon Bay, and I decided that we must land there. We set the bows of the boat towards the bay and ran before the freshening gale. Soon we had angry reefs on either side. Great glaciers came down to the sea and offered no landing-place, the sea spouted on the reefs and thundered against the shore. About noon we sighted a line of jagged reef, like blackened teeth, that seemed to bar the entrance to the bay. Inside, comparatively smooth water stretched eight or nine miles to the head of the bay. A gap in the reef appeared, and we made for it. But the fates had another rebuff for us. The wind shifted and blew from the east right out of the bay. We could see the way through the reef, but we could not approach it directly. That afternoon we bore up, tacking five times in the strong wind. The last tack enabled us to be through, and at last we were in the wide mouth of the bay. Dusk was approaching. A small cove, with a boulder-strewn beach guarded by a reef, made a break in the cliffs on the south side of the bay and we turned in that direction. I stood in the bows directing the steering as we ran through the kelp and made the passage of the reef. The entrance was so narrow that we had to take in the oars, and the swell was piling itself right over the reef into the cove; but in a minute or two we were inside, and in the gathering darkness the *James Caird* ran in on a swell and touched the beach. I sprang ashore with the short painter and held on when the boat went out with the backward surge. When the *James Caird* came in again three of the men got ashore, and they held the painter while I climbed some rocks with another line. A slip on the wet rocks twenty feet up nearly closed my part of the story just at the moment when we were achieving safety. A jagged piece of rock held me and at the same time bruised me sorely. However, I made fast the line, and in a few minutes we were all safe on the beach, with the boat floating in the surging water just off the shore. We heard a gurgling sound that was sweet music in our ears, and peering around, found a stream of fresh water almost at our feet. A moment later we were down on our knees drinking the pure, ice cold water in long draughts that put new life into us. It was a splendid moment.

The next thing was to get the stores and ballast out of the boat, in order that we might secure her for the night. We carried the stores and gear above high-water mark and threw out the bags of sand and the boulders that we knew so well. Then we attempted to pull the empty boat up the beach, and discovered by this effort how weak we had become. Our united strength was not sufficient to get the *James Caird* clear of the water. Time after time we pulled together, but without avail. I saw that it would be necessary to have food and rest before we beached the boat. We made fast a line to a heavy boulder and set a watch to fend the *James Caird* off the rocks of the beach. Then I sent Crean round to the left side of the cove, about thirty yards away, where I had noticed a little cave as we were running in. He could not see much in the darkness, but reported that the place certainly promised some shelter. We carried the sleeping-bags round and found a mere hollow in the rock-face with a shingle floor sloping at a steep angle to the sea. There we prepared a hot meal, and when the food was finished I ordered the men to turn in. The time was now about 8 P.M., and I took the first watch beside the *James Caird,* which was still afloat in the tossing water just off the beach.

Fending the *James Caird* off the rocks in the darkness was awkward work. The boat would have bumped dangerously if allowed to ride in with the waves that drove into the cove. I found a flat rock for my feet, which were in a bad way owing to cold, wetness, and lack of exercise in the boat, and during the next few hours I laboured to keep the *James Caird* clear of the beach. Occasionally I had to rush into the seething water. Then, as a wave receded, I let the boat out on the alpine rope so as to avoid a sudden jerk. The heavy painter had been lost when the sea-anchor went adrift. The *James Caird* could be seen but dimly in the cove, where the high black cliffs made the darkness almost complete, and the strain upon one's attention was great.

After several hours had passed I found that my desire for sleep was becoming irresistible, and at 1 A.M. I called Crean. I could hear him groaning as he stumbled over the sharp rocks on his way down the beach. While he was taking charge of the *James Caird* she got adrift, and we had some anxious moments. Fortunately, she went across towards the cave and we secured her unharmed. The loss or destruction of the boat at this stage would have been a very serious matter, since we probably would have found it impossible to leave the cove except by sea. The cliffs and glaciers around offered no practicable path towards the head of the bay. I arranged for one-hour watches during the remainder of the night and then took Crean's place among the sleeping men and got some sleep before the dawn came.

The sea went down in the early hours of the morning (May 11), and after sunrise we were able to set about getting the boat ashore, first bracing ourselves for the task with another meal. We were all weak still. We cut off the topsides and took out all the movable gear. Then we waited for Byron's "great ninth wave," and when it lifted the *James Caird* in we held her and by dint of great exertion, worked her round broadside to the sea. Inch by inch we dragged her up until we reached the fringe of the tussock-grass. The completion of this job removed our immediate anxieties, and we were free to examine our surroundings and plan the next move. The day was bright and clear.

King Haakon Bay is an eight-mile sound penetrating the coast of South Georgia in an easterly direction. We had noticed that the northern and southern sides of the sound were formed by steep mountain-ranges, their flanks furrowed by mighty glaciers, the outlets of the great ice-sheet of the interior. It was obvious that these glaciers and the precipitous slopes of the mountains barred our way inland from the cove. We must sail to the head of the sound. Swirling clouds and mist-wreaths had obscured our view of the sound when we were entering, but glimpses of snow-slopes had given us hope that an overland journey could be begun from that point. A few patches of very rough, tussocky land, dotted with little tarns, lay between the glaciers along the foot of the mountains, which were heavily scarred with scree-slopes. Several magnificent peaks and crags gazed out across their snowy domains to the sparkling waters of the sound.

Our cove lay a little inside the southern headland of King Haakon Bay. A narrow break in the cliffs, which were about a hundred feet high at this point, formed the entrance to the cove. The cliffs continued inside the cove on each side and merged into a hill which descended at a steep slope to the boulder beach. The slope, which carried tussock-grass, was not continuous. It eased at two points into little peaty swamp terraces dotted with frozen pools and drained by two small streams. Our cave was a recess in the cliff on the left-hand end of the beach. The rocky face of the cliff was undercut at this point, and the shingle thrown up by the waves formed a steep slope, which we reduced to about one in six by scraping the stones away from the inside. Later we strewed the rough floor with the dead, nearly dry underleaves of the tussock-grass so as to form a slightly soft bed for our sleeping-bags. Water had trickled down the face of the cliff and formed long icicles, which hung down in front of the cave to the length of about fifteen feet. These icicles provided shelter, and when we had spread our sails below them, with the assistance of oars, we had quarters that, in the circumstances, had to be regarded as reasonably comfortable. The camp at least was dry, and we moved our gear there with confidence. We built a fireplace and arranged our sleeping-bags and blankets around it. The cave was about 8 ft. deep and 12 ft. wide at the entrance.

While the camp was being arranged Crean and I climbed the tussock slope behind the beach and reached the top of a headland overlooking the sound. There we found the nests of albatrosses, and, much to our delight, the nests contained young birds. The fledgelings were fat and lusty, and we had no hesitation about deciding that they were destined to die at an early age. Our most pressing anxiety at this stage was a shortage of fuel for the cooker. We had rations for ten more days, and we knew now that we could get birds for food; but if we were to have hot meals we must secure fuel. The store of petroleum carried in the boat was running very low, and it seemed necessary to keep some quantity for use on the overland journey that lay ahead of us. A sea-elephant or a seal would have provided fuel as well as food, but we could see none in the neighbourhood. During the morning we started a fire in the cave with wood from the top-sides of the boat, and though the dense smoke from the damp sticks inflamed our tired eyes, the warmth and prospect of hot food were ample compensation. Crean was cook that day, and I suggested to him that he should wear his goggles, which he happened to have brought with him. The goggles helped him a great deal as he bent over the fire and tended the stew. And what a stew it was! The young albatrosses weighted about fourteen pounds each fresh killed, and we estimated that they weighted at least six pounds each when cleaned and dressed for the pot. Four birds went into the pot for six men, with a Bovril ration for thickening. The flesh was white and succulent, and the bones, not fully formed, almost melted in our mouths. That was a memorable meal. When we had eaten our fill, we dried our tobacco in the embers of the fire and smoked contentedly. We made an attempt to dry our clothes, which were soaked with salt water, but did not meet with much success. We could not afford to have a fire except for cooking purposes until blubber or driftwood had come our way.

The final stage of the journey had still to be attempted. I realized that the condition of the party generally, and particularly of McNeish and Vincent, would prevent us putting to sea again except under pressure of dire necessity. Our boat, moreover, had been weakened by the cutting away of the top-sides, and I doubted if we could weather the island. We were still 150 miles away from Stromness whaling-station by sea. The alternative was to attempt the crossing of the island. If we could not get over, then we must try to secure enough food and fuel to keep us alive through the winter, but this possibility was scarcely thinkable. Over on Elephant Island twenty-two men were waiting for the relief that we alone could secure for them. Their plight was worse than ours. We must push on somehow. Several days must elapse before our strength would be sufficiently recovered to allow us to row or sail the last nine miles up to the head of the bay. In the meantime we could make what preparations were possible and dry our clothes by taking advantage of every scrap of heat from the fires we lit for the cooking of our meals. We turned in early that night, and I remember that I dreamed of the great wave and aroused my companions with a shout of warning as I saw with half-awakened eyes the towering cliff on the opposite side of the cove.

Shortly before midnight a gale sprang up suddenly from the north-east with rain and sleet showers. It brought quantities of glacier-ice into the cove and by 2. A.M. (May 12) our little harbour was filled with ice, which surged to and fro in the swell and pushed its way on to the beach. We had solid rock beneath our feet and could watch without anxiety. When daylight came rain was falling heavily, and the temperature was the highest we had experienced for many months. The icicles overhanging our cave were melting down in streams and we had to move smartly when passing in and out lest we should be struck by falling lumps. A fragment weighing fifteen or twenty pounds crashed down while we were having breakfast. We found that a big hole had been burned in the bottom of Worsley's reindeer sleeping-bag during the night. Worsley had been awakened by a burning sensation in his feet, and had asked the men near him if his bag was all right; they looked and could see nothing wrong. We were all superficially frostbitten about the feet, and this condition caused the extremities to burn painfully, while at the same time sensation was lost in the skin. Worsley thought that the uncomfortable heat of his feet was due to the frost-bites, and he stayed in his bag and presently went to sleep again. He discovered when he turned out in the morning that the tussock-grass which we had laid on the floor of the cave had smouldered outwards from the fire and had actually burned a large hole in the bag beneath his feet. Fortunately, his feet were not harmed.

Our party spent a quiet day, attending to clothing and gear, checking stores, eating and resting. Some more of the young albatrosses made a noble end in our pot. The birds were nesting on a small plateau above the right-hand end of our beach. We had previously discovered that when we were landing from the boat on the night of May 10 we had lost the rudder. The *James Caird* had been bumping heavily astern as we were scrambling ashore, and evidently the rudder was then knocked off. A careful search of the beach and the rocks within our reach failed to reveal the missing article. This was a serious loss, even if the voyage to the head of the sound could be made in good weather. At dusk the ice in the cove was rearing and crashing on the beach. It had forced up a ridge of stones close to where the *James Caird* lay at the edge of the tussock-grass. Some pieces of ice were driven right up to the canvas wall at the front of our cave. Fragments lodged within two feet of Vincent, who had the lowest sleeping-place, and within four feet of our fire. Crean and McCarthy had brought down six more of the young albatrosses in the afternoon, so we were well supplied with fresh food. The air temperature that night probably was not lower than 38° or 40° Fahr., and we were rendered uncomfortable in our cramped sleeping quarters by the unaccustomed warmth. Our feelings towards our neighbours underwent a change. When the temperature was below 20° Fahr. we could not get too close to one another—every man wanted to cuddle against his neighbour; but let the temperature rise a few degrees and the warmth of another man's body ceased to be a blessing. The ice and the waves had a voice of menace that night, but I heard it only in my dreams.

The bay was still filled with ice on the morning of Saturday, May 13, but the tide took it all away in the afternoon. Then a strange thing happened. The rudder, with all the broad Atlantic to sail in and the coasts of two continents to search for a resting-place, came bobbing back into our cove. With anxious eyes we watched it as it advanced, receded again, and then advanced once more under the capricious influence of wind and wave. Nearer and nearer it came as we waited on the shore, oars in hand, and at last we were able to seize it. Surely a remarkable salvage! The day was bright and clear; our clothes were drying and our strength was returning. Running water made a musical sound down the tussock slope and among the boulders. We carried our blankets up the hill and tried to dry them in the breeze 300 ft. above sea-level. In the afternoon we began to prepare the *James Caird* for the journey to the head of King Haakon Bay. A noon observation on this day gave our latitude as 54° 10' 47" S., but according to the German chart the position should have been 54° 12' S. Probably Worsley's observation was the more accurate. We were able to keep the fire alight until we went to sleep that night, for while climbing the rocks above the cove I had seen at the foot of a cliff a broken spar, which had been thrown up by the waves. We could reach this spar by climbing down the cliff, and with a reserve supply of fuel thus in sight we could afford to burn the fragments of the *James Caird*'s topsides more freely.

During the morning of this day (May 13) Worsley and I tramped across the hills in a north-easterly direction with the object of getting a view of the sound and possibly gathering some information that would be useful to us in the next stage of our journey. It was exhausting work, but after covering about 2½ miles in two hours we were able to look east, up the bay. We could not see very much of the country that we would have to cross in order to reach the whaling-station on the other side of the island. We had passed several brooks and frozen tarns, and at a point where we had to take to the beach on the shore of the sound we found some wreckage—an 18-ft. pine-spar (probably part of a ship's topmast), several pieces of timber, and a little model of a ship's hull, evidently a child's toy. We wondered what tragedy that pitiful little plaything indicated. We encountered also some gentoo penguins and a young sea-elephant, which Worsley killed.

When we got back to the cave at 3 P.M., tired, hungry, but rather pleased with ourselves, we found a splendid meal of stewed albatross chicken waiting for us. We had carried a quantity of blubber and the sea-elephant's liver in our blouses, and we produced our treasures as a surprise for the men. Rough climbing on the way back to camp had nearly persuaded us to throw the stuff away, but we had held on (regardless of the condition of our already sorely tried clothing), and had a reward at the camp. The long bay had been a magnificent sight, even to eyes that had dwelt on grandeur long enough and were hungry for the simple, familiar things of everyday life. Its green-blue waters were being beaten to fury by the north-westerly gale. The mountains, "stern peaks that dared the stars," peered through the mists, and between them huge glaciers poured down from the great ice-slopes and -fields that lay behind. We counted twelve glaciers and heard every few minutes the reverberating roar caused by masses of ice calving from the parent streams.

On May 14 we made our preparations for an early start on the following day if the weather held fair. We expected to be able to pick up the remains of the sea-elephant on our way up the sound. All hands were recovering from the chafing caused by our wet clothes during the boat journey. The insides of our legs had suffered severely, and for some time after landing in the cove we found movement extremely uncomfortable. We paid our last visit to the nests of the albatrosses, which were situated on a little undulating plateau above the cave amid tussocks, snow-patches, and little frozen tarns. Each nest consisted of a mound over a foot high of tussock-grass, roots, and a little earth. The albatross lays one egg and very rarely two. The chicks, which are hatched in January, are fed on the nest by the parent birds for almost seven months before they take to the sea and fend for themselves. Up to four months of age the chicks are beautiful white masses of downy fluff, but when we arrived on the scene their plumage was almost complete. Very often one of the parent birds was on guard near the nest. We did not enjoy attacking these birds, but our hunger knew no law. They tasted so very good and assisted our recuperation to such an extent that each time we killed one of them we felt a little less remorseful.

May 15 was a great day. We made our hoosh at 7:30 A.M. Then we loaded up the boat and gave her a flying launch down the steep beach into the surf. Heavy rain had fallen in the night and a gusty north-westerly wind was now blowing, with misty showers. The *James Caird* headed to the sea as if anxious to face the battle of the waves once more. We passed through the narrow mouth of the cove with the ugly rocks and waving kelp close on either side, turned to the east, and sailed merrily up the bay as the sun broke through the mists and made the tossing waters sparkle around us. We were a curious-looking party on that bright morning, but we were feeling happy. We even broke into song, and, but for our Robinson Crusoe appearance, a casual observer might have taken us for a picnic party sailing in a Norwegian fiord or one of the beautiful sounds off the west coast of New Zealand. The wind blew fresh and strong, and a small sea broke on the coast as we advanced. The surf was sufficient to have endangered the boat if we had attempted to land where the carcass of the sea-elephant was lying, so we decided to go on to the head of the bay without risking anything, particularly as we were likely to find sea-elephants on the upper beaches. The big creatures have a habit of seeking peaceful quarters protected from the waves. We had hopes, too, of finding penguins. Our expectation as far as the sea-elephants were concerned was not at fault. We heard the road of the bulls as we neared the head of the bay, and soon afterwards saw the great unwieldy forms of the beasts lying on a shelving beach towards the bay-head. We rounded a high, glacier-worn bluff on the north side, and at 12:30 P.M. we ran the boat ashore on a low beach of sand and pebbles, with tussock growing above high-water mark. There were hundreds of sea-elephants lying about, and our anxieties with regard to food disappeared. Meat and blubber enough to feed our party for years was in sight. Our landing-place was about a mile and a half west of the north-east corner of the bay. Just east of us was a glacier-snout ending on the beach but giving a passage towards the head of the bay, except at high water or when a very heavy surf was running. A cold, drizzling rain had begun to fall, and we provided ourselves with shelter as quickly as possible. We hauled the *James Caird* up above high-water mark and turned her over just to the lee or east side of the bluff. The spot was separated from the mountain-side by a low morainic bank, rising twenty or thirty feet above sea-level. Soon we had converted the boat into a very comfortable cabin *à la* Peggotty, turfing it round with tussocks, which we dug up with knives. One side of the *James Caird* rested on stones so as to afford a low entrance, and when we had finished she looked as through she had grown there.

McCarthy entered into this work with great spirit. A sea-elephant provided us with fuel and meat, and that evening found a well-fed and
fairly contented party at rest in Peggotty camp.

Our camp, as I have said, lay on the north side of King
Haakon Bay near the head. Our path towards the whaling-stations
led round the seaward end of the snouted glacier on the east side of
the camp and up a snow-slope that appears to lead to a pass in the
great Allardyce Range, which runs north-west and south-east and
forms the main backbone of South Georgia. The range dipped opposite the bay into a well-defined pass from east to west. An ice-sheet
covered most of the interior, filling the valleys and disguising the
configuration of the land, which, indeed, showed only in big rocky
ridges, peaks, and nunataks. When we looked up the pass from Peggotty Camp the country to the left appeared to offer two easy paths
through to the opposite coast, but we knew that the island was uninhabited at that point (Possession Bay). We had to turn our attention
further east, and it was impossible from the camp to learn much of
the conditions that would confront us on the overland journey. I
planned to climb to the pass and then be guided by the configuration
of the country in the selection of a route eastward to Stromness Bay,
where the whaling-stations were established in the minor bays, Leith,
Husvik, and Stromness. A range of mountains with precipitous slopes,
forbidding peaks, and large glaciers lay immediately to the south of
King Haakon Bay and seemed to form a continuation of the main
range. Between this secondary range and the pass above our camp a
great snow-upland sloped up to the inland ice-sheet and reached a
rocky ridge that stretched athwart our path and seemed to bar the
way. This ridge was a right-angled offshoot from the main ridge. Its
chief features were four rocky peaks with spaces between that looked
from a distance as though they might prove to be passes.

The weather was bad on Tuesday, May 16, and we stayed
under the boat nearly all day. The quarters were cramped but gave full
protection from the weather, and we regarded our little cabin with a
great deal of satisfaction. Abundant meals of sea-elephant steak and

liver increased our contentment. McNeish reported during the day that he had seen rats feeding on the scraps, but this interesting statement was not verified. One would not expect to find rats at such a spot, but there was a bare possibility that they had landed from a wreck and managed to survive the very rigorous conditions.

A fresh west-south-westerly breeze was blowing on the following morning (Wednesday, May 17), with misty squalls, sleet, and rain. I took Worsley with me on a pioneer journey to the west with the object of examining the country to be traversed at the beginning of the overland journey. We went round the seaward end of the snouted glacier, and after tramping about a mile over stony ground and snow-coated debris, we crossed some big ridges of scree and moraines. We found that there was good going for a sledge as far as the north-east corner of the bay, but did not get much information regarding the conditions farther on owing to the view becoming obscured by a snow-squall. We waited a quarter of an hour for the weather to clear but were forced to turn back without having seen more of the country. I had satisfied myself, however, that we could reach a good snow-slope leading apparently to the inland ice. Worsley reckoned from the chart that the distance from our camp to Husvik, on an east magnetic course, was seventeen geographical miles, but we could not expect to follow a direct line. The carpenter started making a sledge for use on the overland journey. The materials at his disposal were limited in quantity and scarcely suitable in quality.

We overhauled our gear on Thursday, May 18, and hauled our sledge to the lower edge of the snouted glacier. The vehicle proved heavy and cumbrous. We had to lift it empty over bare patches of rock along the shore, and I realized that it would be too heavy for three men to manage amid the snow-plains, glaciers, and peaks of the interior. Worsley and Crean were coming with me, and after consultation we decided to leave the sleeping-bags behind us and make the journey in very light marching order. We would take three days' provisions for each man in the form of sledging rations and biscuit. The food was to be packed in three socks so that each member of the party could carry his own supply. Then we were to take the Primus lamp filled with oil, the small cooker, the carpenter's adze (for use as an ice-axe), and the alpine rope, which made a total length of fifty feet when knotted. We might have to lower ourselves down steep slopes or cross crevassed glaciers. The filled lamp would provide six hot meals, which would consist of sledging ration boiled up with biscuit. There were two boxes of matches left, one full and the other partially used. We left the full box with the men at the camp and took the second box, which contained forty-eight matches. I was unfortunate as regarded footgear, since I had given away my heavy Burberry boots on the floe, and had now a comparatively light pair in poor condition. The carpenter assisted me by putting several screws in the sole of each boot with the object of providing a grip on the ice. The screws came out of the *James Caird*.

We turned in early that night, but sleep did not come to me. My mind was busy with the task of the following day. The weather was clear and the outlook for an early start in the morning was good. We were going to leave a weak party behind us in the camp. Vincent was still in the same condition, and he could not march. McNeish was pretty well broken up. The two men were not capable of managing for themselves and McCarthy must stay to look after them. He might have a difficult task if we failed to reach the whaling-station. The distance to Husvik, according to the chart, was no more than seventeen geographical miles in a direct line, but we had very scanty knowledge of the conditions of the interior. No man had ever penetrated a mile from the coast of South Georgia at any point, and the whalers I knew regarded the country as inaccessible. During that day, while we were walking to the snouted glacier, we had seen three wild duck flying towards the head of the bay from the eastward. I hoped that the presence of these birds indicated tussock-land and not snow-fields and glaciers in the interior, but the hope was not a very bright one.

We turned out at 2 A.M. on the Friday morning and had our hoosh ready an hour later. The full moon was shining in a practically cloudless sky, its rays reflected gloriously from the pinnacles and crevassed ice of the adjacent glaciers. The huge peaks of the mountains stood in bold relief against the sky and threw dark shadows on the waters of the sound. There was no need for delay, and we made a start as soon as we had eaten our meal. McNeish walked about 200 yds. with us; he could no more. Then we said good-bye and he turned back to the camp. The first task was to get round the edge of the snouted glacier, which had points like fingers projecting towards the sea. The waves were reaching the points of these fingers, and we had to rush from one recess to another when the waters receded. We soon reached the east side of the glacier and noticed its great activity at this point. Changes had occurred within the preceding twenty-four hours. Some huge pieces had broken off, and the masses of mud and stone that were being driven before the advancing ice showed movement. The glacier was like a gigantic plough driving irresistibly towards the sea.

Lying on the beach beyond the glacier was wreckage that told of many ill-fated ships. We noticed stanchions of teakwood, liberally carved, that must have come from ships of the older type; iron-bound timbers with the iron almost rusted through; battered barrels and all the usual debris of the ocean. We had difficulties and anxieties of our own, but as we passed that graveyard of the sea we thought of the many tragedies written in the wave-worn fragments of lost vessels. We did not pause, and soon we were ascending a snow-slope heading due east on the last lap of our long trail.

The snow-surface was disappointing. Two days before we had been able to move rapidly on hard, packed snow; now we sank over our ankles at each step and progress was slow. After two hours' steady climbing we were 2500 ft. above sea-level. The weather continued fine and calm, and as the ridges drew nearer and the western coast of the island spread out below, the bright moonlight showed us that the interior was broken tremendously. High peaks, impassable cliffs, steep snow-slopes, and sharply descending glaciers were prominent features in all directions, with stretches of snow-plain overlaying the ice-sheet of the interior. The slope we were ascending mounted to a ridge and our course lay direct to the top. The moon, which proved a good friend during this journey, threw a long shadow at one point and told us that the surface was broken in our path. Warned in time, we avoided a huge hole capable of swallowing an army. The bay was now about three miles away, and the continued roaring of a big glacier at the head of the bay came to our ears. This glacier, which we had noticed during the stay at Peggotty Camp, seemed to be calving almost continuously.

I had hoped to get a view of the country ahead of us from the top of the slope, but as the surface became more level beneath our feet, a thick fog drifted down. The moon became obscured and produced a diffused light that was more trying than darkness, since it illuminated the fog without guiding our steps. We roped ourselves together as a precaution against holes, crevasses, and precipices, and I broke trail through the soft snow. With almost the full length of the rope between myself and the last man we were able to steer an approximately straight course, since, if I veered to the right or the left when marching into the blank wall of the fog, the last man on the rope could shout a direction. So, like a ship with its "port," "starboard," "steady," we tramped through the fog for the next two hours.

Then, as daylight came, the fog thinned and lifted, and from an elevation of about 3000 ft. we looked down on what seemed to be a huge frozen lake with its farther shores still obscured by the fog. We halted there to eat a bit of biscuit while we discussed whether we would go down and cross the flat surface of the lake, or keep on the ridge we had already reached. I decided to go down, since the lake lay on our course. After an hour of comparatively easy travel through the snow we noticed the thin beginnings of crevasses. Soon they were increasing in size and showing fractures, indicating that we were traveling on a glacier. As the daylight brightened the fog dissipated; the lake could be seen more clearly, but still we could not discover its east shore. A little later the fog lifted completely, and then we saw that our lake stretched to the horizon, and realized suddenly that we were looking down upon the open sea on the east coast of the island. The slight pulsation at the shore showed that the sea was not even frozen; it was the bad light that had deceived us. Evidently we were at the top of Possession Bay, and the island at that point could not be more than five miles across from the head of King Haakon Bay. Our rough chart was inaccurate. There was nothing for it but to start up the glacier again. That was about seven o'clock in the morning, and by nine o'clock we had more than recovered our lost ground. We regained the ridge and then struck southeast, for the chart showed that two more bays indented the coast before Stromness. It was comforting to realize that we would have the eastern water in sight during our journey, although we could see there was no way around the shoreline owing to steep cliffs and glaciers. Men lived in houses lit by electric light on the east coast. News of the outside world waited us there, and, above all, the east coast meant for us the means of rescuing the twenty-two men we had left on Elephant Island.

An August Day's Sail

From *Spring Tides*

BY SAMUEL ELIOT MORISON

AMERICA'S PREEMINENT NAUTICAL historian, Morison wrote many books, including the official fifteen-volume *History of United States Naval Operations in World War II* and biographies of John Paul Jones and Christopher Columbus, for which he won Pulitzer Prizes. A professor at Harvard and Oxford, he was also the official historian of Harvard.

A retired rear admiral, he had been a passionate sailor throughout his life, and the following is taken from *Spring Tides,* a memoir about his lifelong love affair with the sea.

A LIGHT, CARESSING SOUTHERLY BREEZE is blowing; just enough to heel the yawl and give her momentum. The boy and I get under way from the mooring by the usual ritual. I take in the ensign, hoist the mizzen, cast off main sheet and slack the backstays; he helps me hoist the mainsail, sway the halyards and neatly coil them. I take the wheel and the main sheet in hand, the boy casts off the mooring rode and hoists the jib, and off she goes like a lively dog let off the leash.

We make a long, leisurely beat to windward out of the Western Way, with tide almost dead low; the reefs, sprayed with brown rockweed, show up clearly. We pass the bell buoy and leave to starboard the naked reef known to proper chart makers as South Bunkers Ledge, but to Mount Deserters as "Bunker's Whore."

Now we are in the open sea, nothing between us and Nova Scotia. The day is pleasantly cool and bright, with gathering cirrus clouds that sometimes obscure the sun. Old ocean today is green, heaving with a surge farflung from a blow somewhere between us and Europe. Visibility is so high that the horizon is a clean-cut line over which one can see the masts of fishing draggers whose hulls are concealed by the earth's bulge. Seaward, the Duck Islands seem to float on the emerald waters. Landward, the rocky shores of Great Cranberry Island are misty with the spray from a line of white breakers. One thinks of Heredia's line about Britanny: "Du Raz jusqu´à Penmarc´h la côte entiér fume"—the entire coast is smoky. Ocean swell makes the yawl roll and pitch, not unpleasantly but in harmonious cadence with the sea, the motion starting little snaps and whistles among the cordage, and the tapping of reef-points on the mainsail.

This is the time for the lunch that Priscilla prepared for us— jellied eggs and baby carrots as hors d'oeuvres; mushroom soup in a thermos; succulent ham sandwiches freshly made with lettuce and mayonnaise; chilled beer from the icebox; homemade doughnuts, crisp outside and flaky-soft inside, as you find them only when made by a master hand in Maine.

Now we are off Baker's Island where the long, flat granite ledges, washed clean by winter gales, hang over a reddish-brown apron of kelp and dulse, whirling in the breakers that roar in past the Thumper ledge. We round the groaner, the perpetually whistling buoy, haul our wind and turn northward.

Here we face the superb panorama of Mount Desert Island and Frenchman's Bay. The westering sun kindles the granite summits of Sargent, Green and Newport mountains to rose color; and the ocean between us and them is cobalt blue. Spruce-dark Otter Cliff and bare, brown Great Head thrust out into Frenchman's Bay. Under this luminous northern sky, distant Schoodic stands out bold and clear; miles beyond, the summit of Pigeon Hill appears, and Petit Manan lighthouse tower, entrance post to the Bay of Fundy, pricks the eastern horizon.

We close-haul our sails, round the black can buoy and glide out of the ocean swell into the sheltered anchorage of Baker's Island. Flood tide is only one hour old; and my quest is for fresh mussels in that clear, unpolluted water. We shoot into the wind, avoiding the numerous lobster-pot buoys, hand the jib and mainsail, drop the anchor and pay out scope on the cable. I pull the skiff alongside and row ashore. Spicy late summer fragrance wells out from the sundrenched island—sweet grasses, goldenrod, aster; even some of the white and pink *Rosa rugosa* for which this place is famous are still in bloom. The colorful sea bottom appears; gray sand studded with big smooth pebbles tumbled and polished by millennia of winter gales, when the great combers at high water rip over the reef barrier that now makes this spot a sheltered harbor. Two more strokes of the oars, and the skiff grounds on a rock; bucket in one hand and boat painter in the other, I make a wobbly landing, unlike the fishermen who splash boldly ashore in their rubber boots. Mussels are there in great plenty, their dark blue shells with brown "beards" clinging in clusters to barnacled rocks and to the wooden ways laid years ago for the lighthouse keeper's skiff. In ten minutes' time I have gathered a pailful, then shove the skiff off the rock where she grounded, and row back to the yawl, facing forward to admire her perfect proportions, and the backdrop of mountains.

We make sail once more, weigh anchor, and the yawl pirouettes on her keel to head toward home. My young sailor, blond and lithe as one imagines ancient Greek sailors to have been in the Aegean, gazes, speechless, at sea and mountains. What is he, at nineteen, thinking of it all? Does the beauty of sunwashed shore and granite mountains mean the same to him as to me, four times his age? I respect the youth's right to his own thoughts and do not ask, fearing perhaps to break the spell by some offhand or discordant reply.

Now we close-haul the sails again to pass between Suttons Island and the two Cranberries. I turn my back on the Islesford shore where the summer houses are pretentiously inappropriate, but linger lovingly on the south shore of Suttons, its little cottages built in the good simple taste of a century ago, when Maine men knew how to create as beautiful a house as a ship. Suttons, with its memories of John Gilley and Mary Wheelwright, of picnics long ago, of clumps of blue harebell growing like weeds from the wild grass. In this bight of the Bay we encounter the inevitable spell of calm. The yawl holds her headway for two or three hundred yards, her sails full although the surface of the sea has become a wavy mirror; the ripples from her bows making sweet music. Finally her headway ceases, the sails gently flap, the booms swing from side to side, and the reef points play a tattoo on the mainsail.

What makes this particular day so memorable is its freedom from the mutter of motors. All power yachts are following the annual race in Blue Hill Bay, no snarling outboards are about. The lobstermen have finished hauling their traps and are at home eating supper. There is no sound but the lapping of waves on the shore, the lazy clang of Spurling's Ledge bell buoy, and the distant bark of a dog.

After a breathless calm of a quarter hour, the breeze returns, limp sheets stretch out taut with a clatter of blocks, sails fill, and the yawl heels to the last of the west wind.

Around the western point of Suttons, Bear Island makes out. Its white lighthouse tower and pyramidical bell house seem to look down like benign parents on three tiny sloops that flutter past, having a little race of their own as they did not rate the big cruise. How many thousands of sailing craft have passed that sea mark since 1839 when, at the suggestion of a naval captain, the government built the light station? How many seamen have blessed that winking white eye guiding them through Eastern or Western Way to the snug harbors within, or strained their ears to catch the deep-throated note of the fog bell?

Leaving the cliffs of Bear Island astern on the starboard quarter, we enter Northeast Harbor with the dying breeze, avoiding the ever present "Kimball's Calms" on the port hand. My boy lowers and neatly furls the jib, then stands with boat hook, poised like a classic harpooner, to spear the mooring buoy. Main and mizzen sheets are hauled flat to give the yawl one last graceful curvet before her way is checked in the wind's eye. Then the mooring rode is secured to the forward bitts, and the yacht's white wings are folded for the night.

About *Figaro*

From *On the Wind's Way*

BY WILLIAM SNAITH

THE WINNER OF THE Bermuda-Copenhagen race and a regular member on the American Admiral's Cup team aboard a long line of *Figaros*, Bill Snaith was a literate and sophisticated sailor. In this segment from *On the Wind's Way* during a transatlantic race, he discussed everything from the joys and frustrations of sailing to the choice of a boat name. In the end, however, it's up to you, the reader, to decide what cock-a-snook means.

IT IS HARD TO STAY GLOOMY ABOARD *Figaro,* although events conspire to peg our spirits at the nadir. It is not too farfetched to imagine she exudes happiness, an invisible elixir distilling from her woodwork, making short work of the glums. She's just the opposite of the craggy manors that lady writers of Gothic novels discover on Cornish cliffs or isolated moors in Devon or Transylvania. Whereas these haunted bits of architecture inject their inhabitants with broody gloom, *Figaro* does what she can to chase the blues. Besides, I really don't believe the average man has the stomach for protracted gloom unless he be one who looks for it around every corner like Schopenhauer or wallows in it like Hamlet. Most of us would incline toward hedonism or one of its jolly subdivisions. Unhappily, the events of life intrude and no matter how we stuff the mattress with down, a few nails from the fakir's cot show up in our bed of pleasure.

In response, therefore, to *Figaro's* magic elixir and my own brighter instincts, I awoke after the long and lonely night of wondering and reached eagerly for lightheartedness. From my first waking moment, I felt sure the right decision would be made. That conviction persists despite a look out of the companionway. We are in the murky first ring of a watery purgatory. Somewhere nearby is Vergil waiting to guide us deeper or else the Flying Dutchman ready to rattle his chains. We must elude them both.

Figaro sails in an eerie environment, a world of curdled gray mist. At times, the coils of curd thicken and a deeper murk settles around her. Suddenly the layers thin and the boat sails in a strangely pale crepuscular light. Each droplet in this thinner mist hangs separately against the washed-out yellow eye of the sun; a scummy cataract of varying density veils its burning stare. The chalky green face of the ocean is seen in a short radius around the boat, its heaving surface broken by small, tumbling crests. The waves come out of the mist suddenly, invisible until they are almost on the boat and then as quickly disappear ahead; a rush of energy, hurrying toward an undisclosed rendezvous. Only the bow wave roils the even pattern of the oncoming seas as it falls back diagonally across their path. The churned air imprisoned in foaming bubbles breaks out and hisses in rage as the bubbles clutch fruitlessly at the hull slipping by. Then with a last crackle, no longer sounding angry, like the ultimate gush of gas escaping from stirred champagne or of Alka-Seltzer, the wave expires quietly into the mist, leaving a wake discernible to no one but the two Mother Carey's chickens who have decided to be companions to this voyage. The bow plunges steadily on as though it, and not we, knows where we are going. It is not precisely the morning for hornpipes and chanteys.

As the morning moves on, the weather looks as though it will break clear, even a suspicion of frosty blue tints the muddy blanket overhead. But then the boat enters another area of heavy fog, the sea disappears, all but the bubbles. The bow can no longer be seen, but its wave is still heard in tempo with the rise and fall as it plunges on some-where ahead. *Figaro* carries on steadfastly, unshaken by the lack of visi-bility. I cannot say as much for myself; blind Polyphemus at the mouth of the cave, wondering from which corner the assailant will come.

My son MacLeod stands at the wheel. His watch captain, Bobby Symonette, sits under the dodger smoking a Montecristo No. 1, the size which lasts longer. An unfailing rule on all my *Figaro*s gives the man smoking a good cigar the right to enjoy it under the dodger (except in the case of alarums and excursions). I think it a crime against civilized behavior to let a cigar burn like a torch, hot and hard in the wind. The fact of my liking cigars must have a great deal to do with this sensitivity. Cleody, on the other hand, who does not smoke cigars, feels the rule to be outrageous, especially in view of the fact that Bobby can make the enjoyment of a cigar last more than one hour. To Cleody's mind, this is one hell of a long time to devote to ci-vilities while other men stand out in the wet and cold. In spite of his voiced protest, he steers cheerfully.

I am not the one to thwart the authority of the man in charge, especially in a rule of my own making, so I sit down alongside Bobby and accept a cigar. After carefully lighting up, I ask, "Do you think we can count on catching enough rainwater on the way across to piece out our supply?"

"It's a thought. We've never gone across when we did not have our share of rain. We might as well put it to use."

"I am thinking that way. If we wash in seawater, don't shave, boil as many things as we can in half seawater, except for coffee and soup, we could make it across with water to spare. If we catch rain in addition, we will have built-in insurance."

Monk Farnham, from a position in the galley aft, says, "It sounds good to me."

During the lunch break, at the change of watch, the first time we are all together, I broach the idea to the whole crew. I tell them about the rain catcher made for just such a contingency. It is especially fitted to the boat, a suspended, fabric, bathtublike gizmo lying in the waterway, the tops fastened between the rail and the handgrabs on the cabin top. It is fitted with a spout at the bottom so we can pour off into containers. Knud Reimers, the other watch captain, is a Swedish citizen. He likes the idea of coming home in a sailboat. It is the true Viking (he pronounces it "wicking") return; the only honorable return is to stand up in a boat or be prone on a shield. Once the older and, by inference, wiser men are agreed, the young unhesitatingly go along with the idea. They put their faith in us; we have placed ours in the boat. She has become more than a thing; she is entrusted with our lives. We are committed.

Everyone goes enthusiastically topside to see how the rain catcher fits. We dig it out of its bag. A shock-odor of creosote hits us in the nose, so strong that were it not for the damp sea air our eyes would smart. The cloth is fiberglass. It must still be curing. The smell is so strong we decide to leave it on deck spread out on the cabin housetop to let it air. We are convinced that now having awakened the chemical beast, if we dared put it back in the bag, it would creep in the night.

We are surrounded by fog. The rain catcher and ourselves are soon as wet as if we had been dipped.

Figaro never falters through all this. She plunges along as though she did not have grievously wounded tanks in her vitals and as if the souls on board did not secrete little quaverings of their own. Seeing or not, oblivious of the threat of oncoming or overtaking vessels, she sails on. Occasionally, an out-of-sync wave catches her bow and a shattering of spray shoots diagonally across her deck. Shaking off the water through her freeing ports, she picks up her rhythm as though nothing happened. She's one hell of a boat. How can anything bad happen to you when you are in her!

That's a good question, friend, a real measure of the mythic trust one puts in a creature-thing. Anyway, that's what it is all about and how it stands. We are physically sound, perhaps a bit bruised in spirit, and committed to some two weeks of racing in the open Atlantic. While the crew do not show it, there must be an underlying unease, like that running through an army that has crossed a Rubicon by forced march and wonders if its baggage train will catch up. We have placed our reliance in one another and in the boat. If ever a boat is capable of putting out magic, we could sure as hell use some of it now.

A sport is something special in order to offset an image, which, to the uninitiated, must appear to be an idiot's delight. For those not hooked on ocean racing, yachtsmen must seem to be a web-footed, secular subsection of the Penitentes, a strange order of devotees, each man serving as his own Torquemada and his own subject for trial by water. He allows himself to be torn from his normal habitat and defenses; his usual bodily functions, habits and schedules are upset and in a restlessly rocking shelter at that.

This little vessel, the repository of our faith, in whose fortitude we believe, despite her seeping innards, is the only heroine in an otherwise all-male cast and blessed with a man's name at that—Figaro. Like all beauties who quicken subjective response, she can be given dimensions. Instead of the standard breasts, beam and buttocks, we count her vital statistics as forty-six-foot overall, thirty-two feet six inches on the waterline with a beam of twelve feet. She is a centerboarder and a yawl. Designed by Olin Stephens of Sparkman & Stephens and built in eighteen long months by Joel Johnson, a fine craftsman in Black Rock, Connecticut, in itself a muddy backwater which somehow finds its way into Long Island Sound. She is double planked with Honduras mahogany over ⅜-inch Oregon spruce. Her keelson is white oak, a massive timber, personally selected by Joel. He used a hand adze to achieve the finished shape. It was a great sight to see Joel standing astride the balk and taking off long slivers and short as accurately and fine as with a plane. One rarely sees that sort of skill and craftsmanship anymore. Just to see it is a privilege. Unhappily, the balk lay too long in the building shed during the protracted building period while wonders took place above. It checked badly, being very green in the beginning, and did not dry well. Right after launching, we had trouble with the nagging leaks until another craftsman stopped them. Now the water comes in only at the stuffing box, and that too will be cured. Originally, *Figaro* drew four feet six inches with her board up. With her bronze board down, she drew another three feet six inches. I changed her draft and ballast for this race, but that story deserves a separate telling later on.

Her layout is quite conventional, with her galley aft. The main saloon is handsome. It is paneled in Brazilian rosewood; the forward-bulkhead paneling frames an open fireplace with a white overmantel. This is shaped like a truncated obelisk. It is of white formica into which nautical decorations in imitation of scrimshaw were cut. As part of the decorations, I included a line from Samuel Pepys' *Diary*, "My Lords in discourse discovered a great deal of love to this Ship." Even in her building days, I sensed she would be that kind of boat. I did these engravings myself and have the calluses to prove it. Oval escutcheons on which gimbaled oil lamps are mounted are done in the same technique.

This saloon holds four berths, two regular uppers and two in-extension transoms under which are the wounded and bleeding water tanks. A cabin forward is separated from the saloon by the head on the port side and two hanging lockers across the passageway to port. The roller-coaster movement of this forward cabin is exaggerated when the boat is banging into a head sea. When we are at sea, its use is normally reserved for the ship's acknowledged "Iron Guts."

But a boat should be more than a sterling example of the boat-builder's art and man's desire to embellish her with decorations. Obviously, she means a special thing to the man who sails her. She has the ability to surcharge each event with a special aura, a release of spirit, a feeling of safety and a sense of fellowship.

Consider a single instance when the boat becomes the only secure center of your suddenly changed world—a North Atlantic storm (there is a 75-percent chance of encountering one in a crossing). The usual cyclone system, not a cyclone but the pattern associated with a low-pressure area, lasts an average of two to three days in its coming and going, during which unhappy time a thought threatens to overwhelm all other ideas. It is the question buried in one's mind or expressed to a companion alongside: "How the hell did I get myself into this?" Like as not, the storm will leave bone-tiring repairs in its wake. Yet, if the boat and company are proper, it somehow adds up to a rewarding experience.

Not the least of the various magics which take place is the bond created between a man and the boat in which he sails. It is not necessarily that between a man and a thing. After a time at sea, a boat becomes more than a clever assemblage of insensible matter. I think of a boat as a creature-thing. For me, she is infused with a persona, hovering on the edge of animation. It should not be difficult to understand how a yacht can become imbued with anima and personality. After all, it is a shelter and shield, however frail, and each yacht develops attributes and characteristics peculiar to herself in the way she meets the conditions and hazards of a passage. She can be cranky or sea-kindly, but in the end, the man and boat are made partners in the presence of the antagonist, the sea. To one degree or another, this bond is shared by all who sail in her and is not the sole privilege of the man who pays her yard bills, although somewhere within the Judeo-Christian ethic the idea persists that the degree of love is directly related to the amount of oneself and of one's wealth given. However painful this way to or from love may seem, especially to a man paying alimony, or yard bills, there is no doubt whatever that the bond between the boat and the owner-skipper increases when the burden of a decision which involves his faith in the boat is placed upon him.

Even while the man who sails in her responds to her anima, this creature-thing somehow becomes adapted to his bent and temperament though cherishing idiosyncrasies of her own. Chameleon-like, she takes on the coloration of her owner's needs. Each man uses his boat in his own way to fill certain wants. There are as many roads to Nirvana as boats and men. Nowhere does this show up as precisely as in choosing a name for the darling of his heart. Linguistics and semantics have become important analytical tools in philosophy and behavioral sciences. The choice of a boat's name is the semantic key to his dream, a revealing decision; the clues to his attitude are as clear as the strewn shreds in a paper chase.

The names fall into easily identifiable categories. As an instance, *Mother's Mink* and *String of Pearls* betray certain uxorious guilt feelings. *Press on Regardless, September Song, Last Chance*, speak of the quiet perturbation in the face of onrushing years. *Atomic, Hurricane, Leopard* (usually found on racers) vie with the names chosen for automobiles by automakers in the hunt for virility symbols and a wish-fulfilling longing to identify with tearing power and force. Of quite another order is the desire to relate to the beauty and poetry of the sea. One could let go in Mailerian hyperbole or choose a stanza from a Masefield poem which would dramatically fill a transom and provide inspiring reading for those behind. But timidity, inhibitions and age-old models intrude. A popular device whereby to capture the sea's magic is to choose a name with the prefix *sea*. The waters abound with *Sea Wind*s, *Sea Star*s, *Sea Witch*es, etc. It is my presumption that there are as many names starting with *Sea* in *Lloyd's Register of Yachts*, as listings of *Martinez* in the Madrid phone book, or in the Manhattan directory, for that matter.

In another reaching out for identity with beauty, we encounter *Aphrodite*s, *Apollo*s, and *Circe*s, and for those who wish on a star, there is an *Orion, Vega* or *Arcturus*.

A whole other order of boat names belongs to the dedicated family men. Their boat transoms carry conjunctive family names such as *Joanted* or hyphenated as in *Mar-jac-lou*. It is the bridegroom's last epithalamic song or else a sneaky way to involve the whole family in a sport for which they have little stomach and less enthusiasm.

I do not intend to denigrate any man's choice of name for his ark of dreams but rather to confirm the notion that there is a boat for all seasons in men.

I have made a brief résumé of the origins of boat names because it now falls on me to reveal how I chose the name for my own heart's delight. I have known privilege, joy, rage and frustration as the owner of a string of boats called *Figaro 1* through *Figaro 5*. On the face of it, this redundant choice paints me as an unimaginative clod or one with dynastic dreams. I must profess, "It is not so." My first boat bore the name *Cleody-Skipper*, named for my two eldest sons, MacLeod and Shepperd (Skipper). With the birth of our third son, Jonathan (Jocko), reason returned. The addition of one more child-inspired suffix seemed an empty game. I came to see the shortcomings of the practice. The first seizure on acquiring a new boat is poetic, an anodyne perhaps for signing the check. But my new boat had a smallish transom, incapable of carrying a reasonable stanza in Coast Guard-approved letter size. I did own a beloved dog named Figaro. Immediately one is repelled. What manner of man would exalt a dog over his children or give a dog's name to a thing of beauty like a sailboat (even if the dog is lit by a beauty of his own and if the genus name is that of God spelled backward). It is a tangled tale requiring some explanation. The secret lies in the answer to the question, How did my dog get his name?

A phenomenon that I recognize but can never quite explain is the fact that I instinctively find myself thinking at cross-purposes to any establishment with which I have contact, be it institutional, political, social or esthetic. As an instance: I am emotionally and actively dedicated to contemporary art. I am the head of a leading design firm. For several years running, my paintings had been hung in the Whitney Museum Annual of American Paintings (a practice now discontinued). I was protected from what was happening around me for a time by my recognition of two older polarities of genius— Picasso and Klee. But one day, looking past these two, I wrote a critically polemic book bemoaning certain onrushing antihuman trends. In this, I took my stand alongside Ortega y Gasset and other distinguished voices against the spoilers of the human spirit. But, unlike them, I fell from institutional grace.

In another instance, as a minority liberal ideologue in a tory stronghold, I served for several years as Democratic Party chairman in my town but finally gave way to the fact that I had little admiration or stomach for politics and for several of my party's candidates (and even less for others).

In these various ways, I find myself closer to the quaking edge than the quivering epicenter of a whole order of establishments. It is not by plan—it just turns out that way. It is obvious that being a temperate rebel, never having learned either to make my peace or take to the outer barricades, I have wound up in a mild limbo with undefined geographical borders. There is no home for such.

There may be something in all of the foregoing which harks back to my never-waning admiration for Beaumarchais's antic scamp Figaro—not just for the embellishments added by Mozart and Rossini, but for the character himself.

It is him, the essence of that character, for whom my dog was named and whom my various *Figaro*s honored—a lively scamp thumbing his nose at the establishment around him, left, right and center.

This explanation for my repetitious selection should be enough, but even while recognizing the dangers of "He doth protest too much," there is a very sound, if entirely different, reason for the reiteration. We live in a confused and overly communicated-to world, wandering at a loss in the midst of a traumatic identity crisis. We are witness to the loss of self in the lonely crowd. It is comforting in all this to hold on to a sense of continuity, a something that belongs to you and to which you belong. It may be minimal, but, nevertheless, it is reassuring to be part of a continuing stream, even if it is only the name for boats. This should not be confused with the hollowness of dynastic dreams or substitute clutchings for immortality. Choices like this begin and end with you. This minimal symbol of continuity may be a poor thing, but while it lasts, it is all your own.

Having thus introduced you into one of the pothering muddles that confound and confuse a yachtsman's heart and mind, I can speak glowingly of my joy, rage, frustration in the ownership of my *Figaro*s all in one breath. It is because my normally happy involvement with boats is complete. It is my form of Zen. Beginning with the passive enjoyment of the beauty of sail to the active excitements of competition and through this latter into the theory and self-inflicted practice of do-it-yourself yacht design, I have been enthralled by boats in their many aspects. Through boats, I have made lasting friendships with men who sail with me and whom I sail against.

A boat designed to cock-a-snook must be saucy, pert and nimble on her heels. *Figaro* is all of that and more. She is reliable and gives off confidence that she will take you out and bring you back safely.

The Crystal Coast

From *The Incredible Voyage*

BY TRISTAN JONES

A QUITE REMARKABLE SAILOR and the author of fourteen books, Jones was appropriately born at sea aboard his father's sailing ship, *Star of the West*, off Tristan da Cunha, one of the most remote islands in the world and hence his name. From a long line of Welsh sailors (his grandmother was first mate on a wool-trading ship), he eventually held nine world sailing records, including "the world's longest-distance sailor" since he had sailed more than 450,000 miles at the time of this book, 180,000 of which were solo. Jones sailed the Atlantic more than twenty times, circumnavigated the globe three times, and spent a winter frozen in Arctic ice.

First working at a wage of five cents a week on a sailing barge, he joined the Royal Navy at the outbreak of World War II and was promptly sunk three times before he was eighteen. After the war, he joined the Royal Hydrographic Service, ending in the early 1950s when his survey vessel was blown up by guerrillas, leaving him with a spinal injury that doctors said would leave him paralyzed for life.

The Incredible Voyage is the story of Jones' goal to "set a record that will not be broken until man finds water amongst the stars," in which he planned to sail on the lowest body of water in the world, the Dead Sea in Israel, and the highest, Lake Titicaca in the Andes. During his six-year voyage, he traveled a distance equal to twice the circumference of the world. In the process, he survived a capsize off the Cape of Good Hope, snipers in the Red Sea, and a six-thousand-mile adventure through uncharted rivers after hauling his boat three miles above sea level into the Andes.

At the end of his life, Jones was a double leg amputee, living alone and poor in Thailand, having dedicated his later years to handicapped children. But, when he passed away in 1995, he was planning his next voyage.

In this excerpt, Jones is sailing along the coast of Africa, from Madagascar to Durban, South Africa.

117

AUSTRALIAN SAILORS HAVE A TERM—"seeing the country and meeting the people." What it really means is going on a good run ashore, having a few drinks, visiting different bars, and making friends, mostly with all the pretty girls that cross your bows. That is exactly what we did in Majunga; for I had earned enough cash to have some to spare, and a bored sailor is a bad sailor. We ate well, for the restaurants are cheap; we drank perhaps a little too much, for smuggled booze is cheap; and we made a lot of friends, fair and dusky. So many, in fact, that when we came to leave, Christian, the harbormaster, actually accused me of not having learned one damned thing in fifteen years!

From Majunga we cruised slowly down what is surely the loveliest cruising ground in the world (or so I thought until Lake Titicaca). The air is so clear that it seems you can touch the Massif Centrale, a range of mountains two hundred miles away. In the mornings the limpid sky and the sea appear to be joined together, so that it is impossible to see the horizon, and all the time you are floating in the clearest water I have ever seen. The bottom at sixty feet is as plainly visible as the floor under your feet. It was as if the boat was afloat in a crystal bowl. The silence was so delicate, a shimmering, trembling silence, that it seemed that the slightest noise would shatter the world around you into a million pieces.

Barbara would ghost along in the lightest of zephyrs, and we would creep around the deck, whispering so as not to shatter the magic. There were hundreds of islands off this coast, most of them uninhabited, full of birds and luxurious vegetables. Sandy, untrodden beaches, coral reefs aswarm with fish, safe anchorages, and the best sailing imaginable, all under the lee of Madagascar, with the monsoon coming off the land and a dead flat sea.

We were in no hurry, for ahead of us lay the long, stormy passage around South Africa and the Cape of Good Hope. It was still only September, the southern spring. It would be best to dally until November before tackling one of the roughest sea passages in the world, the thousand-mile run between Durban and Capetown.

I found out a curious thing while we were visiting these islands. It is always my habit when in remote parts to visit the chief elder of any community. At Nosy Vahalia, because I had nothing else suitable, I took the chief one of my old navy shirts—the old collarless type with a tail fore and aft. The chief, an ancient about ninety years old, was beside himself with delight. These folk are Moslems, and he intended to wear the shirt to the mosque. He first gave me coffee and a cheroot to smoke, then sent for chickens for me to take back. When we awoke on board out at anchor the next day, we found the cockpit full of vegetables, fruit, and fish. We had enough food for three weeks and it did not cost one cent. When we went ashore we were escorted like princes to other villages, where we were received as honored guests.

Slowly we ambled down the coast of Madagascar for three hundred miles. This is my favorite kind of cruising, among small remote islands, on a weather shore, with a backdrop of mountains. I have known it in Norway, in Turkey, in Madagascar, and in Panama, and it never fails to enchant me. I could stay in that sort of place forever. Maybe I will end my days somewhere like that, perhaps in southern Chile, an area which has always fascinated me because of its thousands of islands and unspoiled natural beauty. For my last voyage I can head out into Drake's Passage and see and feel the winds of the world as they whistle around the Horn. And my soul can soar like an albatross above the seas of the southern passage, returning north only to seek out the lonely islands and shielings of the Strait of Magellan and Tierra del Fuego.

During this slow passage down the coast of Madagascar we fished a deal and caught many stingrays, the wings of which make delicious eating, something like Dover sole. We also caught dorado, for this is one area where that ocean fish comes in near to shore. The rocky shores were alive with landcrabs, and these, too, made good eating, while on the coral reefs were enough crabs and crayfish to keep us gorged for life. Ashore there were limes, lemons, small oranges, tomatoes, breadfruit, wild pig, and goats. There were few insects, none at all on the islands. Every night we would barbecue on the beach and the glare of the firelight revealed thousands of land-crabs watching our antics with curiosity. But they were harmless, and would scurry away as soon as we moved towards them. They were ugly-looking devils, gray and hairy, and seemed almost obscene to us; then we remembered that we were brown and hairy too, and that the crabs probably thought the same about us, except for Alem, who was very black and almost hairless, and terrified of the crabs.

The Mozambique Channel is a thousand miles wide. At the time we sailed it there was a full-scale civil war going on in the then Portuguese colony of Mozambique. We decided to give that country a wide berth. After our last call in Madagascar, *Barbara* sailed 1,468 miles to Durban, encountering four storms en route, two in the Mozambique Channel and two off the coast of South Africa. The worst one was about one hundred miles northeast of Durban, off the coast of Zululand.

Between storms, which in October are regular in this area (we were passing from the cyclonic system into the temperate zone), we had glorious sailing weather. The Indian Ocean is the bluest of all, a deep aquamarine color, much darker than sky blue. The winds, in between tempests, are steady north of the tropic, and there is much more bird life than in the Pacific or the Atlantic. This is because the many reefs and islets are widely scattered, and while this makes for navigational hazards, it means that there are many isolated specks of coral and land for the birds to visit.

I think the Indian Ocean is probably the most interesting area for tropical cruising. Unfortunately, very few yachtsmen pass through this part of the world. Vast areas of these seas are unknown to western small craft. Most of these isolated pinpricks are natural wildlife re-serves, as, for example, Aldabra, with its huge turtles, and Bassa de India and Europa Island in the Mozambique Channel, two com-pletely untouched and unspoiled coral reefs teeming with sealife. The inhabitants of the area are, in the main, some of the friendliest and most hospitable people that you could possibly wish to meet. The few outsiders living among them are surely amongst the most colorful characters anywhere; most of them operate small cargo schooners and steamers between the islands, collecting copra. In particular, I recall one French lady, skipper of a small steamer in the Comoros, who, pistol at hip, kept the whole male population of Mutsamudu hard at loading her vessel for days on end, with never a murmur of complaint. At the end of the day she would drink a bottle of the best whiskey without turning a hair, at the same time preserving her French savoir-faire and elegance.

The history of this part of the ocean is interesting. The Arabs penetrated as far south as Madagascar in the fourteenth century, looking for gold in the Zambezi River and slaves from Mozambique. In the fifteenth century the Portuguese, led by the courageous Bartholomeu Dias and the indomitable Vasco da Gama, finally, after decades of patient and steady exploration down the west coast of Africa, rounded the Cape of Good Hope to the East Indies and China, establishing an empire which did not dissolve until 1975. The Portuguese also built a chain of forts right up the East African coast and, until the British stumbled into the area after the Napoleonic wars, controlled most of the trade in this huge area.

Until the British defeated the French at Trafalgar, there was a running struggle for control of the sea route around the Cape of Good Hope between these two countries (the Dutch having dropped out in the mid-1700s). Finally, the Cape became a British base for the fleet, another Gibraltar, and the French islands of Mauritius and La Réunion were taken over, thus safeguarding the approaches to and from Europe and allowing the British to take over India.

During this time the Cape of Good Hope became a very important sailing route, with ships richly laden passing to and from the East and Europe. With the trade, as always in the days before the steamer, came the pirates, the freebooters, and for well over a century Madagascar was the lair from which they would pounce on the East Indiamen on their way to and from the Cape. To this day in the Comores and Madagascar, a steamship, indeed any foreign vessel of any kind, is called a "mannowarri," which comes from the old British term, "Man o' War." A foreign seaman is known as a "goddami," for until the nineteenth century "goddamn" was a favorite British expletive. On Madagascar "goddami mannowarri" means a sailor from a foreign ship! This is part of the Swahili language in that area.

On the passage down the Mozambique Channel, which took sixteen days, we blew out the sails a number of times, so that by the time *Barbara* reached Durban, there were more patches on some sails than original sail.

The great storm of Zululand was a lulu. The Agulhas Current runs south down through the Mozambique Channel, but the axis of the current is close to the African shore, about twenty miles offshore, roughly on the 100-fathom line, where the continental shelf drops off into the deeps. Off Cape St. Lucia, in Zululand, however, the axis of the current approaches close to the shore. Now on the axis of the current, and on the seaward side of it, the seas are so steep, with a full gale or storm blowing against the current, that a small craft cannot survive for long, if at all. Therefore, it is wise to stay close to Cape St. Lucia and that is what we did, hoping to slide past before a "southerly buster" came along to shake us up. One hit us smack on the nose just as we reached the Cape—a real beauty, a real ripsnorter. It was the twenty-first of September; later, after we fetched Durban, I found out that the windspeed at the airport that day had registered eighty-two knots.

So there we were, with huge breakers assaulting the coast of Zululand under our quarter a couple of miles off, unable to make much offing because of the tremendous seas of the Agulhas Current. Right through the middle of this hellish mess runs one of the busiest shipping lanes in the world, with huge tankers and cargo vessels passing at the rate of one every half-hour. We couldn't go in, we couldn't go out, and we couldn't stay put.

As the storm increased towards late afternoon, I calculated that if we hove to under mizzen, with the current pushing us one way and the wind pushing the other, we might *just* stay put while the tide was running out. However, as soon as the tide changed, we would be forced to try to make the offing, come what may. So for six hours, until well after dark, we hove to. Then, about midnight, with the wind slacking off a touch, we started to work our way out, slowly and very delicately, against huge seas, across the steamer track at right angles, to the edge of the continental shelf. We had bent on the storm trysail—a small, heavy-canvas, triangular sail rigged in place of the mainsail, except that it is loose-footed, that is, not hanked onto the boom. With this sail and the storm jib, we crept across the face of the wind and sea. I say crept, but in actual fact, in those seas, we bounced around like a bronco, all three of us lashed to sturdy fittings with our safety harnesses. It was useless to try running the engine, for half the time the stern of the boat was clear out of the sea while the other half of the time the bow was digging in deep, so that the sea washed straight over the topsides. We put out a strong light and hoped that the steamers would see us in time to avoid us. To the mariner, and especially the single-handler, the gravest danger in all oceans is other craft, particularly the monster tankers, for they are so large that from the bridge, with the way ahead obscured by a foredeck as big as Yankee Stadium, the helmsman cannot see anything closer than three miles away. At night he can see nothing at all that is not further than three miles away. The tanker trusts to her radar, and in confined seas, such as we were crashing around in, her officers usually pay strict attention to the radar. But human nature being what it is, there is always the chance that for a few minutes the officer of the watch might be drinking coffee, or reading the football results, and not paying attention to his screen. If a tanker like that touched *Barbara*, she would not feel the slightest shock in those seas. We would sink immediately.

But that night off Zululand the tanker sailors were alive and well and at least four of them changed course to avoid us. Watching their radar screens, watching this small mysterious blob out there in the frantic sea, they probably thought we were a small fishing boat that had failed to make port, or that we were stark raving mad. When we had made enough offing (and there was no doubt at all when we had, for the movement was violent, the boat actually being tossed up in the air off the tops of the seas), we started toward shore again, across the steamer track. For three days and nights this nightmare continued until, very weary indeed, we found the wind abating down to about force seven. Handing the mainsail we beat our way into the narrow entrance of Durban harbor, over a hundred miles to the southeast of Cape St. Lucia, down a wild, storm-beaten shore. Finally, we tied up in Durban alongside the Point Yacht Club. The first pint of beer was the best I have ever tasted. The second was even better.

Aloft on the *Flying Cloud*

From *Men at Sea*

BY MORLEY ROBERTS

G OING UP THE MAST ON ANY boat for the first time can be both frightening and exhilarating, but it is almost a rite of passage when climbing the lofty spars of the famed 225-foot square-rigger *Flying Cloud*.

THERE IS SOMETHING INEXPLICABLY SPIRITUAL in a ship, from whatever standpoint she be viewed, whether from the main-deck or from the taffrail under which the divided waters join and bubble joyfully, or from the end of the jibboom, which is nearest to her purpose, as one may say. She is a magnificent creature, a thing complete, visibly complete and austerely adequate (the austerity lying in the nothing beyond her purpose, her splendid economy of means), and her spirituality comes from her completeness; her finite and declared divisions; her lofty silences; her community with the winds and the sea and sky. It comes—ah! who shall say how it comes!—but it is up aloft among the fine tracery of her rigging and her gear that her soul is most manifest. Where indeed, could it be more manifest than from the high places where one sees her gracious dependence on her winds, while her naked body is in the priestlike font of the sea? Oh, most blessed of created things, of the works of man working divinely! Every step of hers in the great waters is a baptism.

It were easy to make her material if, indeed, the vision which perceives her were material, for what is she but iron and timber and cordage? Yet iron is wrought out in fire, and timber sweetens in the great woods, and hemp grows in glory under the same skies as the ship. To go aloft is but to climb by ratlines and the shrouds, to hang in the futtock rigging, to clamber over the rim of the top, and then further by the topmast rigging; a mere catalogue if told in wooden words. But told as it should be (help me, oh, most divine sea and wind that speak together as in an organic psalm!), it becomes a pilgrimage, now of pleasure so sweet that nought can equal if now of tremendous toil that's even sweeter. One leaves the little world of the deck whereon men tread and the sounds of mankind grow dim, and ever dimmer, until they die away like the breaking of the foam about her bows, and so one ascends among the silent, very splendid machinery of the winds; one lies in the very plumage of her wings, thanking God and the divinity within one which with others wrought so lovely and strong a creature.

Now was the wind warm and gentle, but full and clean and steady as a river of crystal. It breathed upon the two that went aloft, on wan white cheek and ruddy, on the one who knew, and on him who was virgin as to his mind of ships, and the heart of the one was haughty pride and the heart of the other eager innocence.

They climb, and to old Mac looking up aloft are but two boys, young and foolish. They were two material objects, two things objective, coloured and visible, tangible objects of the world of sense. They weighed so much, and could talk. But to us they are other than this, something akin to the ship herself on her most spiritual side: part of her very spirit, part of her power of achievement, and this though they chattered as boys will climbing a tree. Yet this was the greatest of all trees, where the very birds of God might nest. One saw their wings and named them as sails. They were vans and pinions, clouds of high Heaven.

By now they've reached the top of the mainrigging and stand under the top itself. Jack, the climber of the tree, this giant tree, this most magnificent Beanstalk into the Cloud Land, stood and breathed. Fear and pain of joy got hold of him and he stared about him open-eyed, open-mouthed, perceiving, without knowing it, that the greatest thing on earth or at sea, or up aloft, is to attain a new point of view. Let us drink to such as climb masts or high mountains, or scale the inmost inaccessible fastnesses of the spirit. The main thing is to climb.

You shall hear Jack say the most commonplace things, in the most natural manner. What of that? Even Dante's visions were strangely material, were they not? Yet had he not been there, been to hell and heaven? How would one expect a youngster devoid of beautiful words, barely furnished with necessary ones, to mouth full-organed the opening divinity of vision in him? It's absurd to ask a babe to describe the Apocalypse. Nevertheless, though he said, "Damn!" it might mean, "This is a real white rose of an hour in my life"; and that hour might remain in his soul's bosom as long as any rose given by Beatrice to an endowed poet and lover.

Indeed, the boy said "Damn" often. It helped; one knows it helped.

"Now, will you come over the rim of the top or go through there?" asked the rare devil the Professor.

"There" was a hole in the top.

"What is it?"

"The Lubber's Hole," said Bram.

The boy flushed and looked at it, and stared overhead and inspected the outward leaning futtock-shrouds and the rim of the top above him. His heart beat fast, but his spirit was monstrously perturbed at such a notion. How could he, on this his first ascent to heaven, go through any passage named the lubber's hole?

But he temporized.

"I'll go the way you go," he said, meekly, but still with a flush on his cheeks.

And he saw Bram climb above, leaning outward, saw him lift himself, grasp the unseen topmast rigging and draw himself over, and kick a haughty heel at conquered space. It was dramatic, very wonderful! No Col de Lion, no shoulder of the Matterhorn, no arête of windy Monte Rosa, no cornice of the Lyskamm, seemed half so awe-inspiring. For it was wholly new, and therein lay its wonder and its power to draw him.

"I'll come," he gasped, and launched himself into the task, feeling that he must necessarily and by all the laws of space and time and matter fall headlong and be converted into pulp. It took courage, and he drew on his youthful heart for it, and found, Heaven be thanked! sufficient at his godlike account, and so drawing, drew himself up and found himself roundly on the top with Bram, who said, "Well done, sonny!"

Now can you or anyone who understands as much as "a, b, c," of the great alphabet of all life, wonder that Jack felt bound with hooks of steel, and grapnels and cables and hawsers to such a man, though he was a debauched young ruffian who knew more Limericks than Latin, and had as little grace as Greek about him? Jack would have blacked his boots, and quite rightly would have blacked them, though they had been seven leagues from heel to toe.

"I say!" said Jack.

He said nothing, though on encouragement he could talk almost as ceaselessly as the spirits that cluster about a vessel's bows. They can be heard most delightfully at night, when the trade wind blows, if the hearer climbs over the head, and, perhaps, out upon the boom where the jibs sleep and work and dream. But now Jack, uplifted from the common ranks of men, had nothing to say, but everything to feel.

He saw the gigantic curve of the mainsail beneath him with the gear lying across its bosom. It was the king of sails, the monarch, the great doer. He inspected it curiously; noted the great spread of the yard, the jackstay to which the sail was made fast, the truss, the great chain slings. Sunlight poured on the sail; he saw shadows on the deck. The air seemed finer already; his lungs filled like big sails; he could go. He was in the middle of the machinery of things: the topsail was before him. Aye, and his hand was on the topmast rigging. Bram slung round and started climbing. Jack followed.

As he climbed he had a sense of losing the ship, of leaving her. There was a magical lightness in her tracery, for all the strength of her proved rigging and well-tried gear. It was the infinite lightness of beauty and simple adequacy that the beholder notes in the loveliest Gothic architecture. She seemed fragile, but was not. The great solidity of the ship lay beneath: the hull narrowed tremendously: aloft the sky opened, the sky still cut by stays, the mizzen t'gallant stay, the mizzen-royal, the sky so heavenly blue over the wrinkled blue sea. He passed the belly of the upper topsail, noting with anxious eyes the spilling lines, the bull's-eyes in the foot of the sail; the topsail-sheets of iron, and gear he could not name. The reef-points were a joy to him; they hung in a steady row; they looked like good workmen, like soldiers of manilla.

So they came to the cross-trees and sat astride them abaft the belly of the t'gallantsail.

"Well?" said Bram, casually. He sat without touching anything. It was a boast. He was a splendid braggart always. But Jack held tight to the mast and the royal-halliards going away down past him.

"Oh!" said Jack. To develop that "Oh!" were a task indeed. For it meant that this was a very wonderful world, a bright, light, splendid world, and that if a ship was a wonder, her lofty spars were astronomy compared with land surveying. She was sheer grace, magical adequacy, and her cross-trees a throne, a great observatory, a peak. It was a joy, a great terrible joy, to think that one might and could fall. It was a risk, and what's so good as that? Life is the more immense as one sees the chance of losing it. Death is the great adventure, after all.

Though the sea was calm and the wind light upon the cross-trees, the Greenhorn felt sweet motions, felt that calmness was but relative. There was a beautiful musical thrill about him; it was as if a far faint organ played, as if spiritual beings touched harps of magic. There was a delicious thrill under and around and in him. His heart responded; he felt the tonic of the open, high world. He looked down and clutched tightly.

That was Mr. Mackintosh! How strange it seemed that he should be so little when at his word strange things might happen. He had clothed the *Flying Cloud* in her majesty, had tended her in her trouble, had stood by her as she slept cradled in the lifting surges when she lay to but a little time ago. The decks looked warm, comfortable, earthlike. A pang went through the boy. This was fine, but it was dreadfully lonely. He desired to go down from aloft. And yet—there was the royal-yard above him and the skysail. Could he?

Bram dangled a careless leg over destruction. But his bright eyes of blue were brighter still.

"How do you like it, Jack?" he asked.

"I'm thinking—"

"What?"

"What it must be up here at night when it's blowing hard."

"Aye, my lad, that's the time!"

For Jack, who had the elements of imagination in him, the sun went down and the wind blew and the sea got up. He looked at the foot-ropes of the t'gallant-yard, and in his mind climbed out upon them, and with the Lascars picked up the sail. He was very much afraid, and still more fearful of showing it.

Then he came back to the cross-trees and saw Bram with a pipe in his mouth.

"Let's go on the royal-yard," said Bram.

Jack's mind, or body perhaps, said that he would much rather not. It was ridiculous to go up there, highly ridiculous. What good would it do? That was what his body wanted to know as he rose carefully and reluctantly and followed. Every step he took was forced now; his reason clamoured against him. He hated Bram very much.

And he found the royal-yard much more hazardously magnificent than the cross-trees. He quite loved Bram for saying "Let's go up to the royal-yard." He even imitated Bram after a moment's pause and sat down on the yard with his heels on the bellying quiet sail. He hugged the mast tightly.

Now he could see under the foot of the skysail. He looked down on the fore-royal and far over it across the open sea. The ship itself was lost; there was no ship, nothing but a little glimpse of the foc's'le head under the roached foot of the lower fore-topsail. A mannikin moved there. He heard a faint far voice speak. The thrill of the rigging was greater yet than it had been in the cross-trees; it was more musical, more vibrant, stronger. A musical ear would have heard subtle tones, overtones, harmonics, and some might have assigned them their stations in the great instrument of the winds.

There came a dissonance.

"Like to go on the skysail-yard, sonny?"

Insatiable beast, the trier of man! Jack looked at him malevolently and saw him staring aloft to where that white bird the lone main-skysail spread its vans to the most heavenly air. The mast itself seemed now but a pole, the yard a thin wand; the backstays and the stays but threads. Jack said he was a vulgarian to bellow there in heaven, at the foot of the great white throne, and yet he knew he was an angel saying "Come." The upward journey was not finished yet and only a recreant would pause now.

There were no more ratlines, but Bram grasped the mast and swarmed it, and said, when he straddled the yard, "Steady does it." It was a saint encouraging a catechumen struggling in faith for sight. Jack drew in his breath and took hold of his young courage and climbed. He swung his leg across the yard and sat shaking and triumphant. Oh, amazing—

Ye Gods of starry depths and the pathless wastes of sunwashed ocean, who shall stand upon the skysail-yard of any *Fishing Cloud* and not declare your glory? There are untouched virgins of the rocks and snows who still baffle mankind's ardours and frown or smile in chastity; but still there's no such height in Alp or Himalaya or Cordillera as the summit that we stand on now. No Golden Throne nor Illimani, nor white Dom, nor Aconcagua, nor Tupungato, lone and glacier-bearing, has a majesty so overpowering as the amazing skysail-yard. Below lies the world itself, the ship, and the world is nothing; here on clouds equal in grace to those of the nigh heaven itself, we float up-borne, and advance into the celestial air that's crystal. We breathe God's air, drink divinest dews, sip from the very bowl of azure that holds the stars and sun, and look down as gods ourselves upon the banded emerald and amethystine pavement of old Ocean.

There's no such glory as the glory of the ship, and no such glory in the ship as when we lift our eyes and hearts upon her nearest reach to heaven. Would it were mine to sing the Swan Song of the great-sailed ships that soon shall be no more, and even now sail over the rim of the great seas to sink and be forever unknown!

The sacred neophyte and the unsacred white-faced wonderful devil who led him there, sat up aloft for an hour. There to my mind they sit yet, brown face and white, debauchee and innocent, half divine and half diabolic. In so pure and holy a spot while the *Flying Cloud* moved before her attendant winds, let us leave them for a while. There should be a new page now. There is a great argument for leaving fair white pages at times in books. Thereon they who are capable should write the unwritten that's in their hearts, in their tears, their joys, their anguish, and their prayers.

The Sea and the Wind That Blows

From *The Sea and the Wind That Blows*

BY E. B. WHITE

A CELEBRATED HUMORIST AND LONGTIME contributor to *The New Yorker* and later *Harper's,* White was also a self-described "salt-water man" who, throughout his life, owned a long succession of small boats. He is perhaps best known for children's stories that have charmed adults as well, such as *Stuart Little* and *Charlotte's Web.*

This essay from his 1963 book, *The Sea and the Wind That Blows,* looks at his passion for sailing with a wry but elegant eye.

WAKING OR SLEEPING, I DREAM OF BOATS—usually of rather small boats under a slight press of sail. When I think how great a part of my life has been spent dreaming the hours away and how much of this total dream life has concerned small craft, I wonder about the state of my health, for I am told that it is not a good sign to be always voyaging into unreality, driven by imaginary breezes.

I have noticed that most men, when they enter a barber shop and must wait their turn, drop into a chair and pick up a magazine. I simply sit down and pick up the thread of my sea wandering, which began more than fifty years ago and is not quite ended. There is hardly a waiting room in the east that has not served as my cockpit, whether I was waiting to board a train or to see a dentist. And I am usually still trimming sheets when the train starts or the drill begins to whine.

If a man must be obsessed by something, I suppose a boat is as good as anything, perhaps a bit better than most. A small sailing craft is not only beautiful, it is seductive and full of strange promise and the hint of trouble. If it happens to be an auxiliary cruising boat, it is without question the most compact and ingenious arrangement for living ever devised by the restless mind of man—a home that is stable without being stationary, shaped less like a box than like a fish or a bird or a girl, and in which the homeowner can remove his daily affairs as far from shore as he has the nerve to take them, close-hauled or running free—parlor, bedroom, and bath, suspended and alive.

Men who ache all over for tidiness and compactness in their lives often find relief for their pain in the cabin of a thirty-foot sailboat at anchor in a sheltered cove. Here the sprawling panoply of The Home is compressed in orderly miniature and liquid delirium, suspended between the bottom of the sea and the top of the sky, ready to move on in the morning by the miracle of canvas and the witchcraft of rope. It is small wonder that men hold boats in the secret place of their mind, almost from the cradle to the grave.

Along with my dream of boats has gone the ownership of boats, a long succession of them upon the surface of the sea, many of them makeshift and crank. Since childhood I have managed to have some sort of sailing craft and to raise a sail in fear. Now, in my sixties, I still own a boat, still raise my sail in fear in answer to the summons of the unforgiving sea. Why does the sea attract me in the way it does? Whence comes this compulsion to hoist a sail, actually or in dream? My first encounter with the sea was a case of hate at first sight. I was taken, at the age of four, to a bathing beach in New Rochelle. Everything about the experience frightened and repelled me: the taste of salt in my mouth, the foul chill of the wooden bath-house, the littered sand, the stench of the tide flats. I came away hating and fearing the sea. Later, I found that what I had feared and hated, I now feared and loved.

I returned to the sea of necessity, because it would support a boat; and although I knew little of boats, I could not get them out of my thoughts. I became a pelagic boy. The sea became my unspoken challenge: the wind, the tide, the fog, the ledge, the bell, the gull that cried help, the never-ending threat and bluff of weather. Once having permitted the wind to enter the belly of my sail, I was not able to quit the helm; it was as though I had seized hold of a high-tension wire and could not let go.

I liked to sail alone. The sea was the same as a girl to me—I did not want anyone else along. Lacking instruction, I invented ways of getting things done, and usually ended by doing them in a rather queer fashion, and so did not learn to sail properly, and still cannot sail well, although I have been at it all my life. I was twenty before I discovered that charts existed; all my navigating up to that time was done with the wariness and the ignorance of the early explorers. I was thirty before I learned to hang a coiled halyard on its cleat as it should be done. Until then I simply coiled it down on deck and dumped the coil. I was always in trouble and always returned, seeking more trouble. Sailing became a compulsion: there lay the boat, swinging to her mooring, there blew the wind; I had no choice but to go. My earliest boats were so small that when the wind failed, or when I failed, I could switch to manual con-trol—I could paddle or row home. But then I graduated to boats that only the wind was strong enough to move. When I first dropped off my mooring in such a boat, I was an hour getting up the nerve to cast off the pennant. Even now, with a thousand little voyages notched in my belt, I still feel a memorial chill on casting off, as the gulls jeer and the empty mainsail claps.

Of late years, I have noticed that my sailing has increasingly become a compulsive activity rather than a source of pleasure. There lies the boat, there blows the morning breeze—it is a point of honor, now, to go. I am like an alcoholic who cannot put his bottle out of his life. With me, I cannot not sail. Yet I know well enough that I have lost touch with the wind and, in fact, do not like the wind any more. It jiggles me up, the wind does, and what I really love are windless days, when all is peace. There is a great question in my mind whether a man who is against wind should longer try to sail a boat. But this is an intellectual response—the old yearning is still in me, belonging to the past, to youth, and so I am torn between past and present, a common disease of later life.

When does a man quit the sea? How dizzy, how bumbling must he be? Does he quit while he's ahead, or wait till he makes some major mistake, like falling overboard or being flattened by an accidental jibe? This past winter I spent hours arguing the question with myself. Finally, deciding that I had come to the end of the road, I wrote a note to the boatyard, putting my boat up for sale. I said I was "coming off the water." But as I typed the sentence, I doubted that I meant a word of it.

If no buyer turns up, I know what will happen: I will instruct the yard to put her in again—"just till somebody comes along." And then there will be the old uneasiness, the old uncertainty, as the mild southeast breeze ruffles the cove, a gentle, steady, morning breeze, bringing the taint of the distant wet world, the smell that takes a man back to the very beginning of time, linking him to all that has gone before. There will lie the sloop, there will blow the wind, once more I will get under way. And as I reach across to the red nun off the Torry Islands, dodging the trap buoys and toggles, the shags gathered on the ledge will note my passage. "There goes the old boy again," they will say. "One more rounding of his little Horn, one more conquest of his Roaring Forties." And with the tiller in my hand, I'll feel again the wind imparting life to a boat, will smell again the old menace, the one that imparts life to me: the cruel beauty of the salt world, the barnacle's tiny knives, the sharp spine of the urchin, the stinger of the sun jelly, the claw of the crab.

Overwhelmed

From *Sufferings in Africa*

BY CAPTAIN JAMES RILEY

I n 1815, young American sea captain James Riley was shipwrecked off the western coast of North Africa, captured by a band of nomadic Arabs, and sold into slavery. His dramatic account of his quest for survival and freedom sold more than a million copies in his day, and was even read by a young and impressionable Abraham Lincoln. In this passage, Riley describes the events that led to the loss of his ship.

AFTER THE CLOSE OF THE WAR, in April 1815, being then in my native state, I was employed as master and supercargo of the brig Commerce of Hartford in Connecticut; a vessel nearly new, and well fitted, of about two hundred and twenty tons burden, belonging to Messrs. Riley & Brown, Josiah Savage & Co. and Luther Savage, of that city. A light cargo was taken on board, and I shipped a crew, consisting of the following persons, namely; George Williams, chief mate, Aaron R. Savage, second mate, William Porter, Archibald Robbins, Thomas Burns, and James Clark, seamen, Horace Savage, cabin boy, and Richard Deslisle, (a black man) cook. This man had been a servant during the late war to Captain Daniel Ketchum, of the 25th regiment of United States' infantry, who distinguished himself by taking prisoner the English Major-General Rial, at the dreadful battle of Bridgewater in Upper Canada, and by several other heroic achievements.

With this crew I proceeded to sea from the mouth of Connecticut River, on the sixth day of May, 1815, bound for New-Orleans. We continued to steer for the Bahama Islands, as winds and weather permitted, until the twentieth of the same month, when we saw the southernmost part of the island of Abaco, and passing the Hole in the Wall, on the twenty-first, entered on the Grand Bahama Bank to the leeward of the northernmost Berri Islands; from thence, with a fair wind and good breeze, we steered W.S.W. twelve leagues; then S.S.W. about forty leagues, crossing the Bank, in from three to four fathoms water. On the morning of the twenty-second we saw the Orange Key on our starboard beam; altered our course and ran off the Bank, leaving them on our starboard hand distant one league. The water on this Great Ban, in most places, appears as white as milk, owing to the white sand at the bottom gleaming through it, and is so clear that an object, the size of a dollar, can be easily seen lying on the bottom in four fathom water, in a still time. Having got off the Bank, we steered W.S.W. for the Double-headed Shot Bank, and at meridian found ourselves, by good observations in the latitude of 24.30. being nearly that of the Orange Keys. In the afternoon it became nearly calm, but a good breeze springing up, we continued our course all night W.S.W. I remained on deck myself, on a sharp look out for the Double-headed Shot Bank, or Keys, until four o'clock A.M. when judging by our distance we must be far past them, and consequently clear of that danger, I ordered the chief mate, who had charge of the watch, to keep a good look out, on all sides, for land, white water and breakers; and after repeating the same to the people, I went below to take a nap. At about five (then fair daylight) I was awakened by a shock and thought I felt the vessel touch bottom. I sprang on deck, put the helm to starboard, had all hands called in an instant, and saw breakers ahead and to southward, close on board; apparently a sound on our right, and land to the northward, at about two leagues distance. The vessel's head was towards the S.W. and she was running on at the rate of ten miles the hour. I instantly seized the helm, put it hard to port, ordered all sails to be let run, and the anchors cleared away. The vessel touched lightly, three or four times; when I found she was over the reef, we let go an anchor, which brought her up in two and a half fathoms, or fifteen feet of water, which was quite smooth. We now handed all the sails, and lowered down the boat. I went in her with four hands, and sounded out a passage; found plenty of water to leeward of the reef; turned and got under way, and at seven o'clock A.M. was in the open sea again, with a fresh breeze.

This being the first time, in the course of my navigating, that any vessel which I was in had struck the bottom unexpectedly, I own I was so much surprised and shocked, that my whole frame trembled, and I could scarcely believe that what had happened was really true, until by comparing the causes and effects of the currents of the Gulph Stream, I was convinced that during the light winds, the day before, when in the Santarem Channel, the vessel had been drifted by the current that runs N.N.W. (and at that time very strong) so far north of the Double-headed Shot Bank; that my course in the night, though the only proper one I could have steered, was such as kept the current on the larboard bow of the vessel, which had horsed her across it sixty miles out of her course in sixteen hours, and would have landed her on the S.W. part of the Carysford Reef in two minutes more, where she must have been totally lost. As so many vessels of all nations who navigate this stream have perished with their cargoes, and oftentimes their crews, I mention this incident to warn the navigator of the danger he is in when his vessel is acted upon by these currents, where no calculation can be depended upon, and where nothing but very frequent castings of the lead, and a good look out, can secure him from their too often fatal consequences.

Having settled this point in my own mind, I became tranquil, and we continued to run along the Florida Keys from W.S.W. to West by South, in from thirty to forty fathoms water, about four leagues distant, seeing from one to two leagues within us many rocks and little sandy islands, just above the waters' edge, with a good depth of water all around them, until noon on the 24th, when we doubled the dry Tortugas Islands in ten fathoms, and on the 26th arrived in the Mississippi River, passed Fort St. Philip at Pluquemines the same night, having shown my papers to the commanding officer of that post (as is customary.)

My previous knowledge of the river and the manner of getting up it, enabled me to pass nearly one hundred sail of vessels that were in before me, and by dint of great and continued exertions, to arrive with my vessel before the city of New-Orleans, on the first day of June. Here we discharged our cargo, and took another on board, principally on freight, in which I was assisted by Messrs. Talcott & Bower, respectable merchants in that city. This cargo consisted of tobacco and flour. The two ordinary seamen, Francis Bliss and James Carrington, now wished for a discharge, and received it. I then shipped in their stead John Hogan and James Barrett, both seamen and natives of the state of Massachusetts.

With this crew and cargo we sailed from New Orleans on the twenty-fourth of June; left the river on the twenty-sixth, and proceeded for Gibraltar, where we arrived on the ninth of August following, and landed our cargo. About the thirteenth the schooner——, Capt. Price of and from New York, in a short passage, came into the

Bay, and the captain on his landing told me he was bound up to Barcelona, and that if I would go on board his vessel, which was then standing off and on in the Bay, he would give me a late New-York Price Current, and some newspapers. I was in great want of a Price Current for my guide in making purchases, and accordingly went on board. The wind blowing strong in, and the vessel far out, I had to take four men with me, namely, James Clark, James Barrett, William Porter, and John Hogan. Having received the Price Current, &c. I left the schooner about sunset, when they immediately filled her sails and stood on. As we were busied in stepping the boat's mast to sail back, a toppling sea struck her, and nearly filled her with water; we all jumped instantly overboard, in the hope of preventing her from filling, but she filled immediately. Providentially the captain of the schooner heard me haloo, though at least a mile from us; put his vessel about, came near us, sent his boat, and saved our lives and our boat, which being cleared of water, and it being after dark, we returned safe alongside of the brig by ten o'clock at night. When the boat filled, we were more than three miles from the Rock, in the Gut, where the current would have set us into the Mediterranean, and we must have inevitably perished before morning, but we were spared, in order to suffer a severer doom and miseries worse than death, on the barbarous shores of Africa.

We now took on board part of a cargo of brandies and wines, and some dollars, say about two thousand, and an old man named Antonio Michel, a native of New-Orleans, who had previously been wrecked on the island of Teneriffe, and was recommended to my charity by Mr. Gavino, who at that time exercised the functions of American Consul at Gibraltar.

We set sail from the bay of Gibraltar on the 23rd of August, 1815, intending to go by way of the Cape de Verd Islands, to complete the lading of the vessel with salt. We passed Capt Spartel on the morning of the 24th, giving it a berth of from ten to twelve leagues, and steered off to the W.S.W. I intended to make the Canary Islands, and pass between Teneriffe and Palma, having a fair wind; but it being very thick and foggy weather, though we got two observations at noon, neither could be much depended upon. On account of the fog, we saw no land, and found, by good meridian altitudes on the twenty-eighth, that we were in the latitude of 27.30.N. having differed our latitude by the force of current, one hundred and twenty miles; thus passing the Canaries without seeing any of them. I concluded we must have passed through the intended passage without discovering the land on either side, particularly, as it was in the night, which was very dark, and black as pitch; nor could I believe otherwise from having had a fair wind all the way, and having steered one course ever since we took our departure from Cape Spartel. Soon after we got an observation on the 28th, it became as thick as ever, and the darkness seemed (if possible) to increase. Towards evening I got up my reckoning, and examined it all over, to be sure that I had committed no error, and caused the mates to do the same with theirs. Having thus ascertained that I was correct in calculation, I altered our course to S.W. which ought to have carried us nearly on the course I wished to steer, that is, for the easternmost of the Cape de Verds; but finding the weather becoming more foggy towards night, it being so thick that we could scarcely see the end of the jib-boom, I rounded the vessel to, and sounded with one hundred and twenty fathoms of line, but found no bottom, and continued on our course, still reflecting on what should be the cause of our not seeing land, (as I never had passed near the Canaries before without seeing them, even in thick weather or in the night.) I came to a determination to haul off to the N.W. by the wind at 10 P.M. as should then be by the log only thirty miles north of Cape Bajador. I concluded on this at nine, and thought my fears had never before so much prevailed over my judgment and my reckoning. I ordered the light sails to be handed, and the steering sail booms to be rigged in snug, which was done as fast as it could be by one watch, under the immediate direction of Mr. Savage.

We had just got the men stationed at the braces for hauling off, as the man at helm cried "ten o'clock." Our try-sail boom was on the starboard side, but ready for jibing; the helm was put to port, dreaming of no danger near. I had been on deck all the evening my-self; the vessel was running at the rate of nine or ten knots, with a very strong breeze, and high sea, when the main boom was jibed over, and I at that instant heard a roaring; the yards were braced up— all hands were called. I imagined at first it was a squall, and was near ordering the sails to be lowered down; but I then discovered breakers foaming at a most dreadful rate under our lee. Hope for a moment flattered me that we could fetch off still, as there were no breakers in view ahead: the anchors were made ready; but these hopes vanished in an instant, as the vessel was carried by a current and a sea directly towards the breakers, and she struck! We let go the best bower an-chor; all sails were taken in as fast as possible: surge after surge came thundering on, and drove her in spite of anchors, partly with her head on shore. She struck with such violence as to start every man from the deck. Knowing there was no possibility of saving her, and that she must very soon bilge and fill with water, I ordered all the provisions we could get at to be brought on deck, in hopes of saving some, and as much water to be drawn from the large casks as possible. We started several quarter casks of wine, and filled them with water. Every man worked as if his life depended upon his present exertions; all were obedient to every order I gave, and seemed perfectly calm;— The vessel was stout and high, as she was only in ballast trim;—The sea combed over her stern and swept her decks, but we managed to get the small boat in on deck, to sling her and keep her from staving. We cut away the bulwark on the larboard side so as to prevent the boats from staving when we should get them out; cleared away the long boat and hung her in tackles, the vessel continuing to strike very heavy, and filling fast. We however, had secured five or six barrels of water, and as many of wine, three barrels of bread, and three or four salted provisions. I had as yet been so busily employed, that no pains had been taken to ascertain what distance we were from the land, nor had any of us yet seen it; and in the meantime all the clothing, chests, trunks, &c. were got up, and the books, charts, and sea instruments, were stowed in them, in the hope of their being useful to us in future.

The vessel being now nearly full of water, the surf making a fair breach over her, and fearing she would go to pieces, I prepared a rope, and put it in the small boat, having got a glimpse of the shore, at no great distance, and taking Porter with me, we were lowered down on the larboard or lee side of the vessel, where she broke the violence of the sea, and made it comparatively smooth; we shoved off, but on clearing away from the bow of the vessel, the boat was overwhelmed with a surf, and we were plunged into the foaming surges: we were driven along by the current, aided by what seamen call the undertow, (or recoil of the sea) to the distance of three hundred yards to the westward, covered nearly all the time by the billows, which, following each other in quick succession, scarcely gave us time to catch a breath before we were again literally swallowed by them, till at length we were thrown, together with our boat, upon a sandy beach. After taking breath a little, and ridding our stomachs of the salt water that had forced its way into them, my first care was to turn the water out of the boat, and haul her up out of the reach of the surf. We found the rope that was made fast to her still remaining; this we carried up along the beach, directly to leeward of the wreck, where we fastened it to sticks about the thickness of handspikes, that had drifted on the shore from the vessel, and which we drove into the sand by the help of other pieces of wood. Before leaving the vessel, I had directed that all the chests, trunks, and everything that would float, should be hove overboard: this all hands were busied in doing. The vessel lay about one hundred fathoms from the beach, at high tide. In order to save the crew, a hawser was made fast to the rope we had on shore, one end of which we hauled to us, and made it fast to a number of sticks we had driven into the sand for the purpose. It was then tautened on board the wreck, and made fast. This being done, the long-boat (in order to save the provisions already in her) was lowered down, and two hands steadied her by ropes fastened to the rings in her stem and stern posts over the hawser, so as to slide, keeping her bow to the surf. In this manner they reached the beach, carried on the top of a heavy wave. The boat was stove by the violence of the shock against the beach; but by great exertions we saved the three barrels of bread in her before they were much damaged; and two barrels of salted provisions were also saved.

We were now, four of us, on shore, and busied in picking up the clothing and other things which drifted from the vessel and carrying them up out of the surf. It was by this time daylight, and high water; the vessel careened deep offshore, and I made signs to have the mast cut away, in the hope of easing her, that she might not go to pieces. They were accordingly cut away, and fell on her starboard side, making a better lee for a boat alongside the wreck, as they projected considerably beyond her bow. The masts and rigging being gone, the sea breaking very high over the wreck, and nothing left to hold on by, the mates and six men still on board, though secured, as well as they could be, on the bowsprit and in the larboard fore-channels, were yet in imminent danger of being washed off by every surge. The long-boat was stove, and it being impossible for the small one to live, my great object was now to save the lives of the crew by means of the hawser. I therefore made signs to them to come, one by one, on the hawser, which had been stretched taut for that purpose. John Hogan ventured first, and having pulled off his jacket, took to the hawser, and made for the shore. When he had got clear of the immediate lee of the wreck, every surf buried him, coming many feet above his head; but he still held fast to the rope with a death-like grasp, and as soon as the surf was passed, proceeded on towards the shore, until another surf, more powerful than the former, unclenched his hands, and threw him within our reach; when he laid hold of him and dragged him to the beach; we then rolled him on the sand, until he discharged the salt water from his stomach, and revived. I kept in the water up to my chin, steadying myself by the hawser, while the surf passed over me, to catch the others as they approached, and thus, with the assistance of those already on shore, was enabled to save all the rest from a watery grave.

Sailing Alone Around the World

From *Sailing Alone Around the World*

BY JOSHUA SLOCUM

THE FIRST MAN TO CIRCUMNAVIGATE alone, Joshua Slocum created a literary masterpiece with his *Sailing Alone Around the World*. It is at once an adventure, a personal achievement, a feat of seamanship, and an example of true understatement. It is the classic tale of a middle-aged has-been who simply refused to let his dreams die.

As Captain Joshua Slocum began his voyage aboard his thirty-seven-foot *Spray,* he had just had his fifty-first birthday. He could look back on two decades of being the master of some of the finest merchant sailing ships, an extremely happy life with his wife, Virginia, who sailed with him and bore him four children, and a life filled with exotic ports and high adventure.

But now middle-aged, his world had crumbled about him. His wife had died suddenly, a second wife was little more than a babysitter for his children, and he was facing the end of the era of sail and the coming of steam—a change to which he could not adapt.

He had nothing when he was given *Spray,* a century-old oyster-fishing sloop, as a joke. But, though it had lain for years on the beach, he set about rebuilding it quixotically and, a year and $553.62 later, he had created a tiny yacht.

With $1.80 in cash and agreements with several newspapers to file stories en route, he set sail with no itinerary or schedule. Thirty-eight months and 46,000 miles later, he sailed into Newport, Rhode Island, and immortality. *Sailing Alone Around The World,* first issued in 1900, became an instant success.

In 1909 at the age of sixty-five, he set off on an expedition to explore the Orinoco and Amazon rivers. He was never seen nor heard from again.

IT WAS THE 3D OF MARCH WHEN the *Spray* sailed from Port Tamar direct for Cape Pillar, with the wind from the northeast, which I fervently hoped might hold till she cleared the land; but there was no such good luck in store. It soon began to rain and thicken in the northwest, boding no good. The *Spray* neared Cape Pillar rapidly, and, nothing loath, plunged into the Pacific Ocean at once, taking her first bath of it in the gathering storm. There was no turning back even had I wished to do so, for the land was now shut out by the darkness of night. The wind freshened, and I took in a third reef. The sea was confused and treacherous. In such a time as this the old fisherman prayed, "Remember, Lord, my ship is small and thy sea is so wide!" I saw now only the gleaming crests of the waves. They showed white teeth while the sloop balanced over them. "Everything for an offing," I cried, and to this end I carried on all the sail she would bear. She ran all night with a tree sheet, but on the morning of March 4 the wind shifted to southwest, then back suddenly to northwest, and blew with terrific force. The *Spray,* stripped of her sails, then bore off under bare poles. No ship in the world could have stood up against so violent a gale. Knowing that this storm might continue for many days, and that it would be impossible to work back to the westward along the coast outside of Tierra del Fuego, there seemed nothing to do but to keep on and go east about, after all. Anyhow, for my present safety the only course lay in keeping her before the wind. And so she drove southeast, as though about to round the Horn, while the waves rose and fell and bellowed their never-ending story of the sea; but the Hand that held these held also the *Spray.* She was running now with a reefed forestaysail, the sheets flat amidship. I paid out two long ropes to steady her course and to break combing seas astern, and I lashed the helm amidship. In this trim she ran before it, shipping never a sea. Even while the storm raged at its worst, my ship was wholesome and noble. My mind as to her seaworthiness was put at ease for aye.

When all had been done that I could do for the safety of the vessel, I got to the fore-scuttle, between seas, and prepared a pot of coffee over a wood fire, and made a good Irish stew. Then, as before and afterward on the *Spray,* I insisted on warm meals. In the tide-race off Cape Pillar, however, where the sea was marvelously high, uneven, and crooked, my appetite was slim, and for a time I postponed cooking. (Confidentially, I was seasick!)

The first day of the storm gave the *Spray* her actual test in the worst sea that Cape Horn or its wild regions could afford, and in no part of the world could a rougher sea be found than at this particular point, namely, off Cape Pillar, the grim sentinel of the Horn.

Farther offshore, while the sea was majestic, there was less apprehension of danger. There the *Spray* rode, now like a bird on the crest of a wave, and now like a waif deep down in the hollow between seas; and so she drove on. Whole days passed, counted as other days, but with always a thrill—yes, of delight.

On the fourth day of the gale, rapidly nearing the pitch of Cape Horn, I inspected my chart and pricked off the course and distance to Port Stanley, in the Falkland Islands, where I might find my way and refit, when I saw through a rift in the clouds a high mountain, about seven leagues away on the port beam. The fierce edge of the gale by this time had blown off, and I had already bent a squaresail on the boom in place of the mainsail, which was torn to rags. I hauled in the trailing ropes, hoisted this awkward sail reefed, the forestaysail being already set, and under this sail brought her at once on the wind heading for the land, which appeared as an island in the sea. So it turned out to be, though not the one I had supposed.

I was exultant over the prospect of once more entering the Strait of Magellan and beating through again into the Pacific, for it was more than rough on the outside coast of Tierra del Fuego. It was indeed a mountainous sea. When the sloop was in the fiercest squalls, with only the reefed forestaysail set, even that small sail shook her from keelson to truck when it shivered by the leech. Had I harbored the shadow of a doubt for her safety, it would have been that she might spring a leak in the garboard at the heel of the mast; but she never called me once to the pump. Under pressure of the smallest sail I could set she made for the land like a race-horse, and steering her over the crests of the waves so that she might not trip was nice work. I stood at the helm now and made the most of it.

Night closed in before the sloop reached the land, leaving her feeling the way in pitchy darkness. I saw breakers ahead before long. At this I wore ship and stood offshore, but was immediately startled by the tremendous roaring of breakers again ahead and on the lee bow. This puzzled me, for there should have been no broken water where I supposed myself to be. I kept off a good bit, then wore round, but finding broken water also there, threw her head again offshore. In this way among dangers, I spent the rest of the night. Hail and sleet in the fierce squalls cut my flesh till the blood trickled over my face; but what of that? It was daylight, and the sloop was in the midst of the Milky Way of the sea, which is northwest of Cape Horn, and it was the white breakers of a huge sea over sunken rocks which had threatened to engulf her through the night. It was Fury Island I had sighted and steered for, and what a panorama was before me now and all around! It was not the time to complain of a broken skin. What could I do but fill away among the breakers and find a channel between them, now that it was day? Since she had escaped the rocks through the night, surely she would find her way by daylight. This was the greatest sea adventure of my life. God knows how my vessel escaped.

The sloop at last reached inside of small islands that sheltered her in smooth water. Then I climbed the mast to survey the wild scene astern. The great naturalist Darwin looked over this seascape from the deck of the *Beagle,* and wrote in his journal, "Any landsman seeing the Milky Way would have nightmare for a week." He might have added, "or seaman" as well.

The *Spray's* good luck followed fast. I discovered, as she sailed along through a labyrinth of islands, that she was in the Cockburn Channel, which leads into the Strait of Magellan at a point opposite Cape Froward, and that she was already passing Thieves' Bay, suggestively named. And at night, March 8, behold, she was at anchor in a snug cove at the Turn! Every heart-beat on the *Spray* now counted thanks.

Here I pondered on the events of the last few days, and, strangely enough, instead of feeling rested from sitting or lying down, I now began to feel jaded and worn; but a hot meal of venison stew soon put me right, so that I could sleep. As drowsiness came on I sprinkled the deck with tacks, and then I turned in, bearing in mind the advice of my old friend Samblich that I was not to step on them myself. I saw to it that not a few of them stood "business end" up; for when the *Spray* passed Thieves' Bay two canoes had put out and followed in her wake, and there was no disguising the fact any longer that I was alone.

Now, it is well known that one cannot step on a tack without saying something about it. A pretty good Christian will whistle when he steps on the "commercial end" of a carpet-tack; a savage will howl and claw the air, and that was just what happened that night about twelve o'clock, while I was asleep in the cabin, where the savages thought they "had me," sloop and all, but changed their minds when they stepped on deck, for then they thought that I or somebody else had them. I had no need of a dog; they howled like a pack of hounds. I had hardly use for a gun. They jumped pell-mell, some into their canoes and some into the sea, to cool off, I suppose, and there was a deal of free language over it as they went. I fired several guns when I came on deck, to let the rascals know that I was home, and then I turned in again, feeling sure I should not be disturbed any more by people who left in so great a hurry.

The Fuegians, being cruel, are naturally cowards; they regard a rifle with superstitious fear. The only real danger one could see that might come from their quarter would be from allowing them to surround one within bow-shot, or to anchor within range where they might lie in ambush. As for their coming on deck at night, even had I not put tacks about, I could have cleared them off by shots from the cabin and hold. I always kept a quantity of ammunition within reach in the hold and in the cabin and in the forepeak, so that retreating to any of these places I could "hold the fort" simply by shooting up through the deck.

Perhaps the greatest danger to be apprehended was from the use of fire. Every canoe carries fire; nothing is thought of that, for it is their custom to communicate by smoke-signals. The harmless brand that lies smoldering in the bottom of one of their canoes might be ablaze in one's cabin if he were not on the alert. The port captain of Sandy Point warned me particularly of this danger. Only a short time before they had fired a Chilean gun-boat by throwing brands in through the stern windows of the cabin. The *Spray* had no openings in the cabin or deck, except two scuttles, and these were guarded by fastenings which could not be undone without waking me if I were asleep.

On the morning of the 9th, after a refreshing rest and a warm breakfast, and after I had swept the deck of tacks, I got out what spare canvas there was on board, and began to sew the pieces together in the shape of a peak for my square-mainsail, the tarpaulin. The day to all appearances promised fine weather and light winds, but appearances in Tierra del Fuego do not always count. While I was wondering why no trees grew on the slope abreast of the anchorage, half minded to lay by the sail-making and land with my gun for some game and to inspect a white boulder on the beach, near the brook, a williwaw came down with such terrific force as to carry the *Spray*, with two anchors down, like a feather out of the cove and away into deep water. No wonder trees did not grow on the side of that hill! Great Boreas! a tree would need to be all roots to hold on against such a furious wind.

From the cove to the nearest land to leeward was a long drift, however, and I had ample time to weigh both anchors before the sloop came near any danger, and so no harm came of it. I saw no more savages that day or the next; they probably had some sign by which they knew of the coming williwaws; at least, they were wise in not being afloat even on the second day, for I had no sooner gotten to work at sail-making again, after the anchor was down, than the wind, as on the day before, picked the sloop up and flung her seaward with a vengeance, anchor and all, as before. This fierce wind, usual to the

Magellan country, continued on through the day, and swept the sloop by several miles of steep bluffs and precipices overhanging a bold shore of wild and uninviting appearance. I was not sorry to get away from it, though in doing so it was no Elysian shore to which I shaped my course. I kept on sailing in hope, since I had no choice but to go on, heading across for St. Nicholas Bay, where I had cast anchor February 19. It was now the 10th of March! Upon reaching the bay the second time I had circumnavigated the wildest part of desolate Tierra del Fuego. But the *Spray* had not yet arrived at St. Nicholas, and by the merest accident her bones were saved from resting there when she did arrive. The parting of a staysail-sheet in a williwaw, when the sea was turbulent and she was plunging into the storm, brought me forward to see instantly a dark cliff ahead and breakers so close under the bows that I felt surely lost, and in my thoughts cried, "Is the hand of fate against me, after all, leading me in the end to this dark spot?" I sprang aft again, unheeding the flapping sail, and threw the wheel over, expecting, as the sloop came down into the hallow of a wave, to feel her timbers smash under me on the rocks. But at the touch of her helm she swung clear of the danger; and in the next moment she was in the lee of the land.

It was the small island in the middle of the bay for which the sloop had been steering, and which she made with such unerring aim as nearly to run it down. Farther along in the bay was the anchorage, which I managed to reach, but before I could get the anchor down another squall caught the sloop and whirled her round like a top and carried her away, altogether to leeward of the bay. Still farther to leeward was a great headland, and I bore off for that. This was retracing my course toward Sandy Point, for the gale was from the southwest.

I had the sloop soon under good control, however, and in a short time rounded to under the lee of a mountain, where the sea was as smooth as a mill-pond, and the sails flapped and hung limp while she carried her way close in. Here I thought I would anchor and rest till morning, the depth being eight fathoms very close to the shore. But it was interesting to see, as I let go the anchor, that it did not reach the bottom before another williwaw struck down from this mountain and carried the sloop off faster than I could pay out cable. Instead of resting, I had to "man the windlass" and heave up the anchor and fifty fathoms of cable hanging up and down in deep water. This was in that part of the strait called Famine Reach. I could have wished it Jericho! On that little crab-windlass I worked the rest of the night, thinking how much easier it was for me when I could say, "Do that thing or the other," than to do it myself. But I hove away on the windlass and sang the old chants that I sang when I was a sailor, from "Blow, Boys, Blow for Californy, O" to "Sweet By and By."

It was daybreak when the anchor was at the hawse. By this time the wind had gone down, and cat's-paws took the place of williwaws. The sloop was then drifting slowly toward Sandy Point. She came within sight of ships at anchor in the roads, and I was more than half minded to put in for new sails, but the wind coming out from the northeast, which was fair for the other direction, I turned the prow of the *Spray* westward once more for the Pacific, to traverse a second time the second half of my first course through the strait.

Down Spinnaker!

From Yachting Bulletin

BY PHILIP HOLLAND

L IGHTWEIGHT TO THE POINT OF flimsy, the spinnaker is a sail that is both loved and hated by sailors. Sailors, particularly racing sailors, love the spinnaker because it adds immense speed downwind, but hate it at the same time because it can be as temperamental and recalcitrant as a mule.

In this story from the short-lived *The Yachtsman* magazine, one crew deals with a spinnaker aboard a racing dinghy in more than enough wind.

WE WERE LATE GETTING ABOARD, which was a pity, because George always has to allow himself time to hoist the mainsail and then lower it again to put the battens in. So we were in a great hurry and the five-minute gun found us with only the foresail set, and the *Mistral* still on her moorings. It was not an uncommon situation for George and myself; we solve it by letting the foresail draw and dropping the mooring over the lee side, if the wind is offshore, so that they can't see us from the club-house. Once under way, nothing very much happened for the next few minutes, so I'd better tell you something about George, so that you'll appreciate the extraordinary events of that race.

George has only once won a race; before the time I'm talking about, that is. That was when all the boats except *Mistral* and *Jeunesse* started on the wrong gun, and *Jeunesse* fouled a mark, so George couldn't help winning. George is one of those chaps who seem to have the average amount of bad luck, but lack the compensating dollop of good luck. If he ever looks like winning a race, something always goes wrong—and when his chances of winning look pretty remote, as they usually do, nothing ever happens to give him that helping hand that other helmsmen sometimes get. Nothing, that is, until the Smythe Cup Race last year.

We were, as I have said, late in getting under way, and for the last few minutes before the gun we were so busy getting things stowed down and set up that the starting-gun found us way down at the leeward end of the line, and some fifty yards away from it. And on the wrong tack. However, this was not unusual, and we were soon pursuing our placid way at the stern of the fleet, untroubled by rights of way or overtaking rules. There was a nice whole-sail breeze, and the sun shone warmly on our necks.

George had suggested reefing about half a minute before the start, but I persuaded him against the idea, although, as he said, we should probably get our transoms beastly wet. I've always crewed for George. I suppose the reason is partly that no one else will do the job, and partly that without me George would probably never get started at all. Furthermore, we are temperamentally suited. George realizes that if he should want to come about while I'm trying to light my pipe, he should defer the maneuver until the weed is drawing nicely. While I, on the other hand, am always ready to sacrifice my handkerchief when George finds he has left the racing flag ashore.

The wind began to freshen as we beat towards the first mark, and by the time we'd rounded it, there was quite a lumpy sea running. The second leg was a reach, and we saw that the others were reefing, for, with the fickleness of summer winds, the breeze was now definitely too much for the whole sail. George, after asking me whether it would be convenient, luffed *Mistral,* and I started to roll down a reef with the patent gear. I'd just managed to get the handle of the rachet unstuck, when there came a sudden free puff. The mainsail caught the weight of it, and the handle snapped in my hand. Of course, there was a fault in the metal, but knowing that didn't help us much.

There was nothing for it but to carry on. We tried reefing the foresail alone, but that made her so unbalanced that she nearly pulled George's arm out. In the midst of our troubles we paused to look around us. We found, to our surprise, that we'd caught up with the rest of the fleet, which was fairly bunched together. We also noticed that the race officer had hoisted a signal which, after much shouting between the boats, was interpreted to mean that the race was shortened to one round.

This was welcome news, for by now several of the boats had reefed again. They argued, wisely, that it was better to lose a race than a mast. For George and me things were more hectic every minute. George started the mainsheet so that the leach was cracking like a machine-gun. We were both lying out as far as we could, not because it was doing much good, but because we felt that it was. The situation was indeed desperate. Ahead of us lay a mark round which we must jibe. After that lay a dead run to the finishing line. With almost the whole mainsail set and the sea now running, it would be almost impossible to hold her, even if we didn't lose the mast. We discussed the situation, and noticed, meanwhile, that we were now fourth, with three boats astern of us.

Finally we decided that the only thing to do was to cut the main halliard and run home under the foresail. Of course, there were other things we could have done, but we didn't think of them till afterwards. It was then we found that we had no knife. It took some time to convince us, but finally we had to face up to it. No knife, nothing that would cut. So we decided to wear ship—but we couldn't. There were three boats close to weather of us, and shout as we might, we couldn't make them understand the situation. It was impossible to luff without hitting them, and traveling as we were, heaven knows what would have happened then.

Before I relate the amazing events of the next few minutes, I'll try and clarify the situation, so that you'll understand how it was that George won the Smythe Cup.

Our boats are half-decked C.B. sloops, 18 ft. l.o.a., and inclined to be a bit tender. On a run we set a parachute spinnaker, which is usually set in stops before the race, as it is not advisable to go for'ard when you're running. *Gypsy* ran under once, so now we have the spinnaker all ready, with the sheets leading aft, so that we can break it out when we want it.

On this memorable occasion, everyone had their kites in stops, in the usual way, only, of course, no one thought of setting them. In that sea, it would have been just damn silly. As we approached the mark, *Mistral* was still fourth, each of us overlapping the other, so that we had the inside berth at the mark. Just before we jibed, George asked me in a harassed voice to let the plate down, to help her round. My hands were cold, and the rope slipped, so that the plate went down with a run. A bight of the spinnaker's starboard sheet fouled the drum, and the parachute burst from its stops with a horrible "whoom-bang." At this moment we jibed. *Mistral* flung herself over like a car taking a bend on two wheels. The bilge-water whooshed across the floorboards as I grabbed the coaming, and hoisted myself up to windward, where I should have been in the first place.

The next few minutes are somewhat blurred. George was yelling like a dervish and trying to set up the port backstay, and let go the starboard one, all in one operation. At the same time he was shoving the tiller to weather with his stern, to stop her from broaching-to. He shouted to me to let the spinnaker halliard go. I fished around in the bilge and found the fall of the halliard, but when I cast it off, the sail came down about a foot, and then stopped. The harder I heaved, the tighter it jammed. I looked aloft, and saw that the spinnaker was on the wrong side of the forestay, which meant that the halliard had a foul lead round the jumper stay. If I let go the one movable sheet, the sail would flog itself to pieces, if it didn't bust the mast first.

So I left it, and came aft to help George. He was somewhat calmer now. In fact he was staring in amazement at the water rushing by. *Mistral* certainly was going like a train. *Josephine,* who had been leading, was now clear astern of us. In fact, if the mast hadn't been whipping about like a trout-rod, we should have been quite happy. The seas coming up astern had a nasty gleam in their eye, but I wouldn't let George look, and we weren't pooped. In fact, *Mistral* behaved in a most ladylike manner, although George kept swearing at her when she seemed inclined to wander from the straight and narrow course.

We won the race by twenty-three seconds, and two seconds after we had crossed the line the mast snapped. Which solved the problem of stopping, anyway.

Rendezvous

From *Yachtsman Magazine*

BY CHARLES RAWLINGS

A SK ANY SAILOR, AND HE'LL TELL YOU that every sailing boat has a soul. This short story tells of one such sailing dinghy whose master left her behind when he went to war.

AT FIRST WE SAID NOTHING ABOUT Pete Howard. Then, after a few weeks, "Any word from Pete Howard?" we wondered. Finally one day I sat across the hexagonal oak table where we always sat in the Yacht Squadron wardroom and sucked a tooth at big Charlie Nichols. "Pete Howard's dead, ain't he?" I asked.

The big harbor was sparkling in a crisp, cold February westerly. It is an important convoy port. "An Eastern Canadian port," will let you by the censors with it. Its wide mouth opens east to sea. Across its narrow neck stretches the submarine boom. Its upper reach is a broad deep anchorage where the rusty anchor chains of fifty deep laden freighters rumble sometimes in a single day's mooring. The Yacht Squadron where we sat was on a small bluff that overlooked the harbor narrows and eastward out to sea. Out there our courses used to be. We'd sailed them hard in the peaceful years that seemed so long ago, when they were clean bold water instead of mine fields. Pete had sailed them better than anybody. He was a splendid character, I had always thought. I would use him sometime, I thought, in a story.

There was something about him like Lucius Quinctius Cincinnatus, the Roman. He was peaceful and contented sailing one of our squadron's little Maritime one-designs. They were eighteen-foot jib and mainsail sloops William J. Roué had designed for us. Pete's was named *Sue*. He could have afforded anything he wanted and sailed it to win. We had a fine fleet of Eight-Metres and a big cutter class and he could have dominated either one of them but he was content with the little *Sue*. She even slept with him. He'd sail her up the harbor in the early evening after the racing and drinking was over and hang her to her home mooring off the big Victorian, red-brick Howard mansion on the upper basin. When we needed Pete for the big racing—to be captain of the Eight-Metre team that met a team from the Eastern from Boston every two years or skipper a defender for an important cup series, he'd toss the *Sue*'s sheets up over her boom and put a hank of gasket around her jib the way Cincinnatus tossed the lines over his plow handles, and come along to do battle for us.

Charlie Nichols shuddered, shaking the red tabs on his tunic collar. Charlie is a Colonel of Engineers.

"Who knows if Pete's dead?" he said. "'Two of our aircraft did not return!' That's all anybody has heard so far. 'Two of our aircraft did not,' said the Air Ministry, 'return.' Pete was at the tiller of one of them. Down in the Ruhr? Down somewhere? That does not mean he's dead. Who can tell? Who—knows—?"

His voice dwindled off and his eyes stared out over my shoulder up the harbor and his mouth slowly gaped under the Anthony Eden moustache he wears. The starkness of his eyes made me turn too and there was the *Sue*. A Norwegian freighter was moored directly in her course and it seemed from our angle that she was going to run her down. Two small pea-jacketed figures on the freighter's after deck started running and we held our breath. But she disappeared behind the big rusty hull and after a moment her tiny bow stuck out and she came on. The breeze was a bowling westerly as I said and it was right on her tail. Tide had her strongly too. Halfway up the stay her jib filled and backed and then jibed and filled again. It had worked itself loose from the gasket and flopped its way up the stay itself. You could see a loop of loose halliard swinging. Over her bow she trailed the broken end of her mooring line like a run-away puppy who had broken his leash. Her canvas was sooted and gray and there was a pitiful small windrow of snow on her tiny bow deck. Steadily, determinedly she came on bound out—bound for sea.

"Say," breathed Charlie, "that poor little crate. Didn't anybody think of hauling her—. Damn it, she's goin' some place, all by herself. Look at her, comin' along straight and true. That's the proper course baby," he said to her, "that's where Pete bears all right—."

Then he stopped and I could hear him breathing as we followed her jogging along so steadily, so determinedly. I rubbed the frost off the easterly window and we squinted at the gate boats on the submarine boom. The gate was open. There was something ready to go out probably, far up the harbor and the gates were open for that. The *Sue* was clear for sea. Then Charlie got up and I could hear his boots slowly creaking as he walked across the room and out the hall to the telephone.

"Yes," he said, "this is Colonel Nichols speaking. Get me through quickly, please. That you, Major? Nichols! Here's a change of orders on that eastern mine field test. We were running it tomorrow, at nine. We'll run it today—right now. Look out your window. There's a small sloop running out toward you. No, there's no one aboard her. She's broken her mooring and sailing herself. That southerly set of tide will bring her down just enough. Let her go. *No I don't want to save her.* Let her go, I said. Let her go merciful and swift, pray God. How's she comin'—?" The rumbling deep throated "bo-o-o-oom" of the mine came then, almost a musical detonation cleansed by a half mile upwind. "Yes," said Charlie, "I knew her. She belonged to a friend of mine. No, he won't be sore. Quite otherwise, I think. He's dead."

Smith Versus *Lichtensteiger*

From *The £200 Millionaire*

BY WESTON MARTYR

AFTER SAILING THE PACIFIC ON A number of boats before World War I, Weston Martyr gave up a job in New York to build a forty-two-foot schooner. Setting sail from Nova Scotia aboard *Southseaman,* Martyr was unable to find Bermuda and only reached Long Island by getting directions from a fleet of rumrunners waiting offshore for their bootleg cargo. He also missed Bermuda the following year in the 1923 Bermuda Race, finally finishing thirty-six hours after the race committee had gone home.

But his enthusiasm for ocean racing caught the attention of English cruising sailors, and he is largely credited with starting the famous Fastnet Race, which led to the Royal Ocean Racing Club.

This story is one of eleven found in *The £200 Millionaire,* an eclectic collection of sailing stories first published in 1932. It is one of the great pieces of short sailing fiction, and to say anything more would be to give away the wonderful twist of an ending.

164

SMITH STOOD 5 FEET 5 INCHES IN HIS boots, weighed nearly 10 stone in his winter clothes and an overcoat, and he had a flat chest and a round stomach. Smith was a clerk in a small branch bank in East Anglia; he was not an athlete or a fighting man, although he followed the fortunes of a professional football team in the newspapers with great interest, and he had fought for a year in France without ever seeing his enemy or achieving a closer proximity to him than one hundred and twenty yards. When a piece of shrapnel reduced his fighting efficiency by abolishing the biceps of one arm, Smith departed from the field of battle and (as he himself would certainly have put it) 'in due course' returned to his branch bank.

For forty-nine weeks each year Smith laboured faithfully at his desk. In his free hours during the winter he read Joseph Conrad, Stevenson and E. F. Knight, and he did hardly anything else. But every year in early April Smith suddenly came to life. For he was a yachtsman, and he owned a tiny yacht which he called the *Kate* and loved with a great love. The spring evenings he spent fitting out, painting and fussing over his boat. Thereafter, as early as possible every Saturday afternoon, he set sail and cruised alone amongst the tides and sandbanks of the Thames Estuary, returning again as late as possible on Sunday night. And every summer, when his three weeks' holiday came round, Smith and his *Kate* would sail away from East Anglia together and voyage afar. One year Smith cruised to Falmouth in the West Countree, and he likes to boast about that cruise still. Once he set out for Cherbourg, which is a port in foreign parts; but that time, thanks to a westerly gale, he got no farther than Dover. The year Smith encountered Lichtensteiger he had sailed as far east as Flushing, and he was on his way back when a spell of bad weather and head winds drove him into Ostend and detained him there three days.

Lichtensteiger was also detained at Ostend; but not by the weather. Lichtensteiger had come from Alexandria, with a rubber tube stuffed full of morphine wound round his waist next his skin, and he was anxious to get to London as quickly as he could. He had already been as far as Dover, but there a Customs official (who had suspicions but no proof) whispered to a friend in the Immigration Department, and Lichtensteiger found himself debarred as an 'undesirable alien' from entering the United Kingdom. He had therefore returned to Ostend in the steamer in which he had left that place.

Lichtensteiger stood 6 feet 1 inch in his socks, weighed 14 stone stripped, and he had a round chest and a flat stomach. He was as strong as a gorilla, as quick in action as a mongoose, and he had never done an honest day's work in his life. There is reason to believe that Lichtensteiger was a Swiss, as he spoke Switzer-Deutsch, which is something only a German-Swiss can do. His nationality, however, is by no means certain, because he looked like a Lombard, carried Rumanian and Austrian passports, and in addition to the various dialects used in those two countries, he spoke French like a Marseillais, German like a Wenrtemberger, and English like a native of the lower Westside of New York.

When Smith and Lichtensteiger first set eyes on each other, Smith was sitting in the *Kate*'s tiny cockpit, smoking his pipe and worrying about the weather. For Smith's holiday was nearly over; he was due at his bank again in three days, and he knew he could not hope to sail back while the strong northwesterly wind continued to blow straight from East Anglia towards Belgium. Said Smith to himself, 'Hang it! I've got to sail to-morrow or get into a nasty fix. And if only I had two sound arms I *would* sail to-morrow and chance it; but a hundred-mile beat to wind'ard and all by myself is going to be no joke. What I need is another man to help me; but there isn't an earthly hope of getting hold of anyone in this filthy hole.'

Lichtensteiger was walking along the quay. He glanced at the *Kate* and her owner with a disdainful eye and passed on, because neither the boat nor the man held any interest for him. But in Lichtensteiger's card-index-like mind, in which he filed without conscious effort most of the things he heard and saw, there were registered three impressions and one deduction: 'A yacht. The British flag. An Englishman. A fool.' Having filed these particulars, Lichtensteiger's mind was about to pass on to the problem of how to get Lichtensteiger to London, when an idea flashed like a blaze of light into his consciousness. To translate Lichtensteiger's multi-lingual thoughts is difficult; a free rendering of them must suffice. Said Lichtensteiger to himself, 'Thunder and lightning. Species of a goose. You poor fish. Of course. It is *that!* If *you* had a yacht—if *you* were a sailor—*there* is the obvious solution. Then there no more need would be to risk placing oneself in the talons of the sacred bureaucrats of Customs or within the despicable jurisdiction of blood-sucking immigration officials. Why, say! If I had a little boat I guess I wouldn't worry myself about smuggling my dope through no Dovers and suchlike places. With a boat of my own then veritably would I be a smuggler classical and complete. But what's the use! I ain't got no boat and I ain't no sailor. But hold! Attention! The English yacht. That fool Englishman. There are possibilities in that direction there. Yes. I guess I go back and take another look at that guy.'

Lichtensteiger's second survey of Smith was detailed and thorough, and it confirmed his previous judgment. 'Easy meat,' said Lichtensteiger to himself, and then, aloud, 'Evening, stranger. Pardon me, but I see you're British, and I guess it'll sound good to me to hear someone talk like a Christian for a change. I'm from Noo York, and Otis T. Merritt's my name. I'm over this side on vacation; but I'll tell you the truth, I don't cotton to these darned Dagos and Squareheads here, not at all. So I reckon to catch the next boat across to your good country, mister, and spend the balance of my trip there with white men. That's a peach of a little yacht you got. I'll say she certainly [illegible]. She's a pippin, and I guess you have a number one first-class time sailing around in her. It's just the kind of game I've always had in mind to try for myself. It 'ud suit me down to the ground, I reckon. If you've no objections I'll step aboard. I'd sure like to look her over. Where are you sailing to next after here?'

'Harwich,' answered Smith. 'Come aboard and look round if you like by all means; but I'm afraid you won't find very much to see here.'

'Why, she's the finest little ship I ever set eyes on,' cried Lichtensteiger a few minutes later, settling himself on the cabin settee. 'And to think you run her all alone. My gracious! Have a cigar?'

'Thanks,' said Smith. 'I do sail her by myself usually, but this time I'm afraid I've bitten off more than I can chew. You see, I've got to get back to Harwich within three days. If I had another man to help me I'd do it easily, but with this wind blowing it's a bit more than I care to tackle alone.'

After that, of course, it was easy for Lichtensteiger. He did not ask Smith if he could sail with him; he led Smith on to make that suggestion himself. Then he hesitated awhile at the unexpectedness of the proposal, and when he finally yielded to persuasion, he left Smith with the impression that he was doing him a favour. It was very beautifully done.

That night Lichtensteiger transferred himself and two suitcases from his hotel and slept aboard the *Kate*. At daybreak next morning they sailed. Once outside the harbour entrance Smith found the wind had fallen to a moderate breeze, but it still blew out of the north-west, making the shaping of a direct course to Harwich impossible. Smith, therefore, did the best he could. He put the *Kate* on the starboard tack and sailed her to the westward along the Belgian coast.

It did not take Smith long to discover that Lichtensteiger was no sailor. He could not steer or even make fast a rope securely. In half an hour it became clear to Smith that Lichtensteiger literally did not know one end of the boat from the other, and within an hour he realised that his passenger, instead of helping him, was going to be a hindrance and an infernal nuisance as well. Lichtensteiger did all those things which must on no account be done if life is to be made livable in the confined space aboard a small boat. In addition to other crimes, Lichtensteiger grumbled at the motion, the hardness of the bunks and the lack of head-room in the cabin. He left his clothes scattered all over the yacht, he used the deck as a spittoon, and he sprawled at ease in the cockpit, so that every time Smith had to move in a hurry he tripped over Lichtensteiger's legs. By mid-day Smith had had as much of Lichtensteiger's company as he felt he could stand. Now that the weather was fine and looked like remaining so, he knew he could easily sail the *Kate* home by himself. He said, 'Look here, Merritt; I'm afraid you don't find yachting in such a small boat is as much fun as you thought it was going to be. See those buildings sticking up on the shore there? Well, that's Dunkerque, and I'll sail in and land you, and then you can catch the night boat over to Tilbury nice and comfortably. I'll run you in there in half an hour.'

Smith's suggestion astounded Lichtensteiger, and produced in him so profound an alarm that he forgot for a moment that he was Merritt. His eyes blazed, the colour vanished from his face, and tiny beads of sweat hopped out upon it. Then Lichtensteiger emitted some most extraordinary sounds which, had Smith but known it, were Switzer-Deutsch curses of a horrid and disgusting kind, coupled with an emphatic and blasphemous assertion that nothing, not even ten thousand flaming blue devils, could force him to set foot upon the suppurating soil of France. In fairness to Lichtensteiger it must be stated that he very rarely forgot himself, or any part he might happen to be playing, and it was also always difficult to frighten him. But the toughest ruffian may be, perhaps, excused if he shrinks from venturing into a country which he has betrayed in time of war. And this is what Lichtensteiger had done to France, or, more precisely, he had twice double-crossed the French Army Intelligence Department, Section Counter-Espionage, Sub-section N.C.D. And the penalty for doing this, as Lichtensteiger well knew, is death. Since 1916, when Lichtensteiger succeeded in escaping from that country by the skin of his teeth, France was a place which he had taken the most sedulous pains to avoid, and at the sudden prospect of being landed there he lost his grip of himself for fifteen seconds. Then he pulled himself together and grinned at Smith and said, 'Dunkerque nix! Nothing doing. I guess not. And don't you make any mistake, brother; I think this yachting stuff's just great. I'm getting a whale of a kick out of it. So we'll keep on a-going for Harwich. Sure, we will. You bet. And no Dunkerque. No, sir. No Dunkerque for mine. Forget it.'

Smith said, 'Oh! All right,' and that was all he said. But he was thinking hard. He thought, 'By God! That was queer. That—was—*damned* queer. The fellow was scared to death. Yes—to *death!* For I'll swear nothing else could make a man look like that so suddenly. He turned absolutely green. And he sweated. And his eyes— He was terrified. And he yammered, panicked, babbled—in German, too, by the sound of it. By Gosh! I wonder who he is? *And what it is he's been up to?* Something damnable, by the look of it. And whatever it was, he did it in Dunkerque—or in France, anyway. That's plain. To look like that at the mere thought of landing in France! My God, he might be a murderer, or anything. Cleared out into Belgium and hanging about, waiting his chance to get away probably. And here I am, helping him to escape. Oh Lord, what a fool I was to let him come! I actually *asked* him to come. Or did I? Yes, I did; but it seems to me now, with *this* to open my eyes, that he meant to come all the time. He did! He led me on to ask him. I can see it all now. He's a clever crafty devil—and he's twice my size! Oh, hang it all. This is *nasty.*'

Smith was so absorbed by his thoughts that he did not notice the change of wind coming. The *Kate* heeled suddenly to the puff, her sheets strained and creaked, and she began to string a wake of bubbles and foam behind her. 'Hullo,' said Smith, 'wind's shifted and come more out of the north. We'll be able to lay our course a little better now; she's heading up as high as nor'-west. I'll just see where that course takes us to if you'll bring up the chart.'

Lichtensteiger brought the chart from the cabin table, and Smith spread it out upon the deck. 'Not so good,' said he, after gazing at it for a while. 'We can't fetch within forty miles of Harwich on this tack. A nor'-west course only just clears the Goodwins and the North Foreland. Look.'

'Then why don't you point the boat straight for Harwich,' said Lichtensteiger, 'instead of going 'way off to the left like that?'

'Because this isn't a steamer, and we can't sail against the wind. But we'll get to Harwich all right, although if this wind holds we won't be there before to-morrow night.'

'To-morrow night,' said Lichtensteiger. 'Well, that suits me. What sort of a kind of a place is this Harwich, anyway? Walk ashore there, I suppose, as soon as we get in, without any messing about?'

'Oh yes. But we'll have to wait till the morning probably, for the Customs to come off and pass us.'

'Customs!' said Lichtensteiger. 'Customs! I thought—you'd think, in a one-hole dorp like Harwich, there wouldn't be no Customs and all that stuff. And, anyways, you don't mean to tell me the Customs'll worry about a little bit of a boat like this?'

'Oh yes, they will,' Smith answered. 'Harwich isn't the hole you seem to think it is. It's a big port. We're arriving from foreign, and if we went ashore before the Customs and harbourmaster and so on passed us there'd be the very devil of a row.'

'Well, crying out loud!' said Lichtensteiger. 'What a hell of a country. Not that the blamed Customs worry me any; but—well, what about all this Free Trade racket you Britishers blow about? Seems to me, with your damned Customs and immigration sharps and passports an' God knows what all, you've got Great Britain tied up a blame sight tighter than the United States.' Saying which, Lichtensteiger spat viciously upon the deck and went below to think things over.

Before Lichtensteiger finished his thinking the sun had set, and when he came on deck again, with his plan of action decided upon, it was night. Said he, 'Gee! It's black. Say, how d'you know where you're going to when you can't see? And where the hell are we now, anyway?'

'A mile or so nor'-west of the Sandettie Bank.'

'That don't mean nothing to me. Where is this Sandettie place?'

'It's about twenty miles from Ramsgate one way and eighteen from Calais the other.'

'Twenty miles from Ramsgate?' said Lichtensteiger. 'Well, listen here, brother. I guess I've kind of weakened on this Harwich idea. It's too far, and it's going to take too long getting there. And I find this yachting game ain't all it's cracked up to be by a long sight.

To tell you the truth, without any more flim-flam, I'm fed right up to the gills with this, and the sooner you get me ashore and out of it the better. See? Twenty miles ain't far, and I reckon Ramsgate, or anywhere around that way, will do me fine. Get me? Now you point her for Ramsgate right away and let's get a move on.'

'But, I say—look here!' protested Smith. 'I don't want to go to Ramsgate. I mean, I've got to get back to Harwich by tomorrow night, and if we put into Ramsgate I'll lose hours and hours. We can't get there till after midnight, and you won't be able to land before daylight at the very earliest, because the Customs won't pass us till then. And—'

'Oh hell!' broke in Lichtensteiger. 'Customs at Ramsgate, too, are there? Well, say, that's all right. I'll tell you what we'll do. We won't trouble no flaming Customs—and save time that way. You land me on the beach, somewheres outside the town, where it's quiet and there's no one likely to be around. I'll be all right then. I'll hump my suitcases into this Ramsgate place and catch the first train to London in the morning. That'll suit me down to the ground.'

'But, look here! I can't do that,' said Smith.

'What d'you mean, you can't? You can. What's stopping you?'

'Well, if you will have it, Merritt,' answered Smith, 'I'll tell you straight, I don't like being a party to landing a man—any man—in the way you want me to. It's illegal. I might get into trouble over it, and I can't afford to get into trouble. If they heard in the bank I'd lose my job. I'd be ruined. I'm sorry, but I can't risk it. Why, if we got caught they might put us in prison!'

'Caught! You poor fish,' said Lichtensteiger. 'How can you get caught! All you've got to do is to put me ashore in the dark in that little boat we're pulling behind us, and then you vamoose and go to Harwich—or Hell if you like. I'll be damned if I care. And you can take it from me, now, brother, you've got to put me ashore whether you like it or not. And if you don't like it, I'm going to turn to right here and make you. See? All this darned shinanyking makes me tired. I'm through with it and it's time you tumbled to who's boss here—you one-armed, mutt-faced, sawn-off little son of a b— you. You steer this boat for Ramsgate, *now*, pronto, and land me like I said, or by *Gor*, I'll scrape that fool face off the front of your silly head and smear the rest of you all over the boat. So—jump to it! Let's see some action, quick!'

If Smith had not been born and bred in the midst of an habitually peaceful and law-abiding community, he might perhaps have understood that Lichtensteiger meant to do what he said. But Smith had never encountered a really *bad* and utterly unscrupulous human being in all his life before. In spite of the feeble imitations of the breed which he had seen inside the cinemas, Smith did not believe in such things as human wolves. It is even doubtful if Smith had ever envisaged himself as being involved in a fight which was not more or less governed by the Marquis of Queensberry's rules. It is a fact that Smith would never have dreamed of kicking a man when he was down or of hitting anyone below the belt, and he made the mistake of believing that Lichtensteiger must, after all, be more or less like himself. Smith believed that Lichtensteiger's threats, though alarming, were not to be taken seriously. He therefore said, 'Here! I say! You can't say things like that, you know. This is my boat and I won't—'

But Smith did not get any further. Lichtensteiger interrupted him. He drove his heel with all his might into Smith's stomach, and Smith doubled up with a grunt and dropped on the cockpit floor. Lichtensteiger then kicked him in the back and the mouth, spat in his face and stamped on him. When Smith came to he heard Lichtensteiger saying, 'You'll be wise, my buck, to get on to the fact that I took pains, that time, not to hurt you. Next time, though, I reckon to beat you up good. So—cut out the grunting and all that sob-stuff and let's hear if you're going to do what I say. Let's hear from you. Or do you want another little dose? Pipe up, you—'

Smith vomited. When he could speak, he said, 'I can't—Ah, God! Don't kick me again. I'll do it. I'll do what you want. But—I can't—get up. Wait—and I'll do it—if I can. I think my back's—broken.'

Smith lay still and gasped, until his breath and his wits returned to him. He explored his hurts with his fingers gingerly, and then he sat up and nursed his battered face in his hands. He was thinking. He was shocked and amazed at Lichtensteiger's strength and brutal ferocity, and he knew that, for the moment, he dare do nothing which might tempt Lichtensteiger to attack him again. Smith was sorely hurt and frightened, but he was not daunted. And deep down in the soul of that under-sized bank clerk there smouldered a resolute and desperate determination to have his revenge. Presently he said, 'Better now. But it hurts me to move. Bring up the chart from the cabin. I'll find out a quiet place to land you and see what course to steer.'

Lichtensteiger laughed. 'That's right, my son,' said he. 'Pity you didn't see a light a bit sooner, and you'd have saved yourself a whole heap of grief.' He brought the chart and Smith studied it carefully for some minutes. Then he put his finger on the coast-line between Deal and Ramsgate and said, 'There, that looks the best place. It's a stretch of open beach, with no houses shown anywhere near. It looks quiet and deserted enough on the chart. Look for yourself. Will that spot suit you?'

Lichtensteiger looked and grunted. He was no sailor, and that small chart of the southern half of the North Sea did not convey very much to him. He said, 'Huh! Guess that'll do. Nothing much doing around that way by the look of it. What's this black line running along here?'

'That's a road. I'll put you on the beach here, and you walk inland till you get to the road and then turn left. It's only two miles to Deal that way.'

'Let her go then,' said Lichtensteiger. 'The sooner you get me ashore the sooner you'll get quit of me, which ought to please you some, I guess. And watch your step! I reckon you know enough now not to try and put anything over on me; but, if you feel like playing any tricks—*look out*. If I have to start in on you again, my bucko, I'll tear you up in little bits.'

'I'll play no tricks,' replied Smith. 'How can I? For my own sake, I can't risk you being caught. You're making me do this against my will, but nobody will believe that if they catch me doing it. I promise to do my best to land you where no one will see you. It shouldn't be hard. In four or five hours we'll be close to the land, and you'll see the lights of Ramsgate on one side and Deal on the other. In between there oughtn't to be many lights showing, and we'll run close inshore where it's darkest and anchor. Then I'll row you ashore in the dinghy, and after that it'll be up to you.'

'Get on with it, then,' said Lichtensteiger, and Smith trimmed the *Kate*'s sails to the northerly wind and settled down to steer the compass course he had decided on. The yacht slipped through the darkness with scarcely a sound. Smith steered and said nothing, while Lichtensteiger looked at the scattered lights of the shipping which dotted the blackness around him and was silent too.

At the end of an hour Lichtensteiger yawned and stretched himself. 'Beats me,' he said, 'how in hell you can tell where you're going to.' And Smith said, 'It's easy enough, when you know how.'

At the end of the second hour Lichtensteiger said, 'Gee, this is slow. Deader'n mud. How long now before we get there?' And Smith replied, 'About three hours. Why don't you sleep? I'll wake you in time.'

Lichtensteiger said, 'Nothing doing. Don't you kid yourself. I'm keeping both eyes wide open, constant and regular. I've got 'em on you. Don't forget it either!'

Another hour went by before Lichtensteiger spoke again. He said, 'What's that light in front there? The bright one that keeps on going in and out.'

'Lighthouse,' said Smith. 'That's the South Foreland light. I'm steering for it. The lights of Deal will show up to the right of it presently, and then we'll pick out a dark patch of coast somewhere to the right of that again and I'll steer for it.'

By 2 A.M. the land was close ahead, a low black line looming against the lesser blackness of the sky. 'Looks quiet enough here,' said Lichtensteiger. 'Just about right for our little job, I reckon. How about it?'

'Right,' said Smith, sounding overside with the lead-line. 'Four fathoms. We'll anchor here.' He ran the *Kate* into the wind, lowered the jib and let go his anchor with a rattle and a splash.

'Cut out that flaming racket,' hissed Lichtensteiger. 'Trying to give the show away, are you, or what? You watch your step, damn you.'

'You watch yours,' said Smith, drawing the dinghy alongside. 'Get in carefully or you'll upset.'

'You get in first,' replied Lichtensteiger. 'Take hold of my two bags and then I'll get in after. And you want to take pains we don't upset. If we do, there'll be a nasty accident—to your neck! I guess I can wring it for you as quick under water as I can here. You watch out now and go slow. You haven't done with me yet, don't you kid yourself.'

'No, not yet,' said Smith. 'I'll put you on shore all right. I'll promise that. It's all I can do under the circumstances; but, considering everything, I think it ought to be enough. I hope so, anyhow. Get in now and we'll go.'

Smith rowed the dingy towards the shore. Presently the boat grounded on the sand and Lichtensteiger jumped out. He looked around him for a while and listened intently; but, except for the sound of the little waves breaking and the distant lights of the town, there was nothing to be heard or seen. Then, 'All right,' said Lichtensteiger. And Smith said nothing. He pushed off from the beach and rowed away silently into the darkness.

Lichtensteiger laughed. He turned and walked inland with a suit-case in each hand. He felt the sand under his feet give way to shingle, the shingle to turf, and the turf to a hard road surface. Lichtensteiger laughed again. It amused him to think that the business of getting himself unnoticed into England should prove, after all, to be so ridiculously easy. He turned to the left and walked rapidly for half a mile before he came to a fork in the road and a signpost. It was too dark for him to see the sign; but he stacked his suit-cases against the post and climbing on them struck a match. He read: 'Calais—1½.'

Being Ashore

From *A Tarpaulin Muster*

BY JOHN MASEFIELD

A N ORPHAN, JOHN MASEFIELD ran away to sea at thirteen and quickly fell under its spell. At sea, he learned the art of story-telling, and after three years ashore in America, he returned to England to become a writer. Hardship followed, but he was encouraged by other writers such as Yeats and Synge, and his works were soon published.

He served as a picket boat commander during World War I, and settled down afterwards to write novels. In 1930, in no small part because King George V was an avid sailor, he was appointed England's poet laureate. He is probably best known for "Sea Fever," whose lines "I must down to the seas again, to the lonely sea and the sky" are known to sailors worldwide.

This piece, which appeared in *A Tarpaulin Muster,* is a remembrance of the joy of running fast and free aboard a square-rigger off South America.

IN THE NIGHTS, IN THE WINTER NIGHTS, in the nights of storm when the wind howls, it is then that I feel the sweet of it. Aha, I say, you howling catamount, I say, you may blow, wind, and crack your cheeks, for all I care. Then I listen to the noise of the elm trees and to the creak in the old floorings, and, aha, I say, you whining rantipoles, you may crack and you may creak, but here I shall lie till daylight.

There is a solid comfort in a roaring storm ashore here. But on a calm day, when it is raining, when it is muddy underfoot, when the world is the colour of a drowned rat, one calls to mind more boisterous days, the days of effort and adventure; and wasn't I a fool, I say, to come ashore to a life like this life. And I was surely daft, I keep saying, to think the sea as bad as I always thought it. And if I were in a ship now, I say, I wouldn't be doing what I'm trying to do. And, ah! I say, if I'd but stuck to the sea I'd have been a third in the Cunard, or perhaps a second in a P.S.N. coaster. I wouldn't be hunched at a desk, I say, but I'd be up on a bridge—up on a bridge with a helmsman, feeling her do her fifteen knots.

It is at such times that I remember the good days, the exciting days, the days of vehement and spirited living. One day stands out, above nearly all my days, as a day of joy.

We were at sea off the River Plate, running south like a stag. The wind had been slowly freshening for twenty-four hours, and for one whole day we had whitened the sea like a battleship. Our run for the day had been 271 knots, which we thought a wonderful run, though it has, of course, been exceeded by many ships. For this ship it was an exceptional run. The wind was on the quarter, her best point of sailing, and there was enough wind for a glutton. Our captain had the reputation of being a "cracker-on," and on this one occasion he drove her till she groaned. For that one wonderful day we staggered and swooped, and bounded in wild leaps, and burrowed down and shivered, and anon rose up shaking. The wind roared up aloft and boomed in the shrouds, and the sails bellied out as stiff as iron. We tore through the sea in great jumps—there is no other word for it. She seemed to leap clear from one green roaring ridge to come smashing down upon the next. (I have been in a fast steamer—a very fast turbine steamer—doing more than twenty knots, but she gave me no sense of great speed.) In this old sailing ship the joy of the hurry was such that we laughed and cried aloud. The noise of the wind booming, and the clack, clack, clack of the sheet-blocks, and the ridged seas roaring past us, and the groaning and whining of every block and plank, were like tunes for a dance. We seemed to be tearing through it at ninety miles an hour. Our wake whitened and broadened, and rushed away aft in a creamy fury. We were running here, and hurrying there, taking a small pull of this, and getting another inch of that, till we were weary. But as we hauled we sang and shouted. We were possessed of the spirits of the wind. We could have danced and killed each other. We were in an ecstasy. We were possessed. We half believed that the ship would leap from the waters and hurl herself into the heavens, like a winged god. Over her bows came the sprays in showers of sparkles. Her foresail was wet to the yard. Her scuppers were brooks. Her swing-ports spouted like cataracts. Recollect, too, that it was a day to make your heart glad. It was a clear day, a sunny day, a day of brightness and splendour. The sun was glorious in the sky. The sky was of a blue unspeakable. We were tearing along across a splendour of sea that made you sing. Far as one could see there was the water shining and shaking. Blue it was, and green it was, and of a dazzling brilliance in the sun. It rose up in hills and in ridges. It smashed into a foam and roared. It towered up again and toppled. It mounted and shook in a rhythm, in a tune, in a music. One could have flung one's body to it as a sacrifice. One longed to be in it, to be a part of it, to be beaten and banged by it. It was a wonder and a glory and a terror. It was a triumph, it was royal, to see that beauty.

And later, after a day of it, as we sat below, we felt our mad ship taking yet wilder leaps, bounding over yet more boisterous hollows, and shivering and exulting in every inch of her. She seemed filled with a fiery, unquiet life. She seemed inhuman, glorious, spiritual. One forgot that she was man's work. We forgot that we were

men. She was alive, immortal, furious. We were her minions and ser-
vants. We were the star-dust whirled in the train of the comet. We
banged our plates with the joy we had in her. We sang and shouted,
and called her the glory of the sea.

There is an end to human glory. "Greatness a period hath, no
sta-ti-on." The end to our glory came when, as we sat at dinner, the
door swung back from its hooks and a mate in oilskins bade us come
on deck "without stopping for our clothes." It was time. She was carrying no longer; she was dragging. To windward the sea was blotted
in a squall. The line of the horizon was masked in a grey film. The
glory of the sea had given place to greyness and grimness. Her beauty
had become savage. The music of the wind had changed to a howl as
of hounds.

And then we began to "take it off her," to snug her down, to
check her in her stride. We went to the clewlines and clewed the royals
up. Then it was, "Up there, you boys, and make the royals fast." My royal
was the mizzen-royal, a rag of a sail among the clouds, a great grey rag,
which was leaping and slatting a hundred and sixty feet above me. The
wind beat me down against the shrouds, it banged me and beat me, and
blew the tears from my eyes. It seemed to lift me up the futtocks into
the top, and up the topmast rigging to the cross-trees. In the cross-trees
I learned what wind was.

It came roaring past with a fervour and a fury which struck
me breathless. I could only look aloft to the yard I was bound for and
heave my panting body up the rigging. And there was the mizzen-
royal. There was the sail I had come to furl. And a wonder of a sight it
was. It was blowing and bellying in the wind, and leaping around
"like a drunken colt," and flying over the yard, and thrashing and
flogging. It was roaring like a bull with its slatting and thrashing. The
royal mast was bending to the strain of it. To my eyes it was buckling
like a piece of whalebone. I lay out on the yard, and the sail hit me in
the face and knocked my cap away. It beat me and banged me, and
blew from my hands. The wind pinned me flat against the yard, and
seemed to be blowing all my clothes to shreds. I felt like a king, like

an emperor. I shouted aloud with the joy of that "rastle" with the sail. Forward of me was the main mast, with another lad, fighting another royal; and beyond him was yet another, whose sail seemed tied in knots. Below me was the ship, a leaping mad thing, with little silly figures, all heads and shoulders, pulling silly strings along the deck. There was the sea, sheer under me, and it looked grey and grim, and streaked with the white of our smother.

Then, with a lashing swish, the rain-squall caught us. It beat down the sea. It blotted out the view. I could see nothing more but grey, driving rain, grey spouts of rain, grey clouds which burst rain, grey heavens which opened and poured rain. Cold rain. Icy-cold rain. Rain which drove the dye out of my shirt till I left blue tracks where I walked. For the next two hours I was clewing up, and furling, and snugging her down. By nightfall we were under our three lower topsails and a reefed forecourse. The next day we were hove-to under a weather cloth.

There are varieties of happiness; and, to most of us, that variety called excitement is the most attractive. On a grey day such as this, with the grass rotting in the mud, the image and memory of that variety are a joy to the heart. They are a joy for this, if for no other reason. They teach us that a little thing, a very little thing, a capful of wind even, is enough to make us exult in, and be proud of, our parts in the pageant of life.

Captain Jim and *Reynard*

From *Yachtsman's Choice*

BY MARJORIE YOUNG BURGESS

THE LOSS OF A SAILBOAT, PARTICULARLY one filled with so many memories, can be as devastating as the passing of a sailor. In this case, the two were intertwined through good times and bad and, in the end, their lives were almost parallel.

SO *REYNARD* HAS GONE. A SINGLE statement in a Rhode Island newspaper after the last hurricane gave the clue: "Also lost was the old catboat *Reynard,* which slipped her mooring and was pounded to pieces on the seawall." I did not need the more accurate confirmation later naming "the fifty-year-old sloop *Reynard.*" She had so often been miscalled "that old catboat" that I recognized her instantly.

Judged by modern standards she was a brute, 40 feet on deck, 11 feet beam, centerboard, about 700 square feet in her gaff mainsail on a long overhanging boom, and about 200 more in the jib on the end of a 6-foot bowsprit. The racing men were none too respectful, but there was something to her style, something about the big, deep oval cockpit with the high coamings, something about the wide old-fashioned stern that made her homelike and comfortable. If you cruised on her, you loved her and, as if she were your grandmother, resented comment on her figure.

She could not take two hurricanes at her age. The one in 1938 almost finished her, but Captain Jim Currier coaxed her back to life. She was not as spry as she had been, and Captain Jim said he would never again take her outside Narragansett Bay after she had gone ashore and been patched up. She had one more summer with him as her skipper before he, too, slipped his mooring. She waited for the next hurricane, but it was really the first that took them both.

She was my school ship, so to speak, for I learned about cruising from her—to hold a straight course and lay out the next, to choose the snuggest anchorage and belay the halliards before turning in, to put away a big breakfast and be ravenous for the next meal, as well as the joys of being dunked from a bowsprit, and the delicious lameness that comes of throwing your whole body into hauling up 700 square feet of mainsail, or trimming it in with a fist-filling mainsheet, and how to relax when someone else is on watch, stretching like a cat and listening to the water slip past her seamy old sides.

She had more than cruising to teach. I saw her first when she was only 40, one wintry day with a great hole gaping in her bottom where the centerboard trunk had been pulled out to make way for new timbers. Before next spring, I knew her through and through—from her linen locker and hard bunks in the forecastle to her marline-smelling lazarette aft between icebox and transom. And I had learned to drill holes two feet long in a straight line, to find her deck beams with a nail from topside when we renailed the whole deck, to slobber canvas and myself with white lead when we recovered the deck, to run a drill press when we made the bolt holes in the bronze rudder stock, to sharpen a plane when we smoothed up the three-inch oak planks of her new barn-door rudder, and to swing pick and shovel when the time came to hang it in place. Then as the warmth of summer drew near and we established a stopping point in our work, I learned the pride that comes when you sweep up the shavings, scrub down the deck, and polish up the brass, for the snowy canvas must lie in spotless cleanliness while the age-old business of bending sail takes place, with marline seizing it to the hoops and lace lines running along gaff and boom, then the first furl when the heavy canvas is soft as linen and begging for the breeze. Life begins at 40, the tale goes, and she was frisky as a kitten with all the good, sound new wood and the loving care we had put into her.

Captain Jim had promised the working crew the first cruise, on which we set out late one soft warm day in early June. The weather had been fair for six weeks, and we had made the most of it. The first cruise after two years ashore was taking place on schedule. The little scudding black cotton clouds around the horizon only amused us. What matter if it should rain? We had done the work before the weekend and had that Friday night and the two following whole days. Where to go?

Captain Jim and his daughter Carolyn chose Potter's Cove on Prudence Island, and promised the rest of us—Harry, Joe, and myself—the most prefect of anchorages when we should arrive. So high were our spirits as we imagined the following weekends of the summer spent in just this way that we would have been content to go just across the bay to Jamestown.

We had a leisurely sail up the bay with a southwest wind over the port quarter, and hauled up on the wind for only the short entrance to the harbor. Then our first meal on board, and our delighted discovery of the miraculous amount of food that thin young Harry could hold, and the astounding combinations of food that appealed to him. Meals were always happy on *Reynard,* if for no other reason than that one had only to catch Harry's eye in the middle of one, and first he and then the whole crew around the big oak table would become convulsed with laughter.

Perhaps we were too gay. We did not then have the proper caution desirable in sailors. We turned in at about 10 o'clock, drowsy as only one can be after a sail, and it was 4 A.M. before the first one awakened. I awoke because my right ear was full of water, my pillow was sopped, and the stream running down the middle of the mattress had just reached my shoulderblade. Rain was drumming overhead. Though we had canvassed her deck and painted her inside and out, we had not gotten around to the seams in the cabin top that had stood uncovered in the hot sun for six weeks on a boat that had not been in the water for two years.

Someone lit a flashlight. Harry, his eyes screwed tightly shut, threw back a blanket and raised his sleepy head, still adorned with his new yachting cap. There was little sleep after that. In fact, there was little sleep the rest of the weekend, for the rain did not stop until Sunday afternoon. We sat on bottom-up saucepans and played with wet cards on the dripping table. We swam in the rain, we rowed in the rain, we hiked in the rain, and we ate well-watered meals.

Sunday afternoon we sailed back down the bay to Newport in a thick fog. It was still fun, and it was a good sail. We forgave *Reynard,* caulked and painted the cabin top, and had our other weekends. Never again did we experience such a wetting. She proudly drew her planks together in the dampness and kept us dry thereafter, relatively speaking.

She had had many such summers before, but that was my first cruising season. A lot of its pleasure sticks with me still.

Captain Jim Currier was chief ordnance engineer of the naval torpedo station in Newport, Rhode Island, and in those days could get away on Friday afternoons. His crew would do the provisioning, fill up the icebox, replenish the water bottle from a spring in the country, and be ready to start the instant he appeared. Each weekend saw *Reynard* in some different harbor of the bay, until August when the peak of the season, the two weeks' cruise, took place.

There were six of us for that cruise, Captain Jim, his wife, their daughters Cons and Carolyn, Harry and I, invading what was to me the virgin cruising ground of Nantucket, Martha's Vineyard, and the Elizabeth Islands, though it was an old story to *Reynard,* these being scenes of many previous holidays.

There were many highlights of the cruise—sailing with full sweep of the tide through Wood's Hole, the "wild horses" of Naushon, the gloriously wet roaring sail across the shoals to Nantucket, the deliciously warm waters of Nantucket Harbor; the choppy pounding beat back to Hadley's Harbor, the grounding on Onset at just the moment I said, "Here, you take her. I don't want to be the one to put her aground." We bent the centerboard on that one and added another job to the list for the winter.

My strongest memory of the cruise is of my first all-night sail from Marion to Wickford, beating down Buzzards Bay with a fresh breeze that got lighter as the full moon sank deeper and deeper into the cloudy fog. About midnight we caught Mischaum light over our stern, due north, just as the fog shut down. The sleepy watch on deck grew less and less alert. The skipper was wrapped in drowsy peace at the wheel, with wind almost imperceptible and *Reynard* ghosting along in the blackness. Suddenly I leaped fully awake from the hardness of the cockpit seat where I lay.

"I smell bayberry bushes!" At just that moment Captain Jim caught the sound of ripples on a beach close aboard. Hard over in that instant went the wheel, over with the surge went the boom and gaff, and down on the cabin sole with a thud rolled the occupants off both port bunks. We dared sail only north to get clear, as we had come. A quick look at the chart showed us that *Reynard* had silently led us into the safety of Robinson's Hole between two islands. Once clear of the land we found the breeze again and shortly picked up the nearest buoy to lay our course for Hen and Chickens lightship.

The breeze was fine once more, and we were close hauled to starboard, passing close aboard the lightship, when we sighted the running lights of a small freighter who threw her impersonal spotlight on us in passing. For an instant we were lifted out of the black void, the sounds of the box wave had another dimension as we saw the white water tossed off to port; the sail, unperceived in the darkness, now towered startlingly above us. We were as self-conscious as if from the vault of heaven the Author of the universe had turned the light of his searching eye down on us alone.

It was gone in a flash. We had a snack all round and changed watches. Heavy-lidded and achingly tired, I stretched out on some wadded blankets to leeward in Stateroom A, the forecastle, and never knew whether I slept or not, so pleasant was the sensation of being cradled in the upsurge of the bow, lightly tossed at the crest of a wave, then gently caught and cradled once more as the bow swept on and down to meet the next upswing. For hours *Reynard* held to this angle of heel and this course, and brought us at dawn to Sakonnet Point.

At Wickford that noon we had a Roman feast, with the choicest of seagoing desserts, watermelon, after which all hands instantly collapsed and slept for several hours. *Reynard* taught us one lesson with her all-night sail. It is a wonderful thing to have done once.

As eventually happens in all cruising, the end of summer arrived. Once more the boat was laid up and worked on, scraped, sanded, and painted. Once more Captain Jim removed the parts he wanted to repair and took them to his workshop cellar. All the crews of the previous summer gathered in the dusty workshop to sand and paint or sit and talk. For Captain Jim was a man who used his hands as well as he used his head. It was a pleasure and an education to pitch in and help him. He had done likewise for all of us. When a new dory was added to our small-boat racing fleet, he was the one who made the bronze tangs, who refitted the rudder with bronze gudgeons and pins of his own fashioning, who showed us how to splice our wire rigging, who made us light racing booms with perfect little outhauls, who adjusted our centerboard pins, and whose own home-built trailer was used to haul and launch the little fleet. He was the heart and spirit of the yacht club, the racing and the cruising, and after he went it was never the same.

When I left the yacht club, the racing, and the *Reynard* cruising to labor in the world, my younger sister inherited my berth on *Reynard,* and wrote me of cruises up the bay and around to Third Beach and the Sakonnet River, while I pictured her learning of boats and growing happier and wiser in the ways of the sea. She will remember her first long cruise as I did mine, though in a quite different way.

The summer of '38 had passed with no cruise of any length. Small-boat racing on weekends, engrossing the crew, and increasing pressure of work at the torpedo station had kept the old vessel close to her mooring. She had gone out on many a summer evening when a willing crew was mustered to take her across the harbor and out into the channel, perhaps to the lightship off Brenton's Reef where the sea breezes play at night, loath to approach the land. Then before the weakening breeze she would ghost homeward, barely carrying steerage way as she lost the last zephyr to come out of Brenton's Cove, and would nestle to her mooring in the glassy black mirror in the leeward corner of the harbor. Her sleepy crew would snug her down for the rest of the night and row ashore, damp, tired, and happy.

Or perhaps on that summer, as on so many others, when the sun had heated the land and the houses ashore to an oven-like temperature, *Reynard* would bear a crew of six across the harbor to anchor in Brenton's Cove and sleep under blankets and awaken to fresh energies in the morning. Midget cruises, these, which left the crew eager for a longer and more memory-enduring one.

The weather was foul later that summer, and one thing and another interfered until the anticipated cruise to Buzzards Bay or Long Island Sound had been postponed several times. At last in mid-

September, after a week of rainy weather, it was decided to seize the first good day (surely the harbinger of fair weather to follow) and set out. At last one such day arrived. The overcast sky began to clear, patches of blue to appear, and the spirits of the restless crew to rise. They did the last bit of provisioning, filled the icebox, and got under way late in the morning. The crew on this memorable voyage were Captain Jim's 22-year-old son Jimmie, his friend Bill of the same age, and two younger girls, Emily, 19, and my sister Connie, 17.

As the weather was still far from settled, Captain Jim decided to take his crew up the bay rather than out to sea, and tucked a double reef into the mainsail, standard procedure in the face of strong winds. They dropped the mooring in the shelter of Newport Harbor, swung around Long Wharf, and headed for the channel between Gull Rock and the Naval War College.

Once out of the shadow of the land, they felt the force of the easterly wind, coming in quick and increasingly heavy gusts. Captain Jim knew immediately that they were in for a real sail, and that there was no turning back. On they leaped, with heavy blasts of beam wind off the easterly shore driving the old vessel through churning seas and heeling her unmercifully. Captain Jim froze to the wheel, staring grimly ahead, hands gripping the spokes, and impressing his young crew with the force of his will to bring his vessel through. Up the bay they charged. The kerosene for the lamps was the first casualty. A five-gallon bottle was thrown across the cockpit, broke, and flooded the bilge with the foul-smelling stuff. The crew was silent. Few orders were given by the rigid man at the wheel, and few were needed. Each watched anxiously for the moment when he or she could be most useful. Jimmie was of course second in command and stood ready for emergency. It soon came. The jib, strained beyond further endurance, blew out of its hooks, and Jimmie and Bill made the remnants fast as best they could.

By now they were approaching Melville, then a naval coaling station with docks but no harbor. Captain Jim told them that he was going to try to work up into the lee and make fast to the dock.

The elements refused to permit him. *Reynard* tried valiantly to bring her bow to the wind, but her mainsail, with a sickening sound, ripped from leech to luff. Some men on the dock shouted unintelligibly down the whipping wind, the crew waved in a comradely way, and *Reynard* tore past, Captain Jim sticking grimly to his wheel, Jimmie and Bill working to secure the slatting gaff and peak of the mainsail. Connie was stationed aft beside Captain Jim to sit on the canvas that dripped from the boom and thus provided a scrap of sail. Once the gaff was lashed down, Bill also came aft to sit on the deck with feet over the transom and shove mightily on the nose of the Dyer dink when she surged forward on the seas to dash her stern against *Reynard's* counter.

The young crew was soaked, hungry, tired, and scared, but Connie said later that the strong figure of Captain Jim at the wheel kept their confidence high. Now and then he would issue a brief order, the details of execution to be worked out by Jimmie. For once he was not interested in the one right way of doing something. Just let it be done. I can see him, too, bending aside to shout a brief remark designed to keep up the spirits of those youngsters under his care, but for the most part the responsibility of getting his ship and the lives aboard her safely into harbor weighed heavily on him. The confidence of my worried parents was a tribute. Through all this day and the following night they did not despair of Connie's safety, assuring each other that with Mr. Currier she must be safe.

Wind and seas were worse as they left the lee of the land and bore off for the north end of Prudence Island. They were dead before the easterly now with only a rag of sail. *Reynard* lumbered with the dinghy constantly trying to ram through her transom. Somehow they managed to dig out the "insurance," the 175-pound anchor under the icebox beneath the cockpit, and secure it forward, and to make ready the heavy reserve rode. The tension eased as they neared Potter's Cove, the little land-locked harbor whose bush covered sandbar curves like a protecting arm around from the north to intercept the easterly winds and seas.

Steadily seas and wind increased, but *Reynard* swung gratefully around the bar and into the empty little harbor. Over went the anchors, the light one and the "insurance." Only then did Captain Jim relax, after he had gone forward to inspect the rodes on the bitts. "Safe at last," he said.

All hands were hungry and sat munching in the cockpit while the wind screamed over them. They pumped the kerosene out of the bilge and put the cabin to rights, then settled down to watch the sea rise and gradually eat away the flat bit of land that spelled safety for the tired old vessel. Up the water crept, cutting the little stretch of sand and bush back and back until it was evident there would soon be no kindly barrier, no shelter whatever from the howling shrieking winds and the merciless seas dashing themselves against the sand and casting their spray tops to the wind. There were several hours of watching and awaiting the inevitable. Then, after the last of the land had crumbled before the onslaught of the waves, *Reynard* began her slow drag to shore.

She was caught on a lee shore, pinned with no chance to escape, no sail, and a roaring, driving hurricane of wind beating her inexorably to a dread hard resting place and destruction ashore. What despair must have filled Captain Jim as he watched the slow shoreward movement as the pitching bows dragged his anchors along, with all the windage of the old gaff-rigged boat aiding the destruction. His thoughts were first for his crew and how best to protect them when she struck. For himself he must have had doubts, for he had a game leg. Infantile paralysis had left one foot paralyzed, and he was a heavy man for others to help. "You must each look out for yourselves," he told his four young companions.

The dinghy had long since parted her painter and vanished downwind into the flying mist. They could no longer even attempt to look into the wind, which picked up salt spray and tried to drive it through them.

The strain of waiting was lightened by Bill's irrepressible Bob Hope-like sense of humor which suffered no pause, unless it was when he begged Captain Jim to allow him to swim ashore with a rope tied to his waist on which the others might pull themselves to safety. Captain Jim would have none of it.

As they approached the land, they took stock of the situation. *Reynard,* shallow with board up, would get very close before striking. The land to leeward was once a sandy bluff about thirty feet high with marshland at its foot. Only the bluff now showed. When they were quite close, they tried to salvage all the articles possible. To the boys' delight they found that all they needed to do was throw things straight in the air, for the wind would whip them ashore.

At last *Reynard* grounded and swung broadside to the wind and the surges at the foot of the bluff whose bush-covered top was halfway up the mast. The poor ship rolled slowly and heavily in the wash and backwash, heeling to the wind, then pounding her leeward bilge with a thud into the muddy bank and sending up a geyser of mud and water between boat and bank.

Connie, being the youngest and but newly awakened to the dubious joys of sailing, was the first ashore. She stood on the gaff clutching the halliard. As *Reynard* took her toll to shore, the boys heaved. Up she went, grabbed for a bush, and scrambled to the top. Here she tried to look back and help Emily, but could not face the wind, let alone open her eyes into it. She could barely crouch, as the force of the wind rolled her again and again into the bushes. Suddenly, over the roar of wind and crash of the boat's side against shore, she heard a scream. Moments later Emily, almost unrecognizable so plastered with mud, came over the bank, dripping. She had slipped and fallen overboard between the boat and the bank. As she fell, one hand caught the gunwale, and Bill, who was nearest, with a single perfect motion, yanked her back to the deck before the boat completed her roll into the mud.

Captain Jim was next, I do not see how, and after him the two boys. They collected the clothing they had heaved to shore and set out across the fields for shelter. A kindly couple, who had watched *Reynard* sweep into the cove, received them and put them up for the sleepless night.

Early the next morning, on a clear blue sunny day, they went back to look for the wreckage. High and dry, several hundred feet from the bluff and from the beach lay *Reynard* on her side, half full of sand and mud, trunk cabin ripped from her deck on one side, and a shambles on deck and below. Jimmie said that the sight was almost too much for him. Over and over through his head hammered the thought, "My father's boat! My father's boat!"

She was in sorry condition, but Jimmie elected to live aboard her, clean her out, and protect her from scavengers until his father could get back to the mainland and investigate salvage possibilities. His Robinson Crusoe life lasted about two weeks before the rescue party arrived.

The comradeship of boats and boatmen is a wonderful thing. Many a power boatman at the club had sniffed his disapproval of "that old box." They could not understand why her crew loved her so on even the calmest days when she could go nowhere, being without power, and many of them could not understand the pleasure in going out for an evening's sail and barely getting back in the small hours of the morning. But they understood a boat and a good skipper in trouble, and turned to. Even the Navy helped. Early that Saturday morning there chugged into Potter's Cove a torpedo station range boat with two sailors to handle her, and about thirty men from the yacht club armed with spades, tackle, and food. They dug manfully around the boat, improvised a railway, dragged her down to the beach, floated her, towed her home, pumping, and made a game of it.

That winter the little cellar workshop was again filled with shavings. At the end of the evening pieces of mellowed and well-salted wood went once more into the living room fireplace while old burning copper paint made rich green and blue plumes in the flames for resting workers to watch and remember. Once more blocks of new wood were pulled out and examined before being declared fit to go into *Reynard*.

I missed that winter's work, and I missed, too, the summer that followed, when *Reynard* was not allowed by Captain Jim to go out of the bay. She had been strained, and might not stand more such punishment. Perhaps Captain Jim realized, too, that his strain had been great, but he never mentioned it. When the sailing summer was over and *Reynard* hauled out, one day as he sat working on the floor with his tools around him, his life ran out and he was gone.

Jimmie dreamed a night or so later that his father came to life for a short space to direct his own funeral, as what skipper would not lay out for his crew the necessary preparations for the longest cruise of all.

Without Captain Jim, *Reynard* was restive. He had recalled her to life when she lay exhausted on the sands, had painfully dragged her back to the water. She missed him keenly the first summer that he was gone. Young Jim was skipper now, but the cruises were not the same. One weekend she almost piled herself up on Halfway Rock in a dense fog. A startled skipper and crew saw the rock go by in the fog barely twenty feet abeam when they had reckoned on a wide berth. Perhaps she could not quite bring herself to risk their lives again.

Young Jim parted with her reluctantly that fall. He felt that things were too different aboard, and sold her up the bay. I almost lost touch with her then. At one time I heard that she had a motor installed and was at East Greenwich.

I was at Quonset Point Naval Air Station in 1944 when the next hurricane roared up Narragansett Bay, and my thoughts were constantly going back to that previous adventure I had missed. As I tried to sleep that night in the Waves' quarters, riding in on the wind was the living vision of that mad sail up the bay and the granite will of Captain Jim to save his boat. It was not until later that I read in the newspapers that *Reynard* had been dashed to pieces on the seawall of the Rhode Island Yacht Club.

She went completely this time, and now her timbers and planks are a part of the ebb and flow of the bay where her life was led. Somehow I think that is what has happened to Captain Jim, too.

Yachtswoman Solo

From *My Ship Is So Small*

BY ANN DAVISON

W OMEN HAVE SAILED FOR CENTURIES on everything from fighting ships to globe-girdling merchant ships, but Ann Davison was the first woman to sail singlehanded across the Atlantic, in 1953. Her book, *My Ship Is So Small* (1956), is an engaging and remarkable story, particularly since her sloop, *Felicity Ann*, was only twenty-three feet long.

It's even more remarkable that Davison would tackle such an adventure, let alone set sail. An accomplished pilot, she and her husband lost their airfield in England when it was requisitioned at the start of World War II. Several business ventures tottered, and they purchased an old fishing vessel, intent on refurbishing it and starting anew. Short on funds, they set sail before the project was completed and it ended in disaster, with her husband drowning before her eyes during a shipwreck.

Yet Davison set out to sail the trade winds on her slow and cramped little boat, with no self steering and an iffy radio, on a quest for a new way of life. In this excerpt, she shows her ability to improvise and to accept help from others, and even a little feminine helplessness.

THE ACTUAL REALIZATION OF A DREAM IS neither better nor worse than imagined. It is entirely different. Before setting out, I thought I had no illusions about the voyage or sailing alone. I expected to be lonely. I expected to be frightened. What I did not expect was the positive panic of emotion that swamped me at the outset of the voyage. I was so lonely that whenever a ship appeared I could not take my eyes off her until she vanished. Once I turned and followed a trawler for nearly an hour, although she was apparently bound for Iceland, because I could not bear the friendless vista of an empty sea. Loneliness does not come from the physical state of being on one's own so much as from fear, the same old fear that stems from ignorance; and having thrust myself out into the unknown with only myself to rely on, I had reverted at once to the primitive. A child with a bogey round every corner. I was not only afraid of the wind and the sea. I was afraid of the ship. I was afraid of reefing the sails, or putting them up or changing them in any way. I was afraid of stopping the engine, and having stopped it, afraid of starting it again . . .

The course I was trying to steer was sou'-westerly but this was hampered by a head wind, so I made in a general southerly direction, plotting estimated positions by dead reckoning on the chart. I made several attempts to take sights with the sextant, and found it a very different proposition in real life, infinitely more difficult than taking a sight from the high cliffs of Devon with the Commander standing by with a stop-watch. The high cliffs of Devon stay put on their nice firm underpinnings, but the deck of a lively little vessel offers a poor support for an inexperienced sight-taker. I concluded it was an impossible undertaking and unreasonable of anyone to think otherwise.

On the fourth day out the log read 230 miles. By then it seemed I had spent a lifetime at sea, and there was another 700 miles to go to Madeira. How embarrassing it would be if Madeira failed to turn up at the appointed time. There was, so far as I could see, very little reason why it should. And what would one do then? Turn right?

Or left? Or keep straight on? Or accost a passing vessel, 'Have you seen Madeira lately?'

Then, as if a kindly Fate interposed to keep me from getting too discouraged, the following night granted a few hours of sheer magic. One of those rare glorious experiences that lift you right out of the commonplace (though God knows there is little of the commonplace about being at sea singlehanded) on to Olympian heights of delight. The wind had backed right round to the North-East, and *Felicity Ann* was flying before it, her boom way out and lifting, tugging at the mainsheet as if she was alive and impatient of restraint. Her mainsail, taut and straining, was silhouetted against the night sky. And the night sky was a black velvet backcloth for countless glittering stars. Wavelets tumbled in a foam of phosphorescence spilling a thousand bright jewels on the sea. A comet spanned the heavens leaving a broad white wake across the sky even as the ship sped over the waves leaving a broad white wake on the water. All the loneliness and the fears were forgotten, dissolved into nothing by an ecstasy of being so pure, so complete, that nothing else mattered or existed. There was no past, no future, only the participation of a brilliant present. An exquisite distillation of the meaning of life.

Then the kind Fate went off duty. Before dawn it was blowing all hell and I was staring in horror at the mounting waves. I reefed the main and, when that was not enough, took it in altogether and changed the staysail for the storm jib. The dawn was scowling and bleak, overhung with a canopy of low cloud. Later, the wind eased a little but left a heavy cross sea for the ship to wallow in. I was in no mood for another bout with the sails, so started the engine and plugged on towards the never-never land of Madeira.

Then the ship began to behave strangely. So much so that it was obvious even to me. She seemed sluggish, rising to the seas with an effort, quite unlike her usual buoyancy, and she rolled with a slow deliberation as if waterlogged. I slid back the hatch and looked into the cabin. She was waterlogged. The cabin was awash, with water way up over the floorboards and slopping from side to side, leaving an oily tidemark on the woodwork. Both bilge pumps were jammed solid when I tried to use them. Anyone else would have pulled up the floorboards, baled the ship out, cleared the pumps, found out why the water was coming in, and taken steps to stop it. I did none of these things. They never occurred to me. I was too stupid with fatigue, too tense and too tired from an excess of experience to think constructively. I was confused, and wanted to stop and take stock of the situation. I wanted to be still and free from the incessant motion. I wanted, most desperately, to sleep. The ship was half full of water which I was unable to get out by the obvious methods, therefore I must find somewhere where I could start thinking again under normal conditions. I looked at the chart and decided to make for Brest, the nearest port, about 70 or 80 miles away if my reckoning was correct.

Later on in the morning the clouds lifted and broke apart, the sun shone and my outlook improved enormously until the colour of the water changed to light green. This was disturbing, as it was different and therefore probably dangerous. Everything was suspect at that stage of my seagoing, which no amount of reassurance from the charts and reckoning could allay.

I passed two fishing boats, very gay and colourful and French, neither of them fishing, but lying to, rolling heavily, evidently waiting for the tide or weather. The fishermen, as colourful as their boats, leant over the side and watched our progress with interest. Some of them waved and I waved back, much heartened by the sight of real live people. Then it occurred to me it would be sensible to ask for a position check, so I turned back to the nearest ship, a bright blue, broad-beamed trawler called *Fends les Vagues,* which seemed a pretty appropriate choice under the circumstances. I motored round and round her trying to convey in basic French and Indian sign language what I wanted. 'Ou est Brest?' I shouted, that being the nearest I could get to expressing my needs. Fishermen crowded to the bulwarks, looking eager, interested, and absolutely blank. I expressed these needs several times on both sides of the fishing boat, upwind and downwind, but succeeded only in throwing the entire crew into a fever of excitement as they threshed from side to side across the deck trying to keep me in sight. I motored round to the stern of the vessel and read the port of registry. Douarnenez. All right then: 'Ou est Douarnenez?' I tried, with no better result, and regretted having started something that was proving difficult to continue and impossible to stop. And I would have gone on my way, but a handsome young man wearing a dashing cap and chewing on a cigarette-end and looking as if he had stepped straight out of a French movie, authoritatively waved me alongside, a manoeuvre I accomplished with a masterly and quite unexpected precision. Several agile men then leapt down on to *FA* and held her off with a dramatic show of strength and dexterity. 'Venez abord, Madame,' invited the handsome young skipper courteously, and completely fascinated by the turn of events, I climbed up on the trawler, a fairly athletic feat, and appreciated as such by the onlookers, as the two ships were rolling wildly and inharmoniously.

'Et maintenant,' said the skipper politely. 'Qu'est-ce que vous desirez, Madame?'

I pointed to *FA,* to the chart I had had the forethought to bring with me, made a sweeping gesture in the general direction of where Brest ought to be, said 'Brest' in a loud clear voice, and hoped it conveyed the general idea. The fishermen crowded round the chart, gazing intently at it as if looking for X marks the spot. 'Douarnenez,' said one of them suddenly, pointing it out triumphantly as if he had found the key to the problem; and the rest nodded wisely. But the skipper tapped me on the shoulder, said something I freely translated into 'Radio,' pointed to the wheelhouse, and beckoned. I followed him into the wheelhouse, down a companionway, and into the main cabin. This compartment, a large piratical-looking affair, managed to give the effect of guttering candles in spite of electric light. There were tiers of berths all round the sides, built-in like the old 'but-and-bens' of Highland cottages, a few wooden kegs at strategic points, and if there had been a roll of parchment on the chart table I would have accepted it unquestioningly; but it was a D.F. chart, and the delicious atmosphere of Treasure Island was thrown off-centre somewhat by the incongruous intrusion of a huge radio, which jutted out into the cabin and occupied most of the forward bulkhead.

The skipper went to this functional-looking machine, handed me a pair of headphones, put on a pair himself, switched on the ship-to-shore apparatus and called up Brest. I could not follow all the moves in the game, but caught the general gist. The shore operator and the skipper held an animated discussion to which I listened with admiration, wondering how they managed to communicate without seeing one another, French conversation being so visual. Then the skipper turned to me, indicating it was question-time and to go ahead. I took fright at once, 'Mais, je ne parle pas Français,' as if he didn't know. And the next thing, there was Land's End at the other end of the phone. Small world. Feeling the situation was getting away from me, I tried to explain.

'I only want to check my position. The, er, ship, my ship—yacht *Felicity Ann,* out of Plymouth—is making a bit of water and the pumps are jammed. I am going into Brest to fix things—just an idea, you know, to get a position check, but my, huh, French isn't up to it.' Nor my English either.

'You are on board the trawler now?' The operator at Land's End sounded puzzled. 'Are they giving you a tow in?'

'Oh, *no,*' I said, very British and liable to give a light laugh any moment. 'It is nothing serious—all I want is a position check—'

'That I can't give you,' said he briskly. 'Ask the skipper—he'll tell you. Good luck.'

Well now, I thought, that had been the idea. Still . . . 'Thanks,' I said, 'I will.'

There was an outbreak of Gallic garrulity on the air and the skipper signed off, looking pleased with himself at having given demonstration of the modern mysteries of science. He leant over the chart table with the expression of a magician about to produce a truly enormous rabbit out of the hat, but the trick was interrupted by a great commotion breaking out on deck. Amidst the general confusion, anguished cries of 'le petit bateau' were recognizable. The skipper's expression changed to one of alarm and he flew up the companionway. I flew after.

Felicity Ann had broken away and was careering off under bare poles with three fishermen aboard. They stood on deck looking helpless and rather woebegone at having been abducted. This escape produced more activity aboard the trawler than a tiger at large in a cattle market. Gesticulating men rushed to and fro, leaping up and down companionways, running into one another, and skipping over fishing gear. Ropes were thrown, orders shouted, bells rung, machinery started, and with a roar of mighty engines the trawler got under way. Cheer-leaders yelled encouragement to the men on *FA*, to me, to one another, and to everyone in earshot. With the maximum of fury and the minimum of effort *FA* was waylaid, captured, and tied up alongside.

The three men immediately climbed back on to the trawler, much relieved for themselves, but very concerned for me, having discovered the water in the cabin. 'Trop de l'eau,' they cried in great agitation. 'Oh, trop,' I agreed. And a passionate discussion took place among the men. Finally the skipper detached himself from the committee meeting to inform me of the findings. Catching about one word in ten, I understood him to say that fishing being what it was, and *FA* being in the state she was, why didn't I let them tow her into Douarnenez? Frankly, it seemed a very good idea. I had never been to Douarnenez, I had never been aboard a French trawler before, and surely one of the reasons for coming to sea was the assimilation of new experiences, so why not? Then I thought of what tows mean in the marine world, and said the only word I knew in the language to cover the situation: 'Combien?' which the skipper brushed aside as an insult to chivalry, and action was taken to put *FA* in tow.

She got away again, by herself this time, and I was really worried for a moment, but once again, amidst fearful tumult, she was caught, and finally lashed up short under the stern so that she had no option but to follow the trawler's every move. When assured that 'le petit bateau' was safe and under control, the men went through a convincing demonstration of eating in mime, and we all trooped below.

Owen Chase's Narrative

From *Shipwreck of the Whaleship Essex*

BY OWEN CHASE

The real-life sinking of the whaleship *Essex* after it was rammed by an angry sperm whale served as the model for Herman Melville's classic *Moby Dick*.

Following the loss of the ship, the stranded crew spent three harrowing months adrift in the South Seas. Of the twenty men who escaped the ship, eight survived, and they did so only by resorting to cannibalism. In the following account, first mate Owen Chase describes the bizarre and frightening attack that precipitated their tragic journey.

I HAVE NOT BEEN ABLE TO RECUR to the scenes which are now to become the subject of description, although a considerable time has elapsed, without feeling a mingled emotion of horror and astonishment at the almost incredible destiny that has preserved me and my surviving companions from a terrible death. Frequently, in my reflections on the subject, even after this lapse of time, I find myself shedding tears of gratitude for our deliverance, and blessing God, by whose divine aid and protection we were conducted through a series of unparalleled suffering and distress, and restored to the bosoms of our families and friends. There is no knowing what a stretch of pain and misery the human mind is capable of contemplating, when it is wrought upon by the anxieties of preservation; nor what pangs and weaknesses the body is able to endure, until they are visited upon it; and when at last deliverance comes, when the dream of hope is realized, unspeakable gratitude takes possession of the soul, and tears of joy choke the utterance. We require to be taught in the school of some signal suffering, privation, and despair, the great lessons of constant dependence upon an almighty forbearance and mercy. In the midst of the wide ocean, at night, when the sight of the heavens was shut out, and the dark tempest came upon us, then it was that we felt ourselves ready to exclaim, "Heaven have mercy upon us, for nought but that can save us now." But I proceed to the recital. On the 20th of November (cruising in latitude 0° 40' S., longitude 119° 0' W.), a shoal of whales was discovered off the lee-bow.

The weather at this time was extremely fine and clear, and it was about 8 o'clock in the morning that the man at the mast-head gave the usual cry of, "There she blows." The ship was immediately put away, and we ran down in the direction for them. When we had got within half a mile of the place where they were observed, all our boats were lowered down, manned, and we started in pursuit of them. The ship, in the meantime, was brought to the wind, and the main-top-sail hove back, to wait for us. I had the harpoon in the second boat; the captain preceded me in the first. When I arrived at the spot where we calculated they were, nothing was at first to be seen. We lay on our oars in anxious expectation of discovering them come up somewhere near us. Presently one rose, and spouted a short distance ahead of my boat; I made all speed towards it, came up with, and struck it; feeling the harpoon in him, he threw himself, in agony, over towards the boat (which at that time was up alongside of him), and, giving a severe blow with his tail, struck the boat near the edge of the water, amidships, and stove a hole in her. I immediately took up the boat hatchet, and cut the line, to disengage the boat from the whale, which by this time was running off with great velocity. I succeeded in getting clear of him, with the loss of the harpoon and line; and finding the water to pour fast in the boat, I hastily stuffed three or four of our jackets in the hole, ordered one man to keep constantly bailing, and the rest to pull immediately for the ship; we succeeded in keeping the boat free, and shortly gained the ship. The captain and the second mate, in the other two boats, kept up the pursuit, and soon struck another whale. They being at this time a considerable distance to leeward, I went forward, braced around the mainyard, and put the ship off in a direction for them; the boat which had been stove was immediately hoisted in, and after examining the hole, I found that I could, by nailing a piece of canvas over it, get her ready to join in a fresh pursuit, sooner than by lowering down the other remaining boat which belonged to the ship.

I accordingly turned her over upon the quarter, and was in the act of nailing on the canvas, when I observed a very large spermaceti whale, as well as I could just about eighty-five feet in length; he broke water about twenty rods off our weather-bow, and was lying quietly, with his head in a direction for the ship. He spouted two or three times, and then disappeared. In less than two or three seconds he came up again, about the length of the ship off, and made directly for us, at the rate of about three knots. The ship was then going with about the same velocity. His appearance and attitude gave us at first no alarm; but while I stood watching his movements, and observing him but a ship's length off, coming down for us with great celerity, I involuntarily ordered the boy at the helm to put it hard up; intending to sheer off and avoid him. The words were scarcely out of my mouth, before he came down upon us with full speed, and struck the ship with his head, just forward of the fore-chains[1]; he gave us such an appalling and tremendous jar, as nearly threw us all on our faces. The ship brought up as suddenly and violently as if she had struck a rock, and trembled for a few seconds like a leaf.

We looked at each other with perfect amazement, deprived almost of the power of speech. Many minutes elapsed before we were able to realize the dreadful accident; during which time he passed under the ship, grazing her keel as he went along, came up alongside of her to leeward, and lay on the top of the water (apparently stunned with the violence of the blow) for the space of a minute; he then suddenly started off, in a direction to leeward. After a few moments reflection, and recovering, in some measure, from the sudden consternation that had seized us, I of course concluded that he had stove a hole in the ship, and that it would be necessary to set the pumps going. Accordingly they were rigged, but had not been in operation more than one minute before I perceived the head of the ship to be gradually settling down in the water; I then ordered the signal to be set for the other boats, which, scarcely had I dispatched, before I again discovered the whale, apparently in convulsions, on the top of the water, about one hundred rods to leeward. He was enveloped in the foam of the sea, that his continual and violent thrashing about in the water had created around him, and I could distinctly see him smite his jaws together, as if distracted with rage and fury. He remained a short time in this situation, and then started off with great velocity, across the bows of the ship, to windward. By this time the ship had settled down a considerable distance in the water, and I gave her up for lost.

I, however, ordered the pumps to be kept constantly going, and endeavoured to collect my thoughts for the occasion. I turned to the boats, two of which we then had with the ship, and with an intention of clearing them away, and getting all things ready to embark

---

[1]Between the platform where the foremast shrouds were secured and the bow of the ship.

in them, if there should be no other resource left; and while my attention was thus engaged for a moment, I was aroused with the cry of a man at the hatchway, "Here he is—he is making for us again." I turned around, and saw him about one hundred rods directly ahead of us, coming down apparently with twice his ordinary speed, and to me at that moment, it appeared with tenfold fury and vengeance in his aspect. The surf flew in all directions about him, and his course towards us was marked by a white foam of a rod in width, which he made with the continual violent thrashing of his tail, his head was about half out of the water, and in that way he came upon, and again struck the ship. I was in hopes when I descried him making for us, that by a dexterous movement of putting the ship away immediately, I should be able to cross the line of his approach, before he could get up to us, and thus avoid what I knew, if he should strike us again, would prove our inevitable destruction.

I bawled out to the helmsman, "Hard up!" but she had not fallen off more than a point, before we took the second shock. I should judge the speed of the ship to have been at this time about three knots, and that of the whale about six. He struck her to windward, directly under the cathead, and completely stove in her bows. He passed under the ship again, went off to leeward, and we saw no more of him. Our situation at this junction can be more readily imagined than described. The shock to our feelings was such, as I am sure none can have an adequate conception of that were not there: the misfortune befell us at a moment when we least dreamt of any accident, and from the pleasing anticipations we had formed, of realizing the certain profits of our labour, we were dejected by a sudden, most mysterious, and overwhelming calamity. Not a moment, however, was to be lost in endeavouring to provide for the extremity to which it was now certain we were reduced. We were more than a thousand miles from the nearest land, and with nothing but a light open boat, as the resource of safety for myself and companions. I ordered the men to cease pumping, and every one to provide for himself; seizing a hatchet at the same time, I cut away the lashings of the spare boat, which lay bottom up across two spars directly over the quarter deck, and cried out to those near me to take her as she came down. They did so accordingly, and bore her on their shoulders as far as the waist of the ship. The steward had in the meantime gone down into the cabin twice, and saved two quadrants, two practical navigators, and the captain's trunk and mine; all of which were hastily thrown into the boat, as she lay on the deck, with the two compasses which I snatched from the binnacle. He attempted to descend again; but the water by this time had rushed in, and he returned without being able to effect his purpose. By the time we had got the boat to the waist, the ship had filled with water, and was going down on her beam-ends: we shoved our boat as quickly as possible from the plank-shear into the water, all hands jumping in her at the same time, and launched off clear of the ship. We were scarcely two boat lengths distant from her, when she fell over to windward, and settled down in the water.

Amazement and despair now wholly took possession of us. We contemplated the frightful situation the ship lay in, and thought with horror upon the sudden and dreadful calamity that had over-taken us. We looked upon each other, as if to gather some consolatory sensation from an interchange of sentiments, but every countenance was marked with the paleness of despair. Not a word was spoken for several minutes by any of us; all appeared to be bound in a spell of stupid consternation; and from the time we were first attacked by the whale, to the period of the fall of the ship, and of our leaving her in the boat, more than ten minutes could not certainly have elapsed! God only knows in what way, or by what means, we were enabled to accomplish in that short time what we did; the cutting away and transporting the boat from where she was deposited would of itself, in ordinary circumstances have consumed as much time as that, if the whole ship's crew had been employed in it. My companions had not saved a single article but what they had on their backs; but to me it was a source of infinite satisfaction, if any such could be gathered from the horrors of our gloomy situation, that we had been fortunate enough to have preserved our compasses, navigators, and quadrants.

After the first shock of my feelings was over, I enthusiastically contemplated them as the probable instruments of our salvation; without them all would have been dark and hopeless. Gracious God! What a picture of distress and suffering now presented itself to my imagination. The crew of the ship were saved, consisting of twenty human souls. All that remained to conduct these twenty beings through the stormy terrors of the ocean, perhaps many thousand miles, were three open light boats.

The prospect of obtaining any provisions or water from the ship, to subsist upon during the time, was at least now doubtful. How many long and watchful nights, thought I, are to be passed? How many tedious days of partial starvation are to be endured, before the least relief or mitigation of our sufferings can be reasonably anticipated. We lay at this time in our boat, about two ship lengths off from the wreck, in perfect silence, calmly contemplating her situation, and absorbed in our own melancholy reflections, when the other boats were discovered rowing up to us. They had but shortly before discovered that some accident had befallen us, but of the nature of which they were entirely ignorant. The sudden and mysterious disappearance of the ship was first discovered by the boat-steerer in the captain's boat, and with a horror-struck countenance and voice, he suddenly exclaimed, "Oh, my God! Where is the ship?"

Their operations upon this were instantly suspended, and a general cry of horror and despair burst from the lips of every man, as their looks were directed for her, in vain, over every part of the ocean. They immediately made all haste towards us. The captain's boat was the first that reached us. He stopped about a boat's length off, but had no power to utter a single syllable: he was so completely overpowered with the spectacle before him that he sat down in his boat, pale and speechless. I could scarcely recognize his countenance, he appeared to be so much altered, awed, and overcome with the oppression of his feelings, and the dreadful reality that lay before him. He was in a short time however enabled to address the inquiry to me. "My God, Mr. Chase, what is the matter?" I answered, "We have been

stove by a whale." I then briefly told him the story. After a few moment's reflection he observed that we must cut away her masts, and
endeavour to get something out of her to eat. Our thoughts were
now all accordingly bent on endeavours to save from the wreck
whatever we might possibly want, and for this purpose we rowed up
and got on to her. Search was made for every means of gaining access
to her hold; and for this purpose the lanyards were cut loose, and with
our hatchets we commenced to cut away the masts, that she might
right up again, and enable us to scuttle her decks. In doing which we
were occupied about three quarters of an hour, owing to our having
no axes, nor indeed any other instruments, but the small hatchets belonging to the boats. After her masts were gone she came up about
two-thirds of the way upon an even keel. While we were employed
about the masts the captain took his quadrant, shoved off from the
ship, and got an observation. We found ourselves in latitude 0° 40' S.,
longitude 119° W. We now commenced to cut a hole through the
planks, directly above two large casks of bread, which most fortunately were between decks, in the waist of the ship, and which being
in the upper side, when she upset, we had strong hopes was not wet.
It turned out according to our wishes, and from these casks we obtained six hundred pounds of hard bread. Other parts of the deck
were then scuttled, and we got without difficulty as much fresh water
as we dared to take in the boats, so that each was supplied with about
sixty-five gallons; we got also from one of the lockers a musket, a
small canister of powder, a couple of files, two rasps, about two
pounds of boat nails, and a few turtles.

In the afternoon the wind came on to blow a strong breeze;
and having obtained every thing that occurred to us could then be
got out, we began to make arrangements for our safety during the
night. A boat's line was made fast to the ship, and to the other end of
it one of the boats was moored, at about fifty fathoms to leeward; another boat was then attached to the first one, about eight fathoms
astern; and the third board, the like distance astern of her. Night came
on just as we had finished our operations; and such a night as it was to

us! so full of feverish and distracting inquietude, that we were deprived entirely of rest. The wreck was constantly before my eyes. I could not, by any effort, chase away the horrors of the preceding day from my mind: they haunted me the live-long night. My companions—some of them were like sick women; they had no idea of the extent of their deplorable situation. One or two slept unconcernedly, while others wasted the night in unavailing murmurs. I now had full leisure to examine, with some degree of coolness, the dreadful circumstances of our disaster. The scenes of yesterday passed in such quick succession in my mind that it was not until after many hours of severe reflection that I was about to discard the idea of the catastrophe as a dream. Alas! It was one from which there was no awaking; it was too certainly true, that but yesterday we had existed as it were, and in one short moment had been cut off from all the hopes and prospects of the living! I have no language to paint out the horrors of our situation. To shed tears was indeed altogether unavailing, and withal unmanly; yet I was not able to deny myself the relief they served to afford me. After several hours of idle sorrow and repining I began to reflect upon the accident, and endeavoured to realize by what unaccountable destiny or design (which I could not at first determine) this sudden and most deadly attack had been made upon us: by an animal, too, never before suspected of premeditated violence, and proverbial for its insensibility and inoffensiveness.

Every fact seemed to warrant me in concluding that it was anything but chance which directed his operations; he made two several attacks upon the ship, at a short interval between them, both of which, according to their direction, were calculated to do us the most injury, by being made ahead, and thereby combining the speed of the two objects for the shock; to effect which, the exact manoeuvres which he made were necessary. His aspect was most horrible, and such as indicated resentment and fury. He came directly from the shoal which we had just before entered, and in which we had struck three of his companions, as if fired with revenge for their sufferings. But to do this it may be observed, that the mode of fighting which they always adopt is either with repeated stroked of their tails, or snapping of their jaws together; and that a case, precisely similar to this one, has never been heard of amongst the oldest and most experienced whalers. To this I would answer, that the structure and strength of the whale's head is admirably designed for this mode of attack; the most prominent part of which is almost as hard and as tough as iron; indeed, I can compare it to nothing else but the inside of a horse's hoof, upon which a lance or harpoon would not make the slightest impression. The eyes and ears are removed nearly one-third the length of the whole fish, from the front part of the head, and are not in the least degree endangered in this mode of attack. At all events, the whole circumstances taken together, all happening before my own eyes, and producing, at the time, impressions in my mind of decided, calculating mischief on the part of the whale (many of which impressions I cannot now recall) induce me to be satisfied that I am correct in my opinion. It is certainly, in all its bearings, a hitherto unheard of circumstance, and constitutes, perhaps, the most extraordinary one in the annals of the fishery.

Kidnapped

From *The Rudder Magazine*

BY WILLIAM ALBERT ROBINSON

R ACING IN THE 1932 BERMUDA Race aboard his thirty-five-foot ketch, *Svaap,* William Albert Robinson had a secret that he hadn't shared with the college chums crewing with him: he planned to continue on around the world in the smallest yacht to ever attempt the journey. Three and a half years later, he completed his journey, publishing accounts of the voyage in *The Rudder Magazine* afterwards, including the one that follows.

A later scientific voyage to the Galapagos would nearly end in disaster when his appendix burst. As a famed sailor, he was saved when the Navy sent a destroyer, and the Army sent a flight of planes. His rescue was covered by national radio. His later life was just as exciting, starting a shipyard to build beautiful sailing ships only to have World War II intervene. At the end of the war, Tahiti called and, with a letter of authorization to enter the Pacific war zone from no less than Admiral Chester Nimitz, he sailed to Tahiti, bought an atoll, and sailed his seventy-foot *Varua* around the Pacific on further adventures.

The following story tells of a frightening adventure while sailing through the Red Sea.

WE PROGRESSED SLOWLY FOR SEVERAL days after leaving the island of Kamaran, groping along through an annoying sand haze from the desert, unable to see reefs or little sandy islets until almost upon them. Nights we anchored in uncharted lagoons or behind offshore reefs, avoiding the few settlements we saw because of the fearsome reputation of the inhabitants. The scorching arid breath of the desert alternated with the saturatingly humid sea wind. Both felt as if they came straight from the door of a blast furnace. Even at night the temperature was 95 degrees or more. Strangely enough, Etera, child of the tropics, felt it worse than I did and was constantly complaining. It was a parched and sunburnt land of endless forlorn sand dunes.

Then one day the barometer tumbled, and from the south came a driving gale. In company with a large cumbersome Arab dhow we flew down the coast seeking shelter. I planned to find a little anchorage called Khor Nohud on the chart. Just before we reached it, the dhow turned in through a different break in the shore reef. Confident that they, with local knowledge, had chosen the best shelter from the storm, I cautiously followed them into a snug little corral-girt basin.

An hour later we were prisoners, not of the swarthy Arabs that manned the dhow, but of the white-robed Emir [an Arabian chieftain] of El Birk—the fantastic Bedouin village of conical brush huts and stone houses that hung beneath a few palms on the barren burnt hillside.

I had seen it coming, when a boatload of heavily armed men put out from shore, but we were trapped. Even if we'd had time to escape it was impossible, for the dhow had shifted to a position that blocked the narrow pass. Resistance was out of the question. It was a hundred to one.

They clambered aboard and indicated by signs that the Emir wished to see me. Taking some of the ship's papers along, I went, not knowing whether I was attending a reception or my funeral. I never saw the papers again.

We climbed to the village and through its disorderly alleys to the Emir's fortified palace, where we entered through an embrasure in the wall. Across the courtyard we went, silently. It was filled with strange, staring Bedouins. Then up a dark stair onto a walled terrace, where the others left their sandals. We entered a small square room with heavily barred windows, and benches covered with Persian rugs around all four sides. There was no other furniture except a bare table with two books and a silver-handled lash.

Facing us from a niche at the opposite side, sat the Emir—enormous in his voluminous robes. Surrounding him all around the walls, sat twenty-four lesser chiefs in picturesque garb. I was presented and seated in a dripping silence. Two riflemen guarded each side of the door.

Through a useless interpreter who knew less than a dozen words of French, I essayed a speech full of blithe lies as to my pleasure at being there. After an extended exchange of compliments I was given to understand that I was being held for ransom. I wrote and signed a letter stating my situation, and they sent it off somewhere by camel courier. I never did learn its destination.

If I am ever kidnapped again I hope I fall into equally hospitable hands. Complaining of the discomfort ashore, I was finally allowed to live aboard the *Svaap* under guard. When I sent word that our prolonged stay meant a food shortage, the Emir at once sent a whole flock of chickens aboard, and the *Svaap* looked like a floating henhouse. I was a model prisoner, behaving as if I enjoyed it all in order to put them off their guard. When the sentries found it tedious and confining aboard the *Svaap*, it was not too difficult to bribe them to watch us from the nearby dhow.

I was full of plans of escape but could do nothing with the dhow in her present position, blocking the only exit. We had two trumps, which the Arabs had overlooked in not searching the *Svaap*. In a locker under my berth lay several guns and plenty of ammunition. Hidden in the gloom beneath the bridge deck was a shapeless object covered with a tarpaulin—the unsuspected engine. Had they so much as dreamed we had power, things would have been different.

Our chance came with the termination of the southerly blow. The wind changed to northwest and necessitated the shifting of anchors since there was not room enough for the boats to swing in the confined little basin. We helped the dhow move hers first, seeing to it that they were placed so as not to interfere with our preconceived plan. Then, ostensibly to keep the *Svaap* from going on the rocks while moving her heavy anchor and chain, we placed a light kedge on a manila line near the pass—just where it would be best for a quick exit. Dropping astern on this line, we hove up on our heavy anchor until it swung clear of the water.

The Arabs on the dhow, not more than fifteen yards away, watched with interest the proceedings whereby two men could execute a maneuver that required half a dozen in their case. From the corner of my eye I studied their faces. No sign of suspicion showed.

"Now is the time!" I whispered to Etera.

Without haste, as if we were merely moving up to place our big anchor, we hove on the manila line. Slowly the *Svaap* swung, until she was heading straight out of the pass. When we were nearly over our light anchor I went below and slipped the guns on deck behind the cabin house.

Then things started to happen. The engine, already primed and coaxed, started with a roar—full speed ahead. I flew on deck, grabbed a gun in each hand, and put a shot or two over the decks of the dhow. Every Arab dropped out of sight behind the bulwarks of the craft amid a confusion of incoherent shouting. Etera got in the small hook as we slid over it, gathering momentum as we went. A second later we were gliding between the narrow jaws of coral that formed the pass. Covering the dhow all the while, we steered for open water, keeping that bulky craft between us and the village as a shield from shore guns.

There was a great hullabaloo on shore and a random shot or two as Arab sheiks in flowing robes rushed about among the crowd on the rocky slopes. The northwest wind prevented the sailing craft from negotiating the pass, so pursuit was impossible. We would not have feared it, anyway, for our high-power rifles would have kept them at a distance.

We were free, but our problems were by no means solved. Our protecting string of offshore reefs had become a prison, confining us to a narrow shoal-infested strip of water close to this piratical coast. More than a hundred miles of this intricate channel remained, and even then, before we could escape to sea we had to get some supplies somewhere. We did have our flock of chickens. I felt that it was adding insult to injury to not only escape from my friend the Emir, but to carry off a dozen of his best chickens besides. Had there been time, I should have returned them to him beforehand.

The only place that offered any chance of getting supplies before we got to Jidda was Lith, a hundred miles north. The pilot book was a bit discouraging about Lith, saying of the inhabitants: "In ordinary times piracy and robbing the few pilgrims who attempt to pass through to Mecca are added to their usual means of gaining a livelihood." It neglects to specify what the "usual means" are, although I strongly suspect it is something nefarious. Pilots and charts are usually unduly discouraging. Half the islands in the South Pacific are called "hostile," whereas their people are the friendliest imaginable. Therefore, I did not take the warning too seriously. Besides, piracy or no piracy, we had to get food.

One evening, after three days of nerve-wracking navigation, we found our way through a winding passage into the inner anchorage of Lith. It was a great disappointment—merely a small settlement of squalid mud houses, instead of the populous town we had expected. As at Khor El Birk, the shore at once disgorged upon us a boatload of truculent Arabs who tried to inveigle me ashore. This time I was not so easily caught, and they finally left. We were tired, and soon turned in for the night, sleeping on deck.

Our ship's clock was just striking the eight bells of midnight. I awoke with a start and thought for a moment I was having a nightmare, for I looked into the muzzles of a motley assortment of firearms. A smoking oil lamp was held on high by a bulky, black-bearded giant with one eye. The flickering light fell on the wildest-looking gang of pirates I ever hope to see. There were more than a dozen of them, and more waiting in the boat which lay alongside. Every man of them was a walking arsenal, bearing rifle, revolver, and one or two knives or a sword.

There was no temporizing with this crowd. I tried to joke it off but instantly realized that these were not the polite captors of El Birk. They simply poked a gun in my ribs and took me along without even letting me dress. I did slip on a bathrobe, but that was all.

Two stayed to guard Etera, who was speechless with fright. As we rowed off, I shouted what I fully believed to be my last instructions to him—to try to escape on some passing dhow and tell the story to the first Europeans he met. Somehow, I felt very melodramatic at that moment. I was certain that I would never see *Svaap* again, and I kept my eyes on her until she faded into the black of night.

Three horses were waiting on shore, beautiful Arabian steeds, without saddles. I have always dreamed of riding a real Arabian under the stars of Asia, but never in my wildest fancies did I imagine such a ride as I had that night as we galloped bareback over the rolling desert sands. In front of me rode the chief, his white mantle fluttering from his head like the wings of a phantom. Immediately behind me rode the guard, brandishing his old French musket toward the middle of my back. I expected a shot at any moment, and curiously enough was quite calm about it, wondering what it would feel like when it came. I believed I was being taken out into the desert to be killed where there would be no trace. Then they would go back and scuttle *Svaap*. I learned that night what a condemned man feels like when he is being led out to the gallows.

My predominant thought was that no one would ever know what had happened. This worried me. People would say, "I told you so; the boat was too small. It was a foolhardy thing to try to sail around the world in that thing." I did very much want to complete the trip successfully, to demonstrate that it was not foolhardy, that a well-designed, well-built small boat could go anywhere safely if properly handled.

On and on we galloped, over the rolling desert dunes. The hot wind was oppressive. The stars shone overhead. My long bathrobe flapped ridiculously in the wind, and I began to have painful reminders that I was unaccustomed to this form of violent exercise, not to mention the fact that I had never before ridden bareback and stirrupless. I longed to reach our destination, whatever it was.

After a while, we came to a lone, grotesquely dwarfed tree, where we stopped. The guard gave a peculiar cry, which was answered from somewhere in the dark. My heart beat rapidly, for I thought that this was to be the spot. But then a man appeared, examined us, and we moved on again. Then we came to an oasis with a considerable settlement. There, grimly commanding its surroundings from a rise, stood a low, square, turreted fortress with round towers at the four corners.

A few minutes later I took stock of my situation from a suffocating low cell in the fortress. There was no window or opening in the wall of any sort except the heavily barred door through which I had entered. There was not a single object in the room. The only break in the monotony of the four walls was a niche cut in the stone of one side, deep and long enough to form a sleeping shelf. A few rays of light from a lamp hung outside filtered through a small aperture in the door. There was no possibility of escape.

In this hopeless condition I languished for what seemed like a week, unable to distinguish day from night. Occasionally some peculiar tough bread-like stuff was passed in with foul water. Eventually some important Emir or Sheik arrived and examined me. We talked for hours, but as there was no interpreter I do not know what it was all about. As a matter of fact, I have never, to this day, understood the whole affair. There was no effort to take *Svaap*. I was never even searched. No effort was made to get ransom. I believe they got cold feet for some reason or other.

I was almost disappointed eventually, that it all ended as tamely as it did.

I was allowed to go back to *Svaap* under guard to get some very important diplomatic papers I claimed in sign talk to have. With the aid of some old bills of health, plenty of red ribbon, and sealing wax, I hurriedly manufactured some of the most awe-inspiring documents ever seen. I had no seal with which to stamp the sealing wax, but used the ornately figured cut-glass stopper from a Coty's Eau de Cologne bottle. This made a very impressive seal. These formidable documents so impressed the Emir (who had not the slightest notion what they were all about) that I was not returned to my cell but was to be detained in port indefinitely, why I don't know.

I soon found that the chief of the guard hated the Emir. Judicious bribery made him my ally, and we were able to get supplies aboard. A large Arab dhow lay alongside with a cutthroat crew of part-time pirates and slave-runners. The captain, an enormous jovial Arab, squeezed himself into all possible corners of the *Svaap*, exclaiming like a child over a new toy at a the curious things he saw. I gave him some charts which delighted him beyond measure. We became great friends, my pirate captain and I.

So everything was prepared for escape number two—probably the best-directed, most thoroughly sure escape ever known. The chief of the guard, in order to repay the Emir for some past injury, agreed not to guard us, although we could not leave openly by daylight, for there were some members of the garrison who were faithful to the Emir. This was where the dhow captain came in. He knew the reefs like the palm of his hand, and it was his job to lead us out in the night.

That last night will always linger in my memory. It was the only time I saw the Arabs throw off all restraint. We were aboard the great clumsy dhow—we three conspirators and the entire crew of the dhow—a wild, fearsome crowd. Drums were produced, and all night long we sang and danced to strange tempos, drinking a peculiar aromatic liquor. Different members of the crew burlesqued as women and performed weird evolutions. Even the gigantic captain did his bit, casting off all but a loincloth and violating his corpulent body with a sword dance something like one I had seen at Makalla. I even felt ashamed that I had my gun in my pocket. It was an unnecessary caution, for these good-natured pirates had accepted me as one of them.

The east was beginning to streak a little with a warning of approaching dawn when the great sail of the dhow creaked its way aloft and I bade farewell to my new-found friends. They got under way before a gentle desert breeze, and we followed close upon their heels in *Svaap*, twisting and turning in a serpentine path through unseen reefs. Dawn was breaking when we left the outer reefs behind. We headed north, and the dhow turned south.

A last farewell came floating across the purple water from that gigantic Arab sailor whose heart was solid gold.

"Salaam, America, Salaam!"

Hornblower and the Man
Who Felt Queer

From *The Saturday Evening Post*

BY C. S. FORESTER

RITISH HISTORICAL NOVELIST, C.S. Forester was the creator of Horatio Hornblower, a swashbuckling hero and naval officer in the Royal Navy of the late eighteenth and early nineteenth centuries. In a dozen books and serialized in *The Saturday Evening Post* (where this tale was published), Hornblower became one of the great mariners of fiction, along with Ahab and Lord Jim. A prolific writer, Forester is perhaps best known for *The African Queen,* which became the Oscar-winning Bogart/Hepburn film.

Not written in sequence, the Hornblower series takes the hero from midshipman to admiral through great sea battles and raging storms, and the books were populated by the likes of the man who felt queer.

THIS TIME THE WOLF WAS PROWLING round outside the sheepfold. H.M. frigate *Indefatigable* had chased the French corvette *Papillon* into the mouth of the Gironde, and was seeking a way of attacking her where she lay anchored in the stream under the protection of the batteries at the mouth. Captain Pellew took his ship into shoal water as far as he dared, until, in fact, the batteries fired warning shots to make him keep his distance, and he stared long and keenly through his glass at the corvette. Then he shut his telescope and turned on his heel to give the order that worked the *Indefatigable* away from the dangerous lee shore—out of sight of land, in fact.

His departure might lull the French into a sense of security which, he hoped, would prove unjustified. For he had no intention of leaving them undisturbed. If the corvette could be captured or sunk, not only would she be unavailable for raids on British commerce but also the French would be forced to increase their coastal defenses at this point and lessen the effort that could be put out elsewhere. War is a matter of savage blow and counterblow, and even a forty-gun frigate could strike shrewd blows if shrewdly handled.

Midshipman Hornblower was walking the lee side of the quarter-deck, as became his lowly station as the junior officer of the watch, in the afternoon, when Midshipman Kennedy approached him. Kennedy took off his hat with a flourish and bowed low, as his dancing master had once taught him, left foot advanced, hat down by the right knee. Hornblower entered into the spirit of the game, laid his hat against his stomach and bent himself in the middle three times in quick succession. Thanks to his physical awkwardness, he could parody ceremonial solemnity almost without trying.

"Most grave and reverend signior," said Kennedy, "I bear the compliments of Captain Sir Ed'ard Pellew, who humbly solicits Your Gravity's attendance at dinner at eight bells in the afternoon watch."

"My respects to Sir Edward," replied Hornblower, bowing to his knees at the mention of the name, "and I shall condescend to make a brief appearance."

"I am sure the captain will be both relieved and delighted," said Kennedy. "I will convey him my felicitations along with your most flattering acceptance."

Both hats flourished with even greater elaboration than before, but at that moment both young men noticed Mr. Bolton, the officer of the watch, looking at them from the windward side, and they hurriedly put their hats on and assumed attitudes more consonant with the dignity of officers holding their warrants from King George.

"What's in the captain's mind?" asked Hornblower.

Kennedy laid one finger alongside his nose. "If I knew that, I should rate a couple of epaulets," he said. "Something's brewing, and I suppose one of these days we shall know what it is. Until then, all that we little victims can do is to play, unconscious of our doom. Meanwhile, be careful not to let the ship fall overboard."

There was no sign of anything brewing while dinner was being eaten in the great cabin of the *Indefatigable*. Pellew was a courtly host at the head of the table. Conversation flowed freely and along indifferent channels among the senior officers present—the two lieutenants, Eccles and Chadd, and the sailing master, Soames. Hornblower and the other junior officer—Mallory, a midshipman of more than two years' seniority—kept silent, as midshipmen should, thereby being able to devote their undivided attention to the food, so vastly superior to what was served in the midshipmen's berth.

"A glass of wine with you, Mr. Hornblower," said Pellew, raising his glass.

Hornblower tried to bow gracefully in his seat while raising his glass. He sipped cautiously, for he had early found that he had a weak head and he disliked feeling drunk.

The table was cleared and there was a brief moment of expectancy as the company awaited Pellew's next move.

"Now, Mr. Soames," said Pellew, "let us have that chart."

It was a map of the mouth of the Gironde with the soundings; somebody had penciled in the positions of the shore batteries.

"The *Papillon*," said Sir Edward—he did not condescend to pronounce it French-fashion—"lies just here. Mr. Soames took the bearings." He indicated a penciled cross on the chart, far up the channel.

"You gentlemen," went on Pellew, "are going in with the boats to fetch her out."

So that was it. A cutting-out expedition.

"Mr. Eccles will be in general command. I will ask him to tell you his plan."

The gray-haired first lieutenant with the surprisingly young blue eyes looked round at the others.

"I shall have the launch," he said, "and Mr. Soames the cutter. Mr Chadd and Mr. Mallory will command the first and second gigs. And Mr. Hornblower will command the jolly boat. Each of the boats except Mr. Hornblower's will have a junior officer second in command."

That would not be necessary for the jolly boat with its crew of seven. The launch and cutter would carry from thirty to forty men each, and the gigs twenty each; it was a large force that was being dispatched—nearly half the ship's company.

"She's a ship of war," explained Eccles, reading their thoughts. "No merchantman. Ten guns a side, and full of men."

Nearer two hundred men than a hundred, certainly—plentiful opposition for a hundred and twenty British seamen.

"But we will be attacking her by night and taking her by surprise," said Eccles, reading their thoughts again.

"Surprise," put in Pellew, "is more than half the battle, as you know, gentlemen. . . . Please pardon the interruption, Mr. Eccles."

"At the moment," went on Eccles, "we are out of sight of land. We are about to stand in again. We have never hung about this part of the coast, and the Frogs'll think we've gone for good. We'll make the land after nightfall, stand in as far as possible, and then the boats will go in. High water tomorrow morning is at four-fifty; dawn is at five-thirty. The attack will be delivered at four-thirty, so that the watch below will have had time to get to sleep. The launch will attack on the starboard quarter, and the cutter on the larboard quarter. Mr. Mallory's gig will attack on the larboard bow, and Mr. Chadd's on the starboard bow. Mr. Chadd will be responsible for cutting the corvette's cable as soon as he has mastered the forecastle and the other boats' crews have at least reached the quarter-deck."

Eccles looked round at the three other commanders of the large boats, and they nodded understanding. Then he went on, "Mr. Hornblower with the jolly boat will wait until the attack has gained a foothold on the deck. He will then board at the main chains, either to starboard or larboard, as he sees fit, and he will at once ascend the main rigging, paying no attention to whatever fighting is going on on deck. He will see to it that the main topsail is loosed, and he will sheet it home on receipt of further orders. I, myself, or Mr. Soames in the event of my being killed or wounded, will send two hands to the wheel and will attend to steering the corvette as soon as she is under way. The tide will take us out, and the *Indefatigable* will be awaiting us just out of gunshot from the shore batteries."

"Any comments, gentlemen?" asked Pellew.

That was the moment when Hornblower should have spoken up—the only moment when he could. Eccles' orders had set in motion sick feelings of apprehension in his stomach. Hornblower was no maintopman, and Hornblower knew it. He hated heights, and he hated going aloft. He knew he had none of the monkey-like agility and self-confidence of the good seaman. He was unsure of himself aloft in the dark even in the *Indefatigable,* and he was utterly appalled at the thought of going aloft in an entirely strange ship and finding his way amid strange rigging. He felt himself quite unfitted for the duty assigned to him, and he should have raised a protest at once, on account of his un-fitness. But he let the opportunity pass, for he was overcome by the matter-of-fact way in which the other officers accepted the plan. He looked round at the unmoved faces; nobody was paying any attention to him, and he jibbed at making himself conspicuous. He swallowed; he even got as far as opening his mouth, but still no one looked at him and his protest died.

"Very well, then, gentlemen," said Pellew....."I think you had better go into the details, Mr. Eccles."

Then it was too late. Eccles, with the chart before him, was pointing out the course to be taken through the shoals and mudbanks of the Gironde, and expatiating on the position of the shore batteries and on the influence of the lighthouse of Cordouan upon the distance to which the *Indefatigable* could approach in daylight. Hornblower listened, trying to concentrate despite his apprehension.

Eccles finished his remarks and Pellew closed the meeting, "Since you all know your duties, gentlemen, I think you should start your preparations. The sun is about to set and you will find you have plenty to do."

The boats' crews had to be told off; it was necessary to see that the men were armed and that the boats were provisioned in case of emergency. Every man had to be instructed in the duties expected of him. And Hornblower had to rehearse himself in ascending the main shrouds and laying out along the main-topsail yard. He did it twice, forcing himself to make the difficult climb up the futtock shrouds, which, projecting outward from the mainmast, made it necessary to climb several feet while hanging back downward, locking fingers and toes into the ratlines.

He could just manage it, moving slowly and carefully, although clumsily. He stood on the foot rope and worked his way out to the yardarm—the foot rope was attached along the yard so as to hang nearly four feet below it. The principle was to set his feet on the rope with his arms over the yard, then, holding the yard in his armpits, to shuffle sideways along the foot rope to cast off the gaskets and loosen the sail.

Twice Hornblower made the whole journey, battling with the disquiet of his stomach at the thought of the hundred-foot drop below him. Finally, gulping with nervousness, he transferred his grip to the brace and forced himself to slide down it to the deck—that would be his best route when the time came to sheet the topsail home. It was a long, perilous descent; Hornblower told himself—as indeed he had said to himself when he had first seen men go aloft—

that similar feats in a circus at home would be received with "Oh's" and "Ah's" of appreciation.

He was by no means satisfied with himself even when he reached the deck, and at the back of his mind was a vivid picture of his missing his hold, when the time came for him to repeat the performance in the *Papillon,* and falling headlong to the deck—a second or two of frightful fear while rushing through the air, and then a shattering crash. And the success of the attack hinged on him as much as on anyone—if the topsail were not promptly set to give the corvette steerageway, she would run aground on one of the shoals in the river mouth, to be ignominiously recaptured, and half the crew of the *Indefatigable* would be dead or prisoners.

In the waist, the jolly boat's crew was formed up for his inspection. He saw to it that the oars were properly muffled, that each man had pistol and cutlass, and made sure that every pistol was at half cock, so that there was no fear of a premature shot giving warning of the attack. He allocated duties to each man in the loosing of the topsail, laying stress on the possibility that casualties might necessitate unrehearsed changes in the scheme.

"I will mount the rigging first," said Hornblower.

That had to be the case. He had to lead—it was expected of him. More than that; if he had given any other order, it would have excited comment . . . and contempt.

"Jackson," went on Hornblower, addressing the coxswain, "you will quit the boat last and take command if I fall."

"Aye, aye, sir."

It was usual to use the poetic expression "fall" for "die," and it was only after Hornblower had uttered the word that he thought about its horrible real meaning in the present circumstances.

"Is that all understood?" asked Hornblower harshly; it was his mental stress that made his voice grate so.

Everyone nodded except one man. "Begging your pardon, sir," said Hales, the young man who pulled stroke oar, "I'm feeling a bit queerlike."

Hales was a lightly built young fellow of swarthy countenance. He put his hand to his forehead with a vague gesture as he spoke.

"You're not the only one to feel queer," snapped Hornblower.

The other men chuckled. The thought of running the gantlet of the shore batteries, of boarding an armed corvette in the teeth of opposition, might well raise apprehension in the breast of any of them. Most of the men detailed for the expedition must have felt qualms to some extent.

"I don't mean that, sir," said Hales indignantly. "'Course I don't."

But Hornblower and the others paid him no attention.

"You just keep your mouth shut," growled Jackson.

There could be nothing but contempt for a man who announced himself sick after being told off on a dangerous duty. Hornblower felt sympathy as well as contempt. He himself had been too much of a coward even to give voice to his apprehensions—too much afraid of what people would say about him.

"Dismiss," said Hornblower. "I'll pass the word for all of you when you are wanted."

There were some hours yet to wait while the *Indefatigable* crept inshore, with the lead going steadily and Pellew himself attending to the course of the frigate. Hornblower, despite his nervousness and his miserable apprehensions, yet found time to appreciate the superb seamanship displayed as Pellew brought the big frigate in through these tricky waters on that dark night. His interest was so caught by the procedure that the little tremblings which had been assailing him ceased to manifest themselves; Hornblower was of the type that would continue to observe and to learn on his deathbed.

By the time the *Indefatigable* had reached the point off the mouth of the river where it was desirable to launch the boats, Hornblower had learned a good deal about the practical application of the principles of coastwise navigation and a good deal about the organization of a cutting-out expedition, and by self-analysis he had learned even more about the psychology of a raiding party before a raid.

He had mastered himself, to all outside appearance, by the time he went down into the jolly boat as she heaved on the inky-black water, and he gave the command to shove off in a quiet, steady voice. Hornblower took the tiller—the feel of that solid bar of wood was reassuring, and it was old habit now to sit in the stern sheets with hand and elbow upon it—and the men began to pull slowly after the dark shapes of the four big boats. There was plenty of time, and the flowing tide would take them up the estuary. That was just as well, for on one side of them lay the batteries of St. Dyé, and inside the estuary on the other side was the fortress of Blaye; forty big guns trained to sweep the channel, and none of the five boats could withstand a single shot from one of them.

He kept his eyes attentively on the cutter ahead of him. Soames had the dreadful responsibility of taking the boats up the channel, while all he had to do was to follow in her wake—all, except to loose that main topsail. Hornblower found himself shivering again.

Hales, the man who had said he felt queer, was pulling stroke oar; Hornblower could just see his dark form moving rhythmically back and forward at each slow stroke. After a single glance, Hornblower paid him no more attention, and was staring after the cuter when a sudden commotion brought his mind back into the boat. Someone had missed his stroke; someone had thrown all six oars into confusion as a result.

"Mind what you're doing, blast you, Hales," whispered Jackson, the coxswain, with desperate urgency.

For answer there was a sudden cry from Hales, loud, but fortunately not too loud, and Hales pitched forward against Hornblower's and Jackson's legs, kicking and writhing.

"The swine's having a fit," growled Jackson.

The kicking and writhing went on. Across the water through the darkness came a sharp, scornful whisper. "Mr. Hornblower," said the voice—it was Eccles putting a world of exasperation into his sotto voce question, "cannot you keep your men quiet?"

Eccles had brought the launch round almost alongside the jolly boat to say this to him, and the desperate need for silence was dramatically demonstrated by the absence of any of the usual blasphemy. Hornblower opened his mouth to make an explanation, but he fortunately realized that raiders in open boats did not make explanations when under the guns of the fortress of Blaye.

"Aye, aye, sir," was all he whispered back, and the launch continued on its mission of shepherding the flotilla in the tracks of the cutter.

"Take his oar, Jackson," he whispered furiously to the coxswain, and he stooped and with his own hands dragged the writhing figure toward him and out of Jackson's way.

"You might try pouring water on 'im, sir," suggested Jackson hoarsely as he moved to the after thwart. "There's the bailer 'andy."

Sea water was the seaman's cure for every ill, his panacea. But Hornblower let the sick man lie. His struggles were coming to an end, and Hornblower wished to make no noise with the bailer. The lives of more than a hundred men depended on silence. Now that they were well into the actual estuary they were within easy reach of cannon shot from the shore, and a single cannon shot would rouse the crew of the *Papillon*, ready to man the bulwarks to beat off the attack, ready to drop cannon balls into the boats alongside, ready to shatter approaching boats with a tempest of grape.

Silently the boats glided up the estuary; Soames in the cutter was setting a slow pace, with only an occasional stroke at the oars to maintain steerageway. Presumably he knew very well what he was doing; the channel he had selected was an obscure one between mudbanks, impracticable for anything except small boats, and he had a twenty-foot pole with him with which to take the soundings—quicker and much more silent than using the lead. Minutes were passing fast, and yet the night was still utterly dark, with no hint of approaching dawn. Strain his eyes as he would, Hornblower could not be sure that he could see the flat shores on either side of him. It would call for sharp eyes on the land to detect the little boats being carried up by the tide.

Hales at his feet stirred and then stirred again. His hand, feeling around in the darkness, found Hornblower's ankle and apparently examined it with curiosity. He muttered something, the words dragging out into a moan.

"Shut up," whispered Hornblower, trying, like the saint of old, to make a tongue of his whole body, so that he might express the urgency of the occasion without making a sound audible at any distance. Hales set his elbow on Hornblower's knee and levered himself up into a sitting position, and then levered himself farther until he was standing, swaying with bent knees and supporting himself against Hornblower.

"Sit down, damn you," whispered Hornblower, shaking with fury and anxiety.

"Where's Mary?" asked Hales in a conversational tone.

"Shut up!"

"Mary!" said Hales, lurching against him. "Mary!"

Each successive word was louder. Hornblower felt instinctively that Hales would soon be speaking in a loud voice, that he might even soon be shouting. Old recollections of conversations with his doctor further stirred at the back of his mind; he remembered that persons emerging from epileptic fits were not responsible for their actions, and might be, and often were, dangerous.

"Mary!" said Hales again.

Victory and the lives of a hundred men depended on silencing Hales, and silencing him instantly. Hornblower thought of the pistol in his belt, and of using the butt, but there was another weapon more conveniently to his hand. He unshipped the tiller, a three-foot bar of solid oak, and he swung it with all the venom and fury of despair. The tiller crashed down on Hales' head, and Hales, an unuttered word cut short in his throat, fell silent in the bottom of the boat.

There was no sound from the boat's crew, save for something like a sigh from Jackson, whether approving or disapproving, Hornblower neither knew nor cared. He had done his duty, and he was certain of it. He had struck down a helpless idiot, most probably he had killed him, but the surprise upon which the success of the expedition depended had not been imperiled. He reshipped the tiller and resumed the silent task of keeping in the wake of the gigs.

Far away ahead—in the darkness it was impossible to estimate the distance—there was a nucleus of greater darkness, close on the surface of the black water. It might be the corvette. A dozen more silent strokes, and Hornblower was sure of it. Soames had done a magnificent job of pilotage, leading the boats straight to that objective. The cutter and launch were diverging now from the two gigs. The four boats were separating in readiness to launch their simultaneous converging attack.

"Easy," whispered Hornblower, and the jolly boat's crew ceased to pull.

Hornblower had his orders. He had to wait until the attack had gained a foothold on the deck. His hand clenched convulsively on the tiller; the excitement of dealing with Hales had driven the thought of having to ascend strange rigging in the darkness clear out of his head, and now it recurred with redoubled urgency. Hornblower was afraid.

Although he could see the corvette, the boats had vanished from his sight, had passed out of his field of vision. The corvette rode to her anchor, her spars just visible against the night sky—that was where he had to climb! She seemed to tower up hugely. Close by the corvette he saw a splash in the dark water—the boats were closing in fast and someone's stroke had been a little careless. At that same moment came a shout from the corvette's deck, and when the shout was repeated, it was echoed a hundredfold from the boats rushing alongside. The yelling was lusty and prolonged, of set purpose. A sleeping enemy would be bewildered by the din, and the progress of the shouting would tell each boat's crew of the extent of the success of the others. The British seamen were yelling like madmen. A flash and a bang from the corvette's deck told of the firing of the first shot; soon pistols were popping and muskets banging from several points of the deck.

"Give way!" said Hornblower. He uttered the order as if it had been torn from him by the rack.

The jolly boat moved forward while Hornblower fought down his feelings and tried to make out what was going on on board. He could see no reason for choosing one side of the corvette in preference to the other, and the larboard side was the nearer, and so he steered the boat to the larboard main chains. So interested was he in what he was doing that he remembered only in the nick of time to give the order, "In oars." He put the tiller over and the boat swirled round and the bowman hooked on.

From the deck just above came a noise exactly like a tinker hammering on a cooking pot; Hornblower noted the curious noise as he stood up in the stern sheets. He felt the cutlass at his side and the pistol in his belt, and then he sprang for the chains. With a mad leap he reached them and hauled himself up. The shrouds came into his hands, his feet found the ratlines beneath them, and he began to climb. As his head cleared the bulwark and he could see the deck, the flash of a pistol shot illuminated the scene momentarily, fixing the struggle on the deck in a static moment, like a picture. Before and below him a British seaman was fighting a furious cutlass duel with a French officer, and he realized with vague astonishment that the kettlemending noise he had heard was the sound of cutlass against cutlass—that clash of steel against steel that poets wrote about. So much for romance.

The realization carried him far up the shrouds. At his elbow he felt the futtock shrouds, and he transferred himself to them, hanging back downward with his toes hooked into the ratlines and his hands clinging like death. That lasted for only two or three desperate seconds, and then he hauled himself on the topmast shrouds and began the final ascent, his lungs bursting with the effort. Here was the topsail yard, and Hornblower flung himself across it and felt with his feet for the foot rope. Merciful God! There was no foot rope—his feet searching in the darkness met only unresisting air. A hundred feet above the deck he hung, squirming and kicking like a baby held up at arm's length in his father's hands. There was no foot rope; it may have been with this very situation in mind that the Frenchmen had removed it. There was no foot rope, so that he could not make his way out to the yardarm. Yet the gaskets must be cast off and the sail loosed—everything depended on that. Hornblower had seen daredevil seamen run out along the yards, standing upright, as though walking a tightrope. That was the only way to reach the yardarm now.

For a moment he could not breathe as his weak flesh revolted against the thought of walking along that yard above the black abyss. This was fear, the fear that stripped a man of his manhood, turning his bowels to water and his limbs to paper. Yet his furiously active mind continued to work. He had been resolute enough in dealing with Hales. Where he personally was not involved he had been brave enough; he had not hesitated to strike down the wretched epileptic with all the strength of his arm. That was the poor sort of courage he was capable of displaying. In the simple vulgar matter of physical bravery he was utterly wanting. This was cowardice, the sort of thing that men spoke about behind their hands to other men. He could not bear the thought of that in himself; it was worse—awful though the alternative might be—than the thought of falling through the night to the deck. With a gasp, he brought his knee up onto the yard, heaving himself up until he stood upright. He felt the rounded, canvas-covered timber under his feet, and his instincts told him not to dally there for a moment.

"Come on, men!" he yelled, and he dashed out along the yard.

It was twenty feet to the yardarm, and he covered the distance in a few frantic strides. Utterly reckless by now, he put his hands down on the yard, clasped it and laid his body across it again, his hands seeking the gaskets. A thump on the yard told him that Oldroyd, who had been detailed to come after him, had followed him out along the yard—he had six feet less to go. There could be no doubt that the other members of the jolly boat's crew were on the yard, and that Clough had led the way to the starboard yardarm. It was obvious from the rapidity with which the sail came loose. Here was the brace beside him. Without any thought of danger now, for he was delirious with excitement and triumph, he grasped it with both hands and jerked himself off the yard. His waving legs found the rope and twined about it, and he let himself slide down it.

Fool that he was! Would he never remember that vigilance and precaution must never be relaxed? He had allowed himself to slide so fast that the rope seared his hands, and when he tried to tighten his grip so as to slow down his progress, it caused him such agony that he had to relax it again and slide on down with the rope stripping the skin from his hands as though peeling off a glove. His feet reached the deck and he momentarily forgot the pain as he looked round him.

There was the faintest gray light beginning to show now, and there were no sounds of battle. It had been a well-worked surprise— a hundred men flung suddenly on the deck of the corvette had swept away the anchor watch and mastered the vessel in a single rush before the watch below could come up to offer any resistance.

Chadd's stentorian voice came pealing from the forecastle, "Cable's cut, sir!"

Then Eccles bellowed from aft, "Mr. Hornblower!"

"Sir!" yelled Hornblower.

"Sheet that topsail home!"

A rush of men came to help—not only his own boat's crew but every man of initiative and spirit. Halyards, sheets and braces; the sail was trimmed round and was drawing full in the light southerly air, and the *Papillon* swung around to go down with the first of the ebb. Dawn was coming up fast, with a trifle of mist on the surface of the water.

Over the starboard quarter came a sullen, bellowing roar, and then the misty air was torn by a series of infernal screams, supernaturally loud. The first cannon balls Hornblower had ever heard were passing him by.

"Mr. Chadd! Set the headsail! Loose the fore-tops'l! Get aloft, some of you, and set the mizzen tops'l."

From the port bow came another salvo—Blaye was firing at them from one side, St. Dyé from the other, now that they could guess what had happened on board the *Papillon*. But the corvette was moving fast with wind and tide, and it would be no easy matter to ripple her in the half-light. It had been a very near-run thing; a few seconds' delay could have been fatal. Only one shot from the next salvo passed within hearing, and its passage was marked by a loud snap overhead.

"Mr. Mallory, get that forestay spliced!"

"Aye, aye, sir!"

It was light enough to look round the deck now; he could see Eccles at the break of the poop, directing the handling of the corvette, and Soames beside the wheel, conning her down the channel. Two groups of red-coated marines, with bayonets fixed, stood guard over the hatchways. There were four or five men lying on the deck in curiously abandoned attitudes. Dead men; Hornblower could look at them with the callousness of youth. But there was a wounded man, too, crouched groaning over his shattered thigh. Hornblower could not look at him as disinterestedly, and he was glad, maybe only for his own sake, when at that moment a seaman asked for and received permission from Mallory to leave his duties and attend to him.

"Stand by to go about!" shouted Eccles from the poop; the corvette had reached the tip of the middle-ground shoal and was about to make the turn that would carry her into the open sea.

The men came running to the braces, and Hornblower tailed on along with them. But the first contact with the harsh rope gave him such pain that he almost cried out. His hands were like raw meat, and fresh-killed at that, for blood was running from them. Now that his attention was called to them, they smarted unbearably.

The headsail sheets came over, and the corvette went handily about.

"There's the old Indy!" shouted somebody.

The *Indefatigable* was plainly visible now, lying to just out of shot from the shore batteries, ready to rendezvous with her prize. Somebody cheered, and the cheering was taken up by everyone, even while the last shots from St. Dyé, fired at extreme range, pitched sullenly into the water alongside. Hornblower had gingerly extracted his handkerchief from his pocket and was trying to wrap it round his hand.

"Can I help you with that, sir?" asked Jackson. Jackson shook his head as he looked at the raw surface. "You was careless, sir. You ought to 'a' gone down 'and over 'and," he said, when Hornblower explained to him how the injury had been caused. "Very careless, you was, beggin' your pardon for saying so, sir. But you young gennelmen often is. You do't 'ave no thought for your necks nor your 'ides sir."

Hornblower looked up at the main-topsail yard high above his head, and remembered how he had walked along that slender stick of timber out to the yardarm in the dark. At the recollection of it, even here with the solid deck under his feet, he shuddered a little.

"Sorry, sir. Didn't mean to 'urt you," said Jackson, tying the knot. "There, that's done, as good as can do it, sir."

"Thank you, Jackson," said Hornblower.

"We got to report the jolly boat as lost, sir," went on Jackson.

"Lost?"

"She ain't towing alongside, sir. You see, we didn't leave no boat keeper in 'er. Wells, 'e was to be boat keeper, you remember, sir. But I sent 'im up the riggin a'ead o' me, seeing that 'Ales couldn't go. We wasn't too many for the job. So the jolly boat must'a' come adrift, sir, when the ship went about."

"What about Hales, then?" asked Hornblower.

"'E was still in the boat, sir."

Hornblower looked back up the estuary of the Gironde. Somewhere up there the jolly boat was drifting about, and lying in it was Hales, probably dead, possibly alive. In either case, the French would find him surely enough, but a cold wave of regret extinguished the warm feeling of triumph in Hornblower's bosom when he thought about Hales back there. If it had not been for Hales, he would never have nerved himself—so, at least, he thought—to run out to the main-topsail yardarm; he would at this moment be ruined and branded as a coward instead of basking in the satisfaction of having capably done his duty.

Jackson saw the bleak look in his face. "Don't you take on so, sir," he said. "They won't 'old the loss of the jolly boat agin' you, not the captain and Mr. Eccles, they won't."

"I wasn't thinking about the jolly boat," said Hornblower. "I was thinking about Hales."

"Oh, 'im?" said Jackson. "Don't you fret about 'im, sir. 'E wouldn't never have made no seaman, not no'ow."

A Pacific Passage

From *Racing Through Paradise*

BY WILLIAM F. BUCKLEY, JR.

K NOWN FAR AND WIDE FOR HIS acerbic wit and conservative stance, Buckley is the founder of *National Review,* a widely syndicated columnist, and the former host of the weekly PBS debate, *Firing Line,* which was the longest-running TV program with the same host when it ended in 1999.

The author of many best-selling nonfiction and fiction books, Buckley started sailing as a teenager and, after college, raced for a decade, including four Bermuda Races. He sailed transatlantic aboard his schooner, *Cyrano,* and turned that experience into his first sailing book, *Airborne.* Later, he sailed his Ocean 71 ketch, *Sealestial,* from St. Thomas to Spain, producing *Atlantic High* as a result. Both books combined high adventure, high spirits, companionship, and as much luxury as they could pack aboard a yacht.

With *Racing Through Paradise,* the story continues as Buckley takes his son, Christopher, and friends on a four-thousand-mile voyage across the Pacific from Hawaii to New Guinea. Each voyage with Buckley is a venture into a range of experiences and not a little comedy, as well as wit and reflection.

In this chapter from early in the book, Buckley talks about sailing in and around his home waters of Long Island Sound, and about how he devised the perfect plan that allowed him the pleasures of overnight cruises with friends in spite of a wife who abhorred sailing.

His plan is the very model of simplicity, and fits neatly into the time available in modern lives.

PATITO IS A GREAT PLEASURE TO ME, but the one trip planned with my wife Pat also aboard proved, as she would put it, "a disaster" (a *Women's Wear Daily* word for uncomfortable). I am being harsh, because setting out from Block Island I decided to go to my destination, Edgartown, by heading northeast, by Chappaquiddick, in order to avoid an adverse current on the westerly route up Martha's Vineyard Sound, which would not turn for five hours in our favor. This decision meant close windward sailing, of the kind that causes a sailboat to lean dramatically to one side, the going bumpy, wet, disagreeable. And the going this day was very choppy, indeed so much so that the mate I had retained to ferry the boat back to Stamford from Nantucket, and who was with us for this leg of our little cruise, was himself a little chagrined at the punishment I permitted *Patito* to take.

Matt Craven was about twenty-seven. We had crossed paths when I cruised on one of the Delta Line's cargo/cruise ships in 1980, from Rio de Janeiro to Valparaiso, an ocean trip I had greatly looked forward to in part because it gave me the time I needed to complete a book, in part because I longed to go through the Strait of Magellan. It was November, midsummer in that part of the world, but Punta Arenas, at 53° 10' latitude, is cold, and the two pilots who board at Rio, one of them Chilean, the second Argentine, are properly tense as they guide the vessel through the narrow strait, a day and a half's anfractuous journey to the open ocean.

To amuse myself I had brought along a sextant and a Plath calculator, my then-current enthusiasm, and every night I took star sights, along with another American passenger also hooked on celestial navigation. The two of us were given the courtesy of the bridge and became familiar with the officers. Matt had had four years' training at Kings Point and I noted with some awe the meticulousness of operations on a modern bridge manned by professional seamen. I had been in the Gulf of Tonkin, aboard the aircraft carrier *Forrestal,* and it was on the order of being inside the clockwork of an atomic timepiece. I have been in the cockpit of a Boeing 747 when it made a mind-dazzling all-blind landing, and I have seen high-tech precision at work. Something of the same sort happens in the belly of an ice-breaker charged with keeping a shipping lane open to McMurdo Station in the Antarctic. There a young man who cannot have been more than eighteen, guided by radar and other instruments that register the least palpability, ordered the icebreaker's hull to rampage forward, shattering the ice; then reverse-engine back, then full-throttle forward; then back, repeating the sequence for about five months, surely the most grueling peacetime assignment in military life. I have been inside an atomic submarine, satisfied that the team of navigators knows the submarine's position within a matter of inches.

All of this engages rapt admiration, but taking the same sights with virtually the same equipment used two hundred years ago is quite another world. Standing fifty feet above the water, with a (gyroscopic) compass and fixed binoculars, predicting with the aid of the tables within a half minute or so the ideal moment to catch the premeditated navigational star—these are laboratory navigational conditions, I thought; but even so, I admired the profitable routinization of the navigational enterprise, making any error almost instantly transparent. Matt, a tall, blond American of Scandinavian background, told me on that cruise that his profession was subject to long layoffs and if ever I needed crew to ferry my little sailboat from anyplace, he would probably be very much available.

So here he was, as I pounded close-hauled against the heavy seas off Block Island. He turned to me, finally, and said that, really, he thought I was asking too much of the vessel. This observation delighted my wife, who thinks I ask too much of a vessel if I hoist a handkerchief up the mainmast. But, to be agreeable, I took a second reef on the mainsail, and reflected that at Kings Point they probably do not expose the cadets to very much ocean racing. I abandoned racing after a number of years in part because I did not have a suitable boat for competitive work; in part because the administrative burden of collecting a crew, weekend after weekend, gets terribly burdensome; in part because the activity is progressively antisocial if your family does not participate. And, also in part, because ocean racing can be protractedly uncomfortable. Necessary discomfort at sea is one thing. Unnecessary discomfort is quite another thing, and I have devoted a substantial measure of my sailing career, if that is the word for it, to distinguishing between the two.

But the major problem, where *Patito* is concerned, is that my wife suffers from arthritis. She has had two hip operations, and that night at Nantucket (from which she flew home) she told me, resolutely, that she would not again sail on *Patito,* and she has not. This is saddening, because one aspires to share all one's pleasures; but it is better that way than the other way—the other way being to take along one's wife on the clear understanding that the passage in prospect will be no more adventurous than sailing across the window of Abercrombie and Fitch. Often it isn't more than that; but one can never tell. And the preeminent anxiety one feels for the biological and temperamental well-being of one's wife quite upsets the experience you seek from sailing.

So then, for four years Pat and I have not sailed together aboard *Patito.* We have sailed a great deal together, but on vessels 70 feet or longer; and, with the single exception of our annual overnight run from Anguilla to Virgin Gorda, no overnights, thank you.

It was then that I developed what has become a practice I most heartily recommend. My friend Peter Flanigan, in the summer of 1985, thought to buy a 45-foot sailboat and to keep it in Essex, Connecticut, even though he lives in Greenwich, Connecticut. This would mean, I pleaded with him, that every time he used the boat it would need to be for a proper cruise. It is hardly worth driving two hours to Essex for a day's sail, followed by two hours' drive back, never mind the hour it requires to reach the Sound from Essex by boat. Why not do as I do?—I asked seductively.

What is that?

Well, I said, I have now a routine, and I do it about fifteen times every year. For one thing (I slip quickly into the didactic mode) you must not think of putting your boat away, as most people do, right after Labor Day. This is a habit associated with children going back to school, children being at once the most convenient menials in a sailing family, as also very often (though by no means always), the greatest enthusiasts. So that when they go off to school the boat tends to sit, forlornly; and is soon put away in the boatyard.

No more! I said. If you have a boat that requires little maintenance, a boat two people can easily operate, why, keep it in the water and use it. But develop your own routine.

I have one, and it suits and pleases me hugely and, I gladly report, gives pleasure to others. It always includes four people, and almost always all male—36-foot boats are inconveniently small for privacy. We meet at my house in Stamford between six-thirty and seven. Danny, who lives a few hundred yards away and who exercises supervision over *Patito,* is always invited; but half the time, and even more these days (he is preoccupied with his wife and three children), he is not free. I then gladly invite Tony Leggett, who sailed across the Atlantic with me in 1980, an Olympic-class sailor also aged about twenty-seven, a splendid companion, bon vivant, and conversationalist who rusticates in a bank vault somewhere in Brooklyn during the week and aches for the mere sight of salt water.

He and I are absolutely all that is needed to sail the boat, leaving room for two jolly good fellows, and it matters not in the least whether they know the difference between the mast and the boom. We serve up a drink and watch the first fifteen minutes of the evening news with Pat and, more often than not, her houseguest, all in my enchanted, littered music room. Before the news is concluded, we go to the station wagon in the rear of which is everything we will need to dine royally. We are at the boat basin in five minutes, the food is stowed in ten minutes. If the wind is severe, I will take a reef. With the roller-furling genoa, we can get exactly as much pull from the headsail as we desire. I rejoice in activating every electric and electronic device I have aboard *Patito,* and these would sink the average boat show. I put on the radar, and show my guests how we can track our way out of the harbor. I pause to note that the new digital radar (I have Raytheon's 200) gives a wonderful clear reading, avoiding the revolving wand that left one, over the years, forgetting what lay out there at one o'clock, by the time the wand had reached eleven o'clock. For fun and instruction, one summer night after a picnic dinner, I made Christopher pledge not to look out from the cockpit. He must stare only at the face of the radar and from there issue me instructions on how to pilot *Patito* back to my slip. He guided me past two beacons, then into the mouth of Stamford Harbor, up the main channel, past the rocky beacon at the north end, into the 50-foot-wide channel leading to the yacht basin. We'd have run aground just at the point where the channel was the narrowest. The radar, in short, guided us almost to our berth.

I turn on my beloved Trimble, which now has an extension on the cockpit bulkhead so that by pushing this button or that you can learn everything you'd have needed, earlier, to go below to learn: your course, the distance to your destination, your drift, your speed made good—all these are sitting in front of you. When you reach the mouth of the harbor, you set your course, first to the little reef one mile south, then—unless the wind is from the southeast, which usually it is not—I sail to my favorite little harbor at Eatons Neck, a nine-mile sail.

Sometimes the passage is completely calm. Sometimes the wind is raging ferociously and with a double reef—once or twice under reduced headsail alone—we travel at hull speed, over 8 knots. We do our best simultaneously to nibble at our foie gras and to drink our spring vinho verde. In an hour and a half we have wended our way through the serpentine channel, always a little bit of a breath-catcher as the sands run erratically, requiring, at low tide, concentration on how you managed the channel a fortnight ago. Occasionally we go aground, and use one of the standard devices to claw our way into navigable water. But then the final northerly undulation and we are in the little harbor, more like a lagoon. The low-profile beach does nothing to protect you from the wind, if it is heavy from the north. But it shields the water, which is wonderfully still, and you throw out the anchor, and feel wonderfully refreshed.

Danny or Tony lights the fire on the grill that hangs out over the rear pulpit, and you go below and attend to a) music (your kind of music), b) lights (your kind of lights—candlelight), c) heat (when it is cold outside you light the kerosene 13,000 BTU heater), d) picture lights (two forward, carefully designed to light up two charming oil paintings by Richard Grosvenor), and e) wines (you open the wines you will have for dinner, and pass about a preview). One of the guests usually volunteers to mix the salad, already prepared, or preheat the corn before it gets its roasting on the grill, or light the oven (careful: lighting an alcohol oven is not the kind of thing one lightly turns over to the amateur to perform), or to heat the dessert.

In a half hour you are eating and drinking and listening to music and conversing. The question eventually arises whether to dip into the ocean. Danny and I once did this on December 13, and have no wish to break that record. But last year I did it on Thanksgiving weekend, and the survival rate is remarkably high. The pain is intense, but only for about five seconds—to be sure, four seconds more than, they tell you, someone being electrocuted experiences pain. But you feel splendid when this is over. You help to make the beds. One guest occupies the quarter berth (a coffin open at one end, stretching aft along the ship's hull; Tom Wendel has the quite extraordinary habit of going into the berth head first, which most vertebrates would find impossibly claustrophobic). Two guests are comfortably ensconced in sleeping bags on either side of the collapsed saloon table, their reading lights on; and I am in my little private cabin, having dutifully checked the strength of the battery bank we are not using, to make certain that when we need the engine the following day we will have it. And if the kerosene heat is left on, however reduced, we must have an opening through the cockpit doors to let in air (otherwise we all die at night).

The most unattractive half hour of boat life is immediately after you wake up. There is so much to do, and the old yo-ho-ho has yet to kindle. You need to get dressed, in cramped quarters. You need to perform your toilette. Probably you will swim. The alcohol stove must be lighted.

I therefore tend to favor the quick getaway. Tony will weigh anchor, while I run the boat forward with the engine, and our two guests below are making toast, coffee, and asking who wants what cold cereal. By the time we are out of the little harbor, as a rule, we have had our breakfast, leaving us only the second cup of coffee to drink, and attention to pay to the sails. Generally in the morning the wind is not brisk, but usually it is enough to take us home at about six knots. At 10:30 you are in the car, the big garbage bag dumped in the boatyard's huge receptacle designed for that, the second plastic bag, containing all the saucers, plates, and utensils used during dinner and breakfast (they will be stuck into the automatic dishwasher), in the car trunk.

We go to the cellar of my house, into the swimming pool, first using the hot shower from the Jacuzzi, then the pool. In twenty minutes we are fresh as the newborn, sitting upstairs reading the Saturday *Times* with fresh coffee. The diaspora, almost by pre-understanding, begins. Your guests take the train to New York, or else drive off if they came by car; you go to your study in the garage and get to work, and you feel . . . They used to remark, in Gstaad when she lived part of the winter there, that Elizabeth Taylor, stretching her arms out in the morning on her porch, looking over the beautiful valley, would sigh and say, "I feel like a new man!"

I don't know how many guests I have taken on these little miniature cruising experiences, but I think they are almost all quite taken with them. There is so little fuss and bother. And yet you have had a genuine experience at sea. Call it a sailing haiku.

I should add that Peter Flanigan's boat rests now in Stamford, fifteen minutes from his house, not in Essex.

Call Me Ishmael

From Moby Dick

BY HERMAN MELVILLE

T HE MOST FAMOUS OPENING line in fiction, "Call me Ishmael" both introduces the character and shows what draws men to set sail on the oceans.

After weaving the spell of the sea, a later chapter tells of life at the masthead watching for whales, an experience that is at once both mystical and meditative.

⚓ ⚓ ⚓ ⚓

CALL ME ISHMAEL. SOME YEARS AGO—never mind how long precisely—having little or no money in my purse, and nothing particular
to interest me on shore, I thought I would sail about a little and see
the watery part of the world. It is a way I have of driving off the
spleen, and regulating the circulation. Whenever I find myself growing grim about the mouth; whenever it is a damp, drizzly November
in my soul; whenever I find myself involuntarily pausing before coffin warehouses, and bringing up the rear of every funeral I meet; and
especially whenever my hypos get such an upper hand of me, that it
requires a strong moral principle to prevent me from deliberately
stepping into the street, and methodically knocking people's hats
off—then, I account it high time to get to sea as soon as I can. This is
my substitute for pistol and ball. With a philosophical flourish Cato
throws himself upon his sword; I quietly take to the ship. There is
nothing surprising in this. If they but knew it, almost all men in their
degree, some time or other, cherish very nearly the same feelings towards the ocean with me.

There now is your insular city of the Manhattoes, belted
round by wharves as Indian isles by coral reefs—commerce surrounds
it with her surf. Right and left, the streets take you waterward. Its extreme downtown is the Battery, where that noble mole is washed by
waves, and cooled by breezes, which a few hours previous were out
of sight of land. Look at the crowds of water gazers there.

Circumambulate the city of a dreamy Sabbath afternoon. Go
from Corlears Hook to Coenties Slip, and from thence, by Whitehall,
northward. What do you see? Posted like silent sentinels all around
the town, stand thousands upon thousands of mortal men fixed in
ocean reveries. Some leaning against the spiles; some seated upon the
pierheads; some looking over the bulwarks of ships from China; some
high aloft in the rigging, as if striving to get a still better seaward
peep. But these are all landsmen; of weekdays pent up in lath and
plaster—tied to counters, nailed to benches, clinched to desks. How
then is this? Are the green fields gone? What do they here?

But look! here come more crowds, pacing straight for the water, and seemingly bound for a dive. Strange! Nothing will content them but the extremest limit of the land; loitering under the shady lee of yonder warehouses will not suffice. No. They must get just as nigh the water as they possibly can without falling in. And there they stand—miles of them—leagues. Inlanders all, they come from lanes and alleys, streets and avenues—north, east, south, and west. Yet here they all unite. Tell me, does the magnetic virtue in the needles of the compasses of all those ships attract them thither?

Once more. Say, you are in the country; in some high land of lakes. Take almost any path you please, and ten to one it carries you down in a dale, and leaves you there by a pool in the stream. There is magic in it. Let the most absentminded of men be plunged in his deepest reveries—stand the man on his legs, set his feet agoing, and he will infallibly lead you to water, if water there be in all that region. Should you ever be athirst in the great American desert, try this experiment, if your caravan happen to be supplied with a metaphysical professor. Yes, as every one knows, meditation and water are wedded forever.

But here is an artist. He desires to paint you the dreamiest, shadiest, quietest, most enchanting bit of romantic landscape in all the valley of the Saco. What is the chief element he employs? There stand his trees, each with a hollow trunk, as if a hermit and a crucifix were within; and here sleeps his meadow, and there sleep his cattle; and up from yonder cottage goes a sleepy smoke. Deep into distant woodlands winds a mazy way, reaching to overlapping spurs of mountains bathed in their hillside blue. But though the picture lies thus tranced, and though this pine tree shakes down its sighs like leaves upon this shepherd's head, yet all were vain, unless the shepherd's eye were fixed upon the magic stream before him. Go visit the Prairies in June, when for scores on scores of miles you wade knee-deep among tiger lilies—what is the one charm wanting?—Water—there is not a drop of water there! Were Niagara but a cataract of sand, would you travel your thousand miles to see it? Why did the poor poet of Tennessee, upon suddenly receiving two handfuls of silver, deliberate whether to buy him a coat, which he sadly needed, or invest his money in a pedestrian trip to Rockaway Beach? Why is almost every robust healthy boy with a robust healthy soul in him, at some time or other crazy to go to sea? Why upon your first voyage as a passenger, did you yourself feel such a mystical vibration, when first told that you and your ship were now out of sight of land? Why did the old Persians hold the sea holy? Why did the Greeks give it a separate deity, and make him the own brother of Jove? Surely all this is not without meaning. And still deeper the meaning of that story of Narcissus, who because he could not grasp the tormenting, mild image he saw in the fountain, plunged into it and was drowned. But that same image, we ourselves see in all rivers and oceans. It is the image of the ungraspable phantom of life; and this is the key to it all.

Now, when I say that I am in the habit of going to sea whenever I begin to grow hazy about the eyes, and begin to be overconscious of my lungs, I do not mean to have it inferred that I ever go to sea as a passenger. For to go as a passenger you must needs have a purse, and a purse is but a rag unless you have something in it. Besides, passengers get seasick—grow quarrelsome—don't sleep of nights—do not enjoy themselves much, as a general thing—no, I never go as a passenger; nor, though I am something of a salt, do I ever go to sea as a commodore, or a captain, or a cook. I abandon the glory and distinction of such offices to those who like them. For my part, I abominate all honorable respectable toils, trials, and tribulations of every kind whatsoever. It is quite as much as I can do to take care of myself, without taking care of ships, barques, brigs, schooners, and whatnot. And as for going as cook—though I confess there is considerable glory in that, a cook being a sort of officer on shipboard—yet, somehow, I never fancied broiling fowls—though once broiled, judiciously buttered, and judgmatically salted and peppered, there is no one who will speak more respectfully, not to say reverentially, of a broiled fowl than I will. It is out of the idolatrous dotings of the old Egyptians upon broiled ibis and roasted river horse, that you see the mummies of those creatures in their huge bakehouses the pyramids.

No, when I go to sea, I go as a simple sailor, right before the mast, plumb down into the forecastle, aloft there to the royal masthead. True, they rather order me about some, and make me jump from spar to spar, like a grasshopper in a May meadow. And at first, this sort of thing is unpleasant enough. It touches one's sense of honor, particularly if you come of an old established family in the land, the Van Rensselaers, or Randolphs, or Hardicanutes. And more than all, if just previous to putting your hand into the tar pot, you have been lording it as a country schoolmaster, making the tallest boys stand in awe of you. The transition is a keen one, I assure you, from a schoolmaster to a sailor, and requires a strong decoction of Seneca and the Stoics to enable you to grin and bear it. But even this wears off in time.

What of it, if some old hunks of a sea captain orders me to get a broom and sweep down the decks? What does that indignity amount to, weighed, I mean, in the scales of the New Testament? Do you think the archangel Gabriel thinks anything the less of me, because I promptly and respectfully obey that old hunks in that particular instance? Who ain't a slave? Tell me that. Well, then, however the old sea captains may order me about—however they may thump and punch me about, I have the satisfaction of knowing that it is all right; that everybody else is one way or other served in much the same way—either in a physical or metaphysical point of view, that is; and so the universal thump is passed round, and all hands should rub each other's shoulder blades, and be content.

Again, I always go to sea as a sailor, because they make a point of paying me for my trouble, whereas they never pay passengers a single penny that I ever heard of. On the contrary, passengers themselves must pay. And there is all the difference in the world between paying and being paid. The act of paying is perhaps the most uncomfortable infliction that the two orchard thieves entailed upon us. But *being paid*—what will compare with it? The urbane activity with which a man receives money is really marvelous, considering that we so earnestly believe money to be the root of all earthly ills, and that on no account can a moneyed man enter heaven. Ah! how cheerfully we consign ourselves to perdition!

Finally, I always go to sea as a sailor, because of the wholesome exercise and pure air of the forecastle deck. For as in this world, head winds are far more prevalent than winds from astern (that is, if you never violate the Pythagorean maxim), so for the most part the commodore on the quarterdeck gets his atmosphere at secondhand from the sailors on the forecastle. He thinks he breathes it first; but not so. In much the same way do the commonalty lead their leaders in many other things, at the same time that the leaders little suspect it. But wherefore it was that after having repeatedly smelled the sea as a merchant sailor, I should now take it into my head to go on a whaling voyage; this the invisible police officer of the Fates, who has the constant surveillance of me, and secretly dogs me, and influences me in some unaccountable way—he can better answer than anyone else. And, doubtless, my going on this whaling voyage, formed part of the grand program of Providence that was drawn up a long time ago. It came in as a sort of brief interlude and solo between more extensive performances. I take it that this part of the bill must have run something like this:

Grand Contested Election for the Presidency of the United States.
Whaling voyage by one Ishmael.
BLOODY BATTLE IN AFFGHANISTAN.

Though I cannot tell why it was exactly that those stage managers, the Fates, put me down for this shabby part of a whaling voyage, when others were set down for magnificent parts in high tragedies, and short and easy parts in genteel comedies, and jolly parts in farces—though I cannot tell why this was exactly; yet, now that I recall all the circumstances, I think I can see a little into the springs and motives which, being cunningly presented to me under various disguises, induced me to set about performing the part I did, besides cajoling me into the delusion that it was a choice resulting from my own unbiased free will and discriminating judgment.

Chief among these motives was the overwhelming idea of the great whale himself. Such a portentous and mysterious monster roused all my curiosity. Then the wild and distant seas where he rolled his island bulk; the undeliverable, nameless perils of the whale; these, with all the attending marvels of a thousand Patagonian sights and sounds, helped to sway me to my wish. With other men, perhaps, such things would not have been inducements; but as for me, I am tormented with an everlasting itch for things remote. I love to sail forbidden seas, and land on barbarous coasts. Not ignoring what is good, I am quick to perceive a horror, and could still be social with it—would they let me—since it is but well to be on friendly terms with all the inmates of the place one lodges in.

By reason of these things, then, the whaling voyage was welcome; the great floodgates of the wonder world swung open, and in the wild conceits that swayed me to my purpose, two and two there floated into my inmost soul, endless processions of the whale, and, midmost of them all, one grand hooded phantom, like a snow hill in the air.

It was during the more pleasant weather, that in due rotation with the other seamen my first masthead came round.

In most American whalemen the mastheads are manned almost simultaneously with the vessel's leaving her port; even though she may have fifteen thousand miles, and more, to sail ere reaching her proper cruising ground. And if, after a three, four, or five years' voyage she is drawing nigh home with anything empty in her—say, an empty vial even—then, her mastheads are kept manned to the last; and not till her skysail poles sail in among the spires of the port, does she altogether relinquish the hope of capturing one whale more.

Now, as the business of standing mastheads, ashore or afloat, is a very ancient and interesting one, let us in some measure expatiate here. I take it, that the earliest standers of mastheads were the old

Egyptians; because, in all my researches, I find none prior to them. For though their progenitors, the builders of Babel, must doubtless, by their tower, have intended to rear the loftiest masthead in all Asia, or Africa either; yet (ere the final truck was put to it) as that great stone mast of theirs may be said to have gone by the board, in the dread gale of God's wrath; therefore, we cannot give these Babel builders priority over the Egyptians. And that the Egyptians were a nation of masthead standers is an assertion based upon the general belief among archaeologists, that the first pyramids were founded for astronomical purposes: a theory singularly supported by the peculiar stairlike formation of all four sides of those edifices; whereby, with prodigious long upliftings of their legs, those old astronomers were wont to mount to the apex, and sing out for new stars; even as the lookouts of a modern ship sing out for a sail, or a whale just bearing in sight. In Saint Stylites, the famous Christian hermit of old times, who built him a lofty stone pillar in the desert and spent the whole latter portion of his life on its summit, hoisting his food from the ground with a tackle; in him we have a remarkable instance of a dauntless stander-of-mastheads; who was not to be driven from his place by fogs or frosts, rain, hail, or sleet; but, valiantly facing everything out to the last, literally died at his post. Of modern standers-of-mastheads we have but a lifeless set; mere stone, iron, and bronze men; who, though well capable of facing out a stiff gale, are still entirely incompetent to the business of singing out upon discovering any strange sight. There is Napoleon; who, upon the top of the column of Vendóme, stands with arms folded, some one hundred and fifty feet in the air; careless, now, who rules the decks below; whether Louis Philippe, Luis Blanc, or Louis the Devil. Great Washington, too, stands high aloft on his towering mainmast in Baltimore, and like one of Hercules' pillars, his column marks that point of human grandeur beyond which few mortals will go. Admiral Nelson, also, on a capstan of gunmetal, stands his masthead in Trafalgar Square; and even when most obscured by that London smoke, token is yet given that a hidden hero is there; for where there is smoke, must be fire. But neither great Washington, nor Napoleon, nor Nelson, will answer a single hail from below, however madly invoked to befriend by their counsels the distracted decks upon which they gaze; however, it may be surmised, that their spirits penetrate through the thick haze of the future, and descry what shoals and what rocks must be shunned.

It may seem unwarrantable to couple in any respect the mast-head standers of the land with those of the sea; but that in truth it is not so, is plainly evinced by an item for which Obed Macy, the sole historian of Nantucket, stands accountable. The worthy Obed tells us, that in the early times of the whale fishery, ere ships were regularly launched in pursuit of the game, the people of that island erected lofty spars along the seacoast, to which the lookouts ascended by means of nailed cleats, something as fowls go upstairs in a hen house. A few years ago this same plan was adopted by the Bay whalemen of New Zealand, who, upon descrying the game, gave notice to the ready-manned boats nigh the beach. But this custom has now be-come obsolete; turn we then to the one proper masthead, that of a whaleship at sea.

The three mastheads are kept manned from sunrise to sunset; the seamen taking their regular turns (as at the helm), and relieving each other every two hours. In the serene weather of the tropics it is exceedingly pleasant—the masthead; nay, to a dreamy meditative man it is delightful. There you stand, a hundred feet above the silent decks, striding along the deep, as if the masts were gigantic stilts, while be-neath you and between your legs, as it were, swim the hugest mon-sters of the sea, even as ships once sailed between the boots of the famous Colossus at old Rhodes. There you stand, lost in the infinite series of the sea, with nothing ruffled but the waves. The tranced ship indolently rolls; the drowsy trade winds blow; everything resolves you into langor. For the most part, in this tropic whaling life, a sublime uneventfulness invests you; you hear no news; read no gazettes; extras with startling accounts of commonplaces never delude you into un-necessary excitements; you hear of no domestic afflictions; bankrupt securities; fall of stocks; are never troubled with the thought of what you shall have for dinner—for all your meals for three years and more are snugly stowed in casks, and your bill of fare is immutable.

In one of those southern whalemen, on a long three or four years' voyage, as often happens, the sum of the various hours you spend at the masthead would amount to several entire months. And it is much to be deplored that the place to which you devote so considerable a portion of the whole term of your natural life, should be so sadly destitute of anything approaching to a cozy inhabitiveness, or adapted to breed a comfortable localness of feeling, such as pertains to a bed, a hammock, a hearse, a sentry box, a pulpit, a coach, or any other of those small and snug contrivances in which men temporarily isolate themselves. Your most usual point of perch is the head of the t'gallant mast, where you stand upon two thin parallel sticks (almost peculiar to whalemen) called the t'gallant crosstrees. Here, tossed about by the sea, the beginner feels about as cozy as he would standing on a bull's horns. To be sure, in coolish weather you may carry your house aloft with you, in the shape of a watch coat; but, properly speaking, the thickest watch coat is no more of a house than the unclad body; for as the soul is glued inside of its fleshly tabernacle, and cannot freely move about in it, nor even move out of it, without running great risk of perishing (like an ignorant pilgrim crossing the snowy Alps in winter); so a watch coat is not so much of a house as it is a mere envelope, or additional skin encasing you. You cannot put a shelf or chest of drawers in your body, and no more can you make a convenient closet of your watch coat.

Concerning all this, it is much to be deplored that the mastheads of a southern whaleship are unprovided with those enviable little tents or pulpits, called *crow's nests,* in which the lookouts of a Greenland whaler are protected from the inclement weather of the frozen seas. In the fireside narrative of Captain Sleet, entitled "A Voyage among the Icebergs, in Quest of the Greenland Whale, and Incidentally for the Rediscovery of the Lost Icelandic Colonies of Old Greenland"; in this admirable volume, all standers of mastheads are furnished with a charmingly circumstantial account of the then recently invented *crow's nest* of the *Glacier,* which was the name of Captain Sleet's good craft. He called it the *Sleet's crow's nest,* in honor of himself; he being the original inventor and patentee, and free from all ridiculous false delicacy, and holding that if we call our own children after our own names (we fathers being the original inventors and patentees), so likewise should we denominate after ourselves any other apparatus we may beget. In shape, the Sleet's crow's nest is something like a large tierce or pipe; it is open above, however, where it is furnished with a movable side-screen to keep to windward of your head in a hard gale. Being fixed on the summit of the mast, you ascend into it through a little trap-hatch in the bottom. On the after side, or side next the stern of the ship, is a comfortable seat, with a locker underneath for umbrellas, comforters, and coats. In front is a leather rack, in which to keep your speaking trumpet, pipe, telescope, and other nautical conveniences. When Captain Sleet in person stood his masthead in this crow's nest of his, he tells us that he always had a rifle with him (also fixed in the rack), together with a powder flask and shot, for the purpose of popping off the stray narwhales, or vagrant sea unicorns infesting those waters; for you cannot successfully shoot at them from the deck, owing to the resistance of the water, but to shoot down upon them is a very different thing. Now, it was plainly a labor of love for Captain Sleet to describe, as he does, all the little detailed conveniences of his crow's nest; but though he so enlarges upon many of these, and though he treats us to a very scientific account of his experiments in this crow's nest, with a small compass he kept there for the purpose of counteracting the errors resulting from what is called the "local attraction" of all binnacle magnets; an error ascribable to the horizontal vicinity of the iron in the ship's planks, and in the *Glacier's* case, perhaps, to there having been so many broken-down blacksmiths among her crew; I say that though the captain is very discreet and scientific here, yet, for all his learned "binnacle deviations," "azimuth compass observations," and "approximate errors," he knows very well, Captain Sleet, that he was not so much immersed in those profound magnetic meditations, as to fail being attracted occasionally towards that well replenished little case bottle, so nicely tucked in on one side of his crow's nest, within easy reach of his hand. Though, upon the whole, I greatly admire and even love the brave, the honest, and learned captain; yet I take it very ill of him that he should so utterly ignore that case bottle, seeing what a faithful friend and comforter it must have been, while with mittened fingers and hooded head he was studying the mathematics aloft there in that bird's nest within three or four perches of the pole.

But if we southern whale-fishers are not so snugly housed aloft as Captain Sleet and his Greenland-men were; yet that disadvantage is greatly counterbalanced by the widely contrasting serenity of those seductive seas in which we southern fishers mostly float. For one, I used to lounge up the rigging very leisurely, resting in the top to have a chat with Queequeg, or anyone else off duty whom I might find there; then ascending a little way further, and throwing a lazy leg over the topsail yard, take a preliminary view of the watery pastures, and so at last mount to my ultimate destination.

Let me make a clean breast of it here, and frankly admit that I kept but sorry guard. With the problem of the universe revolving in me, how could I—being left completely to myself at such a thought-engendering altitude—how could I but lightly hold my obligations to observe all whaleships' standing orders, "Keep your weather eye open, and sing out every time."

And let me in this place movingly admonish you, ye shipowners of Nantucket! Beware of enlisting in your vigilant fisheries any lad with lean brow and hollow eye; given to unseasonable meditativeness; and who offers to ship with the Phaedon instead of Bowditch in his head. Beware of such one, I say; your whales must be seen before they can be killed; and this sunken-eyed young Platonist will tow you ten wakes round the world, and never make you one pint of sperm the richer. Nor are these monitions at all unneeded. For nowadays, the whale fishery furnishes an asylum for many romantic, melancholy, and absentminded young men, disgusted with the carking cares of earth, and seeking sentiment in tar and blubber. Childe Harold not infrequently perches himself upon the masthead of some luckless disappointed whaleship, and in moody phrase ejaculates:

Roll on, thou deep and dark blue ocean, roll!
Ten thousand blubber-hunters sweep over thee in vain.

Very often do the captains of such ships take those absent-minded young philosophers to task, upbraiding them with not feeling sufficient "interest" in the voyage; half-hinting that they are so hopelessly lost to all honorable ambition, as that in their secret souls they would rather not see whales than otherwise. But all in vain; those young Platonists have a notion that their vision is imperfect; they are short-sighted; what use, then, to strain the visual nerve? They have left their opera glasses at home.

"Why, thou monkey," said a harpooneer to one of these lads, "we've been cruising now hard upon three years, and thou hast not raised a whale yet. Whales are scarce as hen's teeth whenever thou art up here." Perhaps they were; or perhaps there might have been shoals of them in the far horizon; but lulled into such an opiumlike listlessness of vacant, unconscious reverie is this absentminded youth by the blending cadence of waves with thoughts, that at last he loses his identity; takes the mystic ocean at his feet for the visible image of that deep, blue, bottomless soul, pervading mankind and nature; and every strange, half-seen, gliding, beautiful thing that eludes him; every dimly-discovered, uprising fin of some undiscernible form, seems to him the embodiment of those elusive thoughts that only people the soul by continually flitting through it. In this enchanted mood, thy spirit ebbs away to whence it came; becomes diffused through time and space; like Wickliff's sprinkled pantheistic ashes, forming at last a part of every shore the round globe over.

There is no life in thee, now, except that rocking life imparted by a gently rolling ship; by her, borrowed from the sea; by the sea, from the inscrutable tides of God. But while this sleep, this dream is on ye, move your foot or hand an inch; slip your hold at all; and your identity comes back in horror. Over Descartian vortices you hover. And perhaps, at midday, in the fairest weather, with one half-throttled shriek you drop through that transparent air into the summer sea, no more to rise forever. Heed it well, ye pantheists!

"100 Tons of Bronze, Son"

From *Yachting*

BY CLEVELAND AMORY

ASELF-DESCRIBED CURMUDGEON, Amory was a famed humorist and humanitarian who founded the Fund for Animals. The youngest editor of *The Saturday Evening Post,* his books ranged from social histories to bestsellers about his cat. A social commentator for *The Today Show,* chief critic of *TV Guide,* and an editor of *Parade* magazine, he devoted much of his life to animal rights.

This piece, from the pages of *Yachting* magazine, is a Walter Mitty-like fantasy about his America's Cup "career."

CUP DEFENDERS! SCHMUP DEFENDERS! Don't talk to me about these modern Defenders. Tenders, that's what they are, landlubbering tenders! Why, boy, before you were born, I shipped on a Defender in the days when they *were* Defenders. A J-boat, that's what she was, son, the *Vanitie*. And as a matter of fact, if I do say so myself, she was the largest J-boat ever built.

And would you like to know how old I was, boy, when I took the helm of *Vanitie?* Twelve, son, that's what I was, *twelve.* And don't think I was just out for the air, either. I was out for the Auld Mug, that's what I was out for. And not just against one other boat either—like these modern trials. "Boat-to-boat," they say. Children, I say. Those aren't races, boy, those are yacht club dances. No, boy, I was up against five other boats—you count 'em, *five*—*Resolute, Yankee, Enterprise,* never mind the others. And do you know who won, son? Do you know who won?

But I am getting ahead of my story. It all started one morning off ol' Marblehead. We were lying at anchor, there—on the good ship *Leonore*. A Q-boat she was, built in ol' Norway. I had shipped on that summer to give my father and brother the benefit of my experience. I had taught my father as much as I could and I was bringing my brother along nicely. Regular doses at regular intervals regularly repeated, that's the way I saw it. Not too much at any one time.

And, if I do say so myself, I ran a taut ship. They were coming along fine. Ship-shape. Then, lo and behold, that morning, if young Gerry Lambert doesn't heave by on his big launch *Utilitie*, tender of the *Vanitie*. "On board *Leonore*," he hollers over his megaphone. "Ahoy there."

"Ahoy there yourself, Gerry my lad," I hollers back. And then, out of the clear blue, he asks the question, "Any body on board can sail a J?" he wants to know. "I'm shy a skipper."

Well, it called for some quick thinking. I took a look at my father. Much as I loved him as a man and had high hopes for him as a sailor, I just didn't think he was ready. A Q, yes—50 feet overall. But *Vanitie*, 84 on the line and 126 overall, no. Then I looked at my brother. Why the little shaver had just turned 15. I couldn't take the chance. No, this was one for the old man. It had to be me.

All this thinking, of course, took far less time than it takes to tell it. A good sailor man, I've always said, thinks in seconds. But with a good racing man, it's split seconds. I picked up the megaphone. "I'll go, Ger," I volunteered.

In a moment the big *Utilitie* was hard by. They were going to lower a boat, but I stopped them. "It's blowin' pretty pert," I said matter-of-factly, "fer to lower"—and, with a quick vault, I was on *Utilitie's* deck. I landed lightly. In a moment Lambert was at my side. "Have you had much experience," he asked, "in J's?"

"Enough," I said quietly. "What's your trouble?"

On the way over to *Vanitie,* Gerry gave me a brief rundown of our situation. It was not good. But I'll always be grateful to Ger that he gave me the bad along with the good. The skipper never lived, I've always said, who was any better than the mate on the watch ahead of him.

In a word, the story was this. We were to be up against the Big Five that day—and for all the marbles. This was the big one—the one we had to win for the Big Skipper Upstairs—I mean, of course, On Deck.

Four of the boats were obviously newer than *Vanitie*—and just built for this—and one of them, *Yankee,* had the best skipper in the business at the wheel. "Charles Francis Adams?" I asked grimly. Lambert nodded. I didn't say anything, but to myself I was thinking, "Well, good ol' Charlie Ad is going to have a fight to the finish this day." As for the rest of them—we went rapidly down the list—they were all trouble. *Enterprise,* backed by New York money and sailed by Mike Vanderbilt—there was no soft touch there. *Whirlwind* was comparatively untested, it is true, but *Weetamoe!* Well, the sardine in the scuppers there was that Gerry himself had been part of the Syndicate that built her.

Again I didn't say anything, but I did plenty of thinking—to myself. "Ger, my lad," I thought, "it looks like today you're going to beat yourself."

Finally there was *Resolute*—as tough as her name implied. And here, as if things weren't tough enough, we had to give her a time allowance. "We've got to give her," Lambert told me nervously, "2:11."

I calculated quickly. "All right," I told myself, "we'll beat her by 2:12."

By now we had reached *Vanitie*. The crew was all lined up, but I permitted no piping the skipper on board. Instead I shook my head and once more leaped lightly to the deck. But, as I did so, I caught the eye of every man jack of that crew—man by man, mate by mate, even the boatswain's mate. "Aha," I thought, "Norwegians all."

"Captain," I joshed, "you're pretty pronounced toward the Norwegians, aren't you—for a Yay-boat?"

The crew got it, as well as the captain, of course. There's nothing to ease the tension of a Norwegian sailor, I always say, like a skipper that knows when to yoke.

But now there would be no more jokes. "Let's go, boys," I said quietly. "Pass the *Utilitie* forward. Mind the tow line."

That did it. That crew might have thought when they first saw me that I didn't know a jib from a jibe or a beat from a batten. But once they got their first order, they knew. A crew just knows those things, that's all. It's the habit of command, I've always said.

I went aft and took the helm. I don't mind saying a lot of green water had gone over the side since I'd had a wheel like that in my hand. But the years seemed to roll away the minute I put thumb and forefinger on her.

"Head 'er up," I said. "Ready on the main halyard." And while I barked out the commands, 23 of those 26 men pulled up that main as if she were a baby. "Clear away," I shouted. "Let go *Utilitie*." And then, as I spun the wheel, I shouted, "Let go the boom crotch."

I put her over on the port tack. But before we came up on the wind again, and I gave orders to hoist the headsails, I took a moment to size up my opposition. First, Mike Vanderbilt. I could see him, out of the corner of my eye, watching me even as I watched him. And then I saw him look at his watch. "Aha," I thought, "the best starter in the business. Well, today he's going to be the second best." And then I spied Charlie Adams. Lambert had warned me—I knew how he loved to bluff—even when he didn't have right of way. "Well," I thought, "if there's any bluffing in this race he'd better have right of way—or Mrs. Charles Ad's a widow tonight."

By now we had the headsails up. And just as the jib started to draw—bang, went the warning gun. I jockeyed up wind, paying no attention. All the time before the second gun I just rode easy, testing and getting the feel of her. And all this time the others couldn't for the life of them figure what I was doing—which was, of course, exactly what I wanted. What I was doing was testing that starting line. "Aha," I thought, "a better fetch on the port tack. They'll all try that. Well, now."

Bang, went the second gun. Now they were all four of them pulling off—I could see all four skippers with their watches. They were crowding each other—jockeying for the same position.

"Let go the mainsheet," I hollered. The Captain looked up. The crew hesitated. Everyone thought I had lost my senses. "I believe, Captain," I said quietly, "I said something about letting go the mainsheet."

The captain repeated the command and the crew hopped to. I sawed off and ran down on the port tack and away from the line. By now they thought I was really crazy. There was one minute left. Out of the corner of my eye I could see all five boats now and on the port tack.

"Ready about," I hollered. We came around. And then, with just 20 seconds left, we were bearing down on five boats—all by ourselves—on the starboard tack. "My God," muttered the boatswain's mate, "ol' Cleve is sweeping the line on the starboard tack."

But I had more important things to think about. "Right of way," I shouted, "right of W-A-Y." You could hear the groans as one by one *Whirlwind, Weetamoe, Enterprise* and *Resolute* had to tack away from the line. Finally there was just old Charlie Adams left. "Right of way," I holler again. Charlie seemed to be pretending he didn't hear me. By now there wasn't 50 feet between us. At last he looked. "You wouldn't," he shouted.

"Charlie," I said quietly, "I've got 100 tons of bronze that says I would."

At the last possible second, Charlie came about—the starting gun went off—and the race was on. But by then, of course, we had such a lead that, almost from that moment, we had nothing but clear sailing.

I should say clear sailing except for one incident. It happened on the second leg, when we were close reaching for the second mark—and we were caught by a wicked puff.

I should explain here that in a light breeze, *Vanitie* handled, as Gerry himself had said, like a violin. But in a breeze of wind, off wind, she could be a wild beast—it took plenty of strength to handle her.

In any case, when that puff caught her, even my strength wasn't enough. It was some puff—one of those green ones that blows the tops right off the waves. And when it hit us, we had green water right up to the companionway and we started to have bad lee helm. I kept slammin' it to her and I never changed expression. I was trying, obviously, not to let the crew know that even the old man himself had doubts about this one.

But I did have doubts and I knew we were in trouble. We had to let that jib sheet off to make her head up. But how to do it? Worst of all, those other boats astern had seen what had happened to us. They were heading up to avoid the squall, and if we couldn't get *Vanitie* headed up, too, we'd never get near that second mark. Every darn one of those tugs would go by us as if we were tied to a mooring. It was good bye Auld Mug.

The crew was willing, I'll say that for them. They knew how important it was to let that jib sheet go, and one after another they tried. But those cleats were four feet under green water—the best crew who ever sailed couldn't get near them. I remember the last kid who was going to try. I just couldn't let him. "Watch out for that damn kid," I heard myself say.

I was cracking. But I couldn't. It was now or never. With a sigh I reached in my pocket and took out my knife. "Captain," I said, "take the wheel." "My God, Cleve," he says, "you're not going to cut that sheet. We'll lose that way too." "No, Captain," I smiled, "I'm not." And in a twinkling I dove down there into that hell, green water and all, and cut—not the sheet, of course, but the jib *whip*.

That was all there was to it. The crew cheered, but it wasn't anything really—nothing any one of them couldn't have done if they'd had the guts and the know how and the experience and set their mind to it and kept moving. In any case, immediately the jib eased, and we headed up and—but, well, there's no need to tell the rest. It's all there, in the books. For the record, though, we beat *Resolute,* as I remember, by 2:23 and not, as some have it, 2:13.

And on the run home, for a brief moment, I allowed Gerry to take the wheel. For one thing, by that time we had the race won 40 ways to Sunday—and, for another . . . well, I just knew it was something he'd remember all the rest of his life.

Service in the Mediterranean

From *The Autobiography of a Seaman*

BY ADMIRAL LORD COCHRANE

A s one of England's most famous naval heroes, Admiral Lord Cochrane's inspired the likes of Patrick O'Brian and C. S. Forester. Called "the sea wolf" by Napoleon, Cochrane was a dashing, brilliant young sailor and well as a fearless campaigner against incompetence and corruption in the navy and politics. In this section, from his *Autobiography of a Seaman,* Cochrane describes his duties as a junior officer and the tensions and politics aboard ship.

TOWARDS THE CLOSE OF THE AUTUMN OF 1798, Lord Keith was appointed to relieve Lord St. Vincent in the command of the Mediterranean fleet, and kindly offered to take me with him as a supernumerary. I therefore embarked, by his lordship's invitation, in the flag-ship.

We arrived at Gibraltar on the 14th of December, and found Lord St. Vincent residing on shore, his flag flying on board the *Souverain* sheer-hulk.

His lordship's reception of me was very kind, and on the 24th of December, at Lord Keith's request, he gave an order for my appointment to the *Barfleur,* to which ship Lord Keith had shifted his flag. This appointment, from a certain dissatisfaction at my having received such a commission after being so short a time at sea, afterwards brought me into trouble.

Lord St. Vincent did not, as was expected, immediately transfer to Lord Keith the command of the Mediterranean fleet, but remained at Gibraltar, giving orders to his lordship to blockade the Spanish fleet in Cadiz.

The first part of the year was spent in this employment, Lord Keith's force varying from eleven to fifteen sail of the line, but without frigates, though the commander-in-chief had a considerable number under his orders. The omission was the more remarkable, as the blockaded Spanish force numbered upwards of twenty ships of the line, with frigates and smaller vessels in proportion.

The British force, for upwards of four months, was anchored some seven or eight miles from Cadiz, but without rousing the national spirit of the Spaniards, who manifested no disposition to quit their shelter, even though we were compelled from time to time to leave our anchorage for the purpose of procuring water and cattle from the neighbouring coast of Africa. It was during one of these trips in the *Barfleur* that an absurd affair involved me in serious disaster.

Our first lieutenant, Beaver, was an officer who carried etiquette in the wardroom and on deck almost to despotism. He was laudably particular in all matters visible to the eye of the admiral, but permitted an honest penny to be turned elsewhere by a practice as reprehensible as revolting. On our frequent visits to Tetuan, we purchased and killed bullocks on board the *Barfleur,* for the use of the whole squadron. The reason was, that raw hides, being valuable, could be stowed away in her hold in empty beef-casks, as especial perquisites to certain persons connected with the flag-ship; a natural result being, that, as the fleshy parts of the hides decomposed, putrid liquor oozed out of the casks, and rendered the hold of the vessel so intolerable, that she acquired the name of "The stinking Scotch Ship."

As junior lieutenant, much of the unpleasantness of this fell to my share, and as I always had a habit of speaking my mind without much reserve, it followed that those interested in the raw hide speculation were not very friendly disposed towards me.

One day, when at Tetuan, having obtained leave to go ashore and amuse myself with shooting wild-fowl, my dress became so covered with mud, as to induce me not to come off with other officers in the pinnace which took me on shore, preferring to wait for the launch, in which the filthy state of my apparel would be less apparent. The launch being delayed longer than had been anticipated, my leave of absence expired shortly before my arrival on board—not without attracting the attention of Lieutenant Beaver, who was looking over the gangway.

Thinking it disrespectful to report myself on the quarter-deck in so dirty a condition, I hastened to put on clean uniform, an operation scarcely completed when Lieutenant Beaver came into the wardroom, and in a very harsh tone demanded the reason of my not having reported myself. My reply was, that as he saw me come up the side, he must be aware that my dress was not in a fit condition to appear on the quarter-deck, and that it had been necessary to change my clothes before formally reporting myself.

Lieutenant Beaver replied to this explanation in a manner so offensive that it was clear he wanted to surprise me into some act of insubordination. As it would have been impossible to be long cool in opposition to marked invective, I respectfully reminded him that by attaching me in the wardroom he was breaking a rule which he had himself laid down; viz. that "Matters connected with the service were not there to be spoken of." The remark increased his violence, which, at length, became so marked as to call forth the reply, "Lieutenant Beaver, we will, if you please, talk of this in another place." He then went on deck, and reported to Captain Elphinstone that in reply to his remarks on a violation of duty, he had received a challenge!

On being sent for to answer the charge, an explanation of what had really taken place was given to Captain Elphinstone, who was kindly desirous that the first lieutenant should accept an apology, and let so disagreeable a matter drop. This was declined on my part, on the ground that, in the conversation which had passed, I had not been in the wrong, and had therefore no apology to make. The effect was, that Beaver demanded a court-martial on me, and this, after manifest reluctance on the part of Lord Keith, was ordered accordingly; the decision of which was an admonition to be "more careful in future"—a clear proof that the court thought great provocation had been given by my accuser, or their opinion would have been more marked.

The Jude-Advocate on this occasion was the admiral's secretary, one of those who had taken offence about the raw hides before mentioned! After the business of the court was concluded, Lord Keith, who was much vexed with the whole affair, said to me privately: "Now, Lord Cochrane, pray avoid for the future all flippancy towards superior officers." His secretary overhead and embodied the remark in the sentence of the court-martial; so that shortly afterwards his officiousness or malice formed an impediment to my promotion, though the court had actually awarded no censure.

Lord Keith, who had in vain used every endeavour to induce the Spaniards to risk an engagement, began to get tired of so fruitless an operation as that of watching an enemy at anchor under their batteries, and resolved to try if he could not entice or force them to quit their moorings. With this view, the British force, though then consisting of twelve ships only, without a single frigate to watch the enemy meanwhile, proceeded to water, as usual, at Tetuan, so as to be in readiness for any contingencies that might arise. As the events which followed have been incorrectly represented by naval historians, if not in once instances misrepresented, it is necessary, in order to do justice to Lord Keith, to detail them at some length.

Immediately after our return from Tetuan, the *Childers* arrived with intelligence that five Spanish sail of the line had got out of Ferrol, and she was followed on the same day by the *Success* frigate, which had been chased by a French fleet off Oporto. Lord Keith at once dispatched the *Childers* to Gibraltar, to inform Lord St Vincent, as it was understood in the squadron, that he intended, if the French fleet came to Cadiz, to engage them, notwithstanding the disparity of numbers. Lord Keith's force, by the arrival of three additional ships of the line and one frigate, now amounted to sixteen sail; viz. one 112-gun ship, four 98's, one 90, two 80's, seven 74's, and one frigate, and these were immediately got under weight and formed in order of battle, standing off and on in front of the harbour.

About 8 A.M. on the 6th of May the French fleet was signaled in the offing, and was made out to consist of thirty-three sail, which, with the twenty-two sail, of Spaniards in Cadiz, made fifty-five, besides frigates, to be encountered by the comparatively small British force. The French fleet was on the larboard tack, and our ships immediately formed on the same tack to receive them. To our surprise they soon afterwards wore and stood away to the south-west; though from our position between them and the Spaniards they had a fair chance of victory had the combined fleets acted in concert. According to Lord Keith's pithily pressed opinion, we lay between "the devil and the deep sea."

Yet there was nothing rash. Lord Keith calculated that the Spaniards would not move unless the French succeeded in breaking through the British line, and this he had no doubt of preventing. Besides which, the wind, though not dead on shore, as has been said, was unfavourable for the Spaniards coming out with the necessary rapidity. The great point to be gained was to prevent the junction of the enemies' fleets, as was doubtless intended; the attempt, was, however, completely frustrated by the bold interposition of Lord Keith, who, strange to say, never received for this signal service the acknowledgment of merit which was his due.

It has been inferred by naval historians that a gale of wind, which was blowing on the first appearance of the French fleet, was the cause of their standing away. A better reason was their disinclination to encounter damage, which they knew would defeat their ultimate object of forming a junction with the Spanish fleet elsewhere.

At daylight on the 7th we were still standing off and on before Cadiz, expecting the enemy to return; when shortly afterwards four of their ships were seen to windward of the British force, which immediately gave chase; but the enemy outstripping us, we returned to the coast, to guard every point by which they might get into Cadiz. Seeing no symptoms of the main body of the French fleet, Lord Keith concluded that the four ships just noticed had been left as a decoy to draw his attention from their real object of running for Toulon, now that they had been foiled in their expectation of carrying with them the Spanish fleet. We accordingly made all sail for Gibraltar.

From the intelligence forwarded by the *Childers,* there was reason to suppose that Lord St Vincent would have prepared for instant pursuit. To our surprise, the signal was made to anchor and obtain water and provision. Three entire days were consumed in this operation; with what effect as regarded the other ships I do not know, but so far as the *Barfleur* was concerned, and as far as I know of the other ships, the delay was unnecessary. The fleet was greatly disappointed at being thus detained, as the enemy would thereby reach Toulon without molestation, and for any good which could be effected we might as well remain where we lay.

This impatience was, after a lapse of three days, ended by Lord St Vincent hoisting his flag on board the *Ville de Paris;* when, reinforced by the *Edgar,* 74, the fleet shaped its course by the Mediterranean.

After we had proceeded as far as the Bay of Rosas, Lord St Vincent, having communicated with Lord Keith, parted company in the Ville de Paris for Minorca, leaving Lord Keith to pursue the enemy with the remaining ships. We now made straight for Toulon, where we learned from some fishing boats that the enemy's fleet had embarked spars, cordage, anchors, and other heavy articles for the equipment of their ships of war built or building at Spezzia—and had sailed to the eastward.

After burning some merchant vessels working into Toulon we again started in chase. It was now of even greater importance to overtake the French fleet, in order to frustrate a double mischief; first, their escape; and secondly, their getting to Spezzia with the materials for so important an addition to their force. With this object the British ships crowded all sail in the direction the enemy had taken, and at length came in sight of their look-out frigates between Corsica and Genoa.

Just as we were upon the point of seeing the fleet also, a fast-sailing transport arrived from Lord St Vincent, with orders to return to Port Mahon; intelligence of the sailing of the French fleet having reached that port, which, Lord St Vincent feared, might become the object of attack. Lord Keith, however, knowing exactly the position of the enemy, within reach of whom we now virtually were, persevered in the pursuit.

Shortly afterwards another fast-sailing transport hove in sight, firing guns for Lord Keith to bring-to, which having done, he received peremptory orders to repair immediately to Minorca; Lord St Vincent still imagining that as the enemy had left Toulon they might catch him in Port Mahon; the fact of their having gone to Spezzia, though known to us, being unknown to him. Compliance with this unseasonable order was therefore compulsory, and Lord Keith made the signal for all captains, when, as reported by those officers, his lordship explained that the bearing up was no act of his, and the captains having returned on board their respective ships, reluctantly changed the course for Minorca, leaving the French fleet to proceed unmo-lested to Spezzia.

On Lord Keith receiving this order, I never saw a man more irritated. When annoyed, his lordship had a habit of taking aloud to himself. On this occasion, as officer of the watch, I happened to be in close proximity, and thereby became an involuntary listener to some very strong expressions, imputing jealousy on the part of Lord St Vin-cent as constituting the motive for recalling him. The actual words of Lord Keith not being meant for the ear of anyone, I do not think proper to record them. The above facts are stated as coming within my own personal knowledge, and are here introduced in conse-quence of blame being cast on Lord Keith to this day by naval histo-rians, who could only derive their authority from *data* which are certainly untrue—even if official. Had the command been surren-dered to Lord Keith on his arrival in the Mediterranean, or had his lordship been permitted promptly to pursue the enemy, they could not have escaped.

The French fleet, after we were compelled to relinquish the chase (when in sight of their look-out frigates), were reported to have landed 1000 men at Savona, and convoyed a supply of wheat to Genoa, as well as having landed their naval stores at Spezzia, not one of which services could have been effected had it not been for the unfortunate delay at Gibraltar and the before-mentioned recall of the pursuing fleet.

Immediately after our departure from Gibraltar, the Spanish fleet quitted Cadiz for the Mediterranean, and as no force remained to watch the Straits, they were enabled to pass with impunity; the whole, after suffering great damage by a gale of wind, succeeded in reaching Carthagena.

On our arrival at Minorca, Lord St Vincent resumed the command, and proceeded for some distance towards Toulon. On the 2nd of June, his lordship again quitted the fleet for Mahon, in the *Ville de Paris*. On the 14th Lord Keith shifted his flag from the *Barfleur* to the *Queen Charlotte,* a much finer ship, to which I had the honour to accompany him.

We once more proceeded in quest of the French fleet, and on the 19th the advance ships captured three frigates and two brigs of war on their way from Egypt to Toulon, but learned nothing of the fleet we were in search of. On the 23rd of June, Lord St Vincent at length resigned the Mediterranean command and sailed for England, so that Lord Keith had no alternative but to return to Port Mahon to make the necessary arrangements.

Scarcely had we come to an anchor when we received intelligence that the French fleet had passed to the westward to join the Spanish fleet at Carthagena!

Without even losing time to fill up with water, every exertion was made for immediate pursuit, and on the 10th we started for Carthagena, but finding the enemy gone, again made sail, and on the 26th reached Tetuan, where we completed our water. On the 29th Lord Keith communicated with Gibraltar, but as nothing was heard of the combined fleets, it was evident they had gone through the Straits in the dark; we therefore followed and examined Cadiz, where they were not. Pursuing our course without effect along the Spanish and Portuguese coasts—on the 8th of August we fell in with a Danish brig off Cape Finisterre, and received from her information that she had two days before passed through the combined French and Spanish fleets. We then directed our course for Brest, hoping to be in time to intercept them, but found that on the day before our arrival they had effected their object, and were then safely moored within the harbour. We now shaped our course for Torbay, and there found the Channel fleet under Sir Alan Gardner—the united force being nearly fifty ships of the line.

On our arrival at Torbay, Lord Keith sent me with dispatches on board the commander-in-chief's ship, where, after executing my commission, it was imperiously demanded by her captain whether I was aware that my coming on board was an infringement of quarantine regulations! Netted at the overbearing manner of an uncalled-for reprimand to an inferior officer, my reply was that, having been directed by Lord Keith to deliver his despatches, his lordship's orders had been executed accordingly; at the same time, however, assuring my interrogator that we had no sickness in the fleet, nor had we been in any contagious localities. From the captain's manner, it was almost evident that, for being thus plain spoken, he intended to put me under arrest, and I was not sorry to get back to the *Queen Charlotte;* even a show of resistance to an excess of authority being in those days fatal to many an officer's prospects.

I shall not enter in detail as to what occurred in the Channel; suffice it to say that despite the imposing force laying at Torbay, the combined French and Spanish fleets found no difficulty in getting out of Brest, and that on the 6th of December Lord Keith returned in pursuit to Gibraltar, where he resumed the Mediterranean command, administered by Lord Nelson during his absence.

It is beyond the province of this work to notice the effectual measures taken by Lord Nelson in the Mediterranean during our absence, as they are matters in which I bore no part. But whilst Nelson and Lord Keith had been doing their best there, little appeared to be done at home to check the enemy's operations.

From Gibraltar we proceeded to Sicily, where we found lord Nelson surrounded by the *élite* of Neapolitan society, amongst whom he was justly regarded as a deliverer. It was never my good fortune to serve under his lordship, either at that or any subsequent period. During our stay at Palermo, I had, however, opportunities of personal conversation with him, and from one of his frequent injunctions, "Never mind manoeuvres, always go at them," I subsequently had reason to consider myself indebted for successful attacks under apparently difficult circumstances.

The impression left on my mind during these opportunities of association with Nelson was that of his being an embodiment of dashing courage, which would not take much trouble to circumvent an enemy, but being confronted with one would regard victory so much a matter of course as hardly to deem the chance of defeat worth consideration.

This was in fact the case; for though the enemy's ships were for the most part superior to ours in build, the discipline and seamanship of their crews was in that day so inferior as to leave little room for doubt of victory on our part. It was probably with the object of improving his crews that Admiral Bruix had risked a run from the Mediterranean to Brest and back, as just now detailed. Had not Lord Keith been delayed at Gibraltar, and afterwards recalled to Minorca, the disparity of numbers of our side would not have been of any great consequence.

Trafalgar itself is an illustration of Nelson's peculiar dash. It has been remarked that Trafalgar was a rash action, and that had Nelson lost it and lived he would have been brought to a court-martial for the way in which that action was conducted. But such cavillers forget that, from previous experience, he had calculated both the nature and amount of resistance to be expected; such calculation forming as essential a part of his plan of attack as even his means for making it. The result justified his expectations of victory, which were not only well founded but certain.

The fact is, that many commanders in those days committed the error of overrating the French navy, just as, in the present day, we are nationally falling into the still more dangerous extreme of underrating it. Steam has, indeed, gone far towards equalizing seamanship and the strenuous exertions of the French Department of Marine have perhaps rendered discipline in their navy as good as in ours. They moreover keep their trained men, whilst we thoughtlessly turn ours adrift whenever ships are paid off—to be replaced by raw hands in case of emergency!

To return from this digression. After quitting Palermo, and when passing the Straits of Messina, Lord Keith placed me as prize-master in command of the *Genereux,* 74—shortly before captured by Lord Nelson's squadron—with orders to carry her to Port Mahon. A crew was hastily made up of sick and invalided men drafted from the ships of the fleet, and with these we proceeded on our voyage, but only to find ourselves in imminent danger from a gale of wind. The rigging not having been properly set up, the masts swayed with every roll of the ship to such a degree that it became dangerous to go aloft; the shrouds alternately straining almost to breaking, or hanging in festoons, as the masts jerked from side to side with the roll of the vessel. It was only by going aloft myself together with my brother Archibald, whom Lord Keith had permitted to accompany me, that the men could be induced to furl the mainsail. Fortunately the weather moderated, or the safety of the ship might have been compromised; but by dint of hard work, as far as the ill-health of the crew would allow, we managed, before reaching Mahon, to put the *Genereux* into tolerable order.

It has been stated that Lord Keith permitted my brother to accompany me in the *Genereux*. By this unexpected incident both he and myself were, in all probability, saved from a fate which soon afterwards befell most of our gallant shipmates.

On our quitting the *Queen Charlotte,* Lord Keith steered for Leghorn, where he landed, and ordered Captain Todd to reconnoiter the island of Cabrera, then in possession of the French. Whilst on his way, some hay, hastily embarked and placed under the half-deck, became ignited, and the flame communicating with the mainsail set the ship on fire aloft and below. All exertions to save her proved in vain, and though some of the officers and crew escaped, more than three-fourths miserably perished, including Captain Todd, his first lieutenant, Bainbridge, three other lieutenants, the captain of marines, surgeon, more than twenty master's mates and petty officers, and upwards of 600 marines and seamen.

On our return from England to Gibraltar I had been associated with poor Bainbridge in an affair which—except as a tribute to his memory—would not have been worth mentioning. On the evening of the 21st of September, 1799, we observed from the *Queen Charlotte,* lying in Gibraltar Bay, the 10-gun cutter *Lady Nelson,* chased by some gun-vessels and privateers, all of which simultaneously commenced an attack upon her. Lord Keith instantly ordered out boats, Bainbridge taking command of the barge, whilst another of the boats was put under my orders. Lord Keith's intention was, by this prompt aid, to induce the *Lady Nelson* to make a running fight of it, so as to get within range of the garrison guns; but before the boats could come up she had been captured; Lieutenant Bainbridge, though with sixteen men only, dashed at her, boarded, and retook her, killing several and taking prisoner seven French officers and twenty-seven men; but not without himself receiving a severe sabre cut on the head and several other wounds.

The boat under my command was the cutter with thirteen men. Seeing two privateers which had chiefly been engaged in the attack on the *Lady Nelson* running for Algesiras, we made at the nearest, and came up with her at dark. On laying the cutter alongside, I jumped on board, but the boat's crew did not follow, this being the only time I ever saw British seamen betray symptoms of hesitation. Regaining the cutter, I upbraided them with the shamefulness of their conduct, for the privateer's crew had run below, and helmsman alone being at his post. Their excuse was that there were indications of the privateer's men having there fortified themselves. No reasoning could prevail on them to board. If this boat's crew perished in the *Queen Charlotte,* their fate is not nationally to be regretted.

On the destruction of the *Queen Charlotte* Lord Keith hoisted his flag in the *Audacious*. His lordship was so well satisfied with my conduct of the *Genereux* as to write home to the Admiralty recommending my promotion, at the same time appointing me to the command of the *Speedy,* then lying at Port Mahon.

The vessel originally intended for me by Lord Keith was the *Bonne Citoyenne,* a fine corvette of eighteen guns; but the brother of his lordship's secretary happening at the time to arrive from Gibraltar, where he had been superseded in the command of the sheer-hulk, that functionary managed to place his brother in one of the finest sloops then in the service, leaving to me the least efficient craft on the station.

Permissions Acknowledgments